SCHOOL INTERVENTIONS FOR CHILDREN OF ALCOHOLICS

The Guilford School Practitioner Series

EDITORS

STEPHEN N. ELLIOTT, Ph.D.　　**JOSEPH C. WITT, Ph.D.**
University of Wisconsin—Madison　　*Louisiana State University, Baton Rouge*

SCHOOL INTERVENTIONS
for
CHILDREN OF ALCOHOLICS

BONNIE K. NASTASI, Ph.D.
University at Albany, State University of New York

DENISE M. DeZOLT, Ph.D.
University of Rhode Island

THE GUILFORD PRESS
New York   London

© 1994 The Guilford Press
A Division of Guilford Publications, Inc.
72 Spring Street, New York, NY 10012

Printed in the United States of America

This book is printed on acid-free paper

Last digit is print number: 9 8 7 6 5 4 3 2 1

Library of Congress cataloging-in-publication data is available from the Publisher

ISBN 0-89862-367-7

Illustrations by Kathryn Mott

We dedicate this book to those who made it necessary, to those who made it possible, and to children everywhere whose lives are affected by alcohol.

B. N. & D. D.

Acknowledgments

We extend our gratitude to the students and school personnel who provided the contexts for the development of the ESCAPE program, and to those individuals whose stories are told herein.

B. N. & D. D.

Preface

Alcoholism affects the lives of millions of children and families. Children growing up in families affected by alcohol are an at-risk and, until recent years, also a hidden population. Unlike those children whose lives are unaffected by alcohol, these children (commonly referred to as children of alcoholics, COAs) are more likely to experience family disharmony and dysfunctional family relationships, to develop social–emotional and academic–occupational problems, and to become alcoholics. Because of the denial of alcohol-related problems within families and our society, COAs often go unrecognized and untreated. Schools provide opportune contexts for identification and intervention with this population.

This book tells the story of children and families whose lives are affected by alcohol, and provides a guide to school personnel who are interested in developing programs for COAs. We take primarily a prevention approach which is focused on creating school cultures that foster the development of social competence and personal efficacy of all children, with particular attention to the needs of COAs. The ESCAPE (Enhancing Social Competence and Personal Efficacy) program we describe is designed to be integrated into existing school curricula in order to address social–emotional as well as cognitive–academic needs of children. Our approach is based on psychological and educational theory and research. The ESCAPE program thus reflects an application of theory and research to practice. The book is written to provide school personnel, including administrative, teaching, and mental health staff, with information about the effects of alcoholism on families and children, and with a theoretical and empirical model for understanding these effects and for designing school-based prevention and intervention programs for COAs. The prevention program we describe, however, is not limited to the COA population. We expect that school personnel will find this text useful for developing programs to enhance the personal–social competence of children and adolescents in general. Because our program relies heavily on the use of existing curricula, it is applicable to a wide range of settings. We strongly advise the collaboration of teaching and mental health staff in the design and implementation of such programs.

The content of this book provides a theoretical, empirical, and practical guide for developing programs to enhance the personal–social competence of school-age populations, particularly COAs. Chapter 1 provides the theoretical model that guided our exploration of family alcoholism and the development of the ESCAPE Program. In Chapter 2, we review research about the characteristics of children and families affected by alcohol, and the efficacy of school-based prevention and intervention programs. We also provide the empirical basis for the intervention strategies inherent in the ESCAPE Program. Chapter 3 provides the practical and ethical guidelines for the development, implementation, and evaluation of school-based programs. In Chapter 4, we present the ESCAPE program, a curriculum-based prevention and intervention program. Chapters 5 and 6 provide additional resource materials that will assist school personnel in the implementation of the ESCAPE Program and in the development of similar programs.

Contents

1

Theoretical Model and Rationale

Maggie's Story

Maggie was the perfect child. She was an excellent student and popular with her peers. She excelled in nonacademic endeavors as well. She was the type of student that teachers valued. At home, she helped with household tasks and with the care of younger siblings. She had many friends in her neighborhood and also enjoyed helping neighbors and other family members to care for their children. She was well liked by children and adults. On the outside, it appeared that Maggie had an ideal life. But no one, it seemed, knew what life was like at home. Maggie's father was an alcoholic. He did not spend much time at home and often came home late at night. Maggie knew this because his arrival home was usually followed by a great deal of yelling. Maggie and her siblings awoke to the conflict often. At these times, Maggie often tried to comfort her younger siblings who seemed frightened by the yelling. But the next day, she and her siblings would go off to school as if nothing had happened.

No one seemed to know what Maggie felt like inside most of the time. From a young age, she often felt sad and scared for no apparent reason. You see, no one talked about what was going on at home and she was also told that she was not to talk to others about her home life. So she remained silent and pretended that all was well. As Maggie reached adolescence, she felt sadder and more anxious. She finally decided to tell someone how she felt, although by this time she was not sure why she felt so sad and scared. She told counselors at school and clergy at church. But to no avail. You see, no one believed that Maggie had a reason to feel sad or scared. After all, she was the perfect child, so she must have the perfect life. So she stopped telling people how she felt. She continued to excel in school, to be active in extracurricular activities, and to make friends—to hide her feelings and pretend that nothing was wrong.

Maggie is an adult now, a very successful adult, at least on the outside. Inside, she still feels sad and scared and lonely much of the time. But she has found a way to be heard. There are professionals now who know about family alcoholism and who listen when she talks about her feelings. They understand how she feels, in spite of the appearance of a successful adult life. She knows there is help and hope. Although the journey is not easy, there are others who can help her find the way to a happier existence.

Robert's Story

Robert is 10 years old. His parents divorced 2 years ago. He now lives with his father and visits his mother every other weekend. He's confused by his mother's behavior and does not like going to her home. Sometimes she drinks a lot and criticizes and hits Robert for no apparent reason. At other times, she is playful and loving. Robert has told his father this but he tells Robert that the judge says he has to go. In school, Robert is experiencing academic difficulties. Although his teachers describe him as intelligent, he often fails to complete assignments and is receiving poor grades. Robert is well liked by children and adults, yet he does not view himself in the same way. He does not think he has any friends and in general does not feel good about himself. He feels sad and lonely much of the time. The school psychologist was asked to evaluate Robert to determine the cause of his learning difficulties. Robert was able to tell her how he felt.

The school psychologist was knowledgeable about family alcoholism and questioned Robert's father about the family history. Not only is Robert's mother an alcoholic, but so are his maternal and paternal grandfathers, two uncles, and an aunt. Robert's father expressed relief that he finally had someone to tell about his own family experiences with alcohol. His attempts to seek help as a child were similar to Maggie's. In addition to recommending academic interventions, the school psychologist referred the family to a community agency that worked with families affected by alcohol and to child protective services to determine alternatives to the current visitation arrangements. As a result, Robert and his family are receiving help in coping with the effects of his mother's alcoholism.

Maggie and Robert are two of approximately 28 million individuals from families affected by alcohol (commonly referred to as "children of alcoholics" or COAs), including over 7 million school-age children (Roosa, Gensheimer, Short, Ayers, & Shell, 1989). They come from both rural and urban areas (Sarvela, Pope, Odylana, & Bajracharya, 1990) and from a variety of cultural and ethnic backgrounds (National Institute on Alcohol Abuse and Alcoholism, 1987). In this chapter, we describe our theoretical framework, define alcoholism, and discuss alcoholism as a family phenomenon. We conclude with a brief commentary on the role of the school in addressing the needs of COAs.

THEORETICAL MODEL

In this section we present an ecological–developmental framework for understanding the influence of alcoholism on the family and for conceptualizing interventions. In addition, we present our model of personal–social competence and the social construction perspective of socialization and learning, which together provide the basis for design of school-based interventions for COAs. This model is exemplified in the ESCAPE (*En*hancing *S*ocial *C*ompetence *A*nd *P*ersonal *E*fficacy) Program detailed in Chapter 4.

Ecological–Developmental Perspective

Child adjustment in an alcoholic family may be examined best from an ecological–developmental perspective. An ecological approach to studying human development assumes a progressive, mutual accommodation throughout the life span between the individual and the environment, taking into account the sociocultural and historical contexts (Bronfenbrenner, 1989). Thus, consideration must be given to the immediate ecological context within which the child develops, for example, the alcoholic family. Viewing the family as an interactive system facilitates understanding of the implicit and explicit family rules, the roles that children and parents assume in alcoholic families, the reciprocal nature of these roles, and the interaction patterns that develop. In addition, we need to consider the contexts in which the family unit is embedded, including the extended family, the community, and the sociocultural history. A life-span perspective to studying human development provides a framework for linking childhood experiences to adjustment in adolescence and adulthood.

From an ecological perspective, an individual's current interactions with the environment are influenced not only by the immediate setting, but also by personal characteristics that in part were influenced by previous interactions with the same or similar environments. Development of personal–social competencies within the family involves an ongoing process of mutual accommodation to the rules, demands, and needs of family members. Behaviors that help to maintain the stability of the system are likely to be reinforced and to perpetuate the system. Thus, over time family members develop behavior patterns that facilitate the maintenance of the alcoholic family. In addition, experiences within the family context provide children with a frame of reference for interpreting other social environments and for guiding social interactions in other contexts. As the individual seeks or elicits similar experiences across contexts, the cognitions and behaviors initially learned within the alcoholic family are reinforced and become characteristic patterns for interpreting and interacting within social contexts. Unless other frames of reference and interpersonal experiences are provided for the developing child, the experiences within the alcoholic family are expected to have long-term influence on the individual's adjustment both within and outside of the family system. Thus, the adult child of the alcoholic is likely to recreate ecological systems (e.g., friendships, family relationships) analogous to the alcoholic family system that maintain the cognitions and behaviors learned during childhood. In this manner, the dynamics of the alcoholic family are transmitted across generations.

A full understanding of the immediate family context requires that we consider the wider contexts in which the nuclear family is embedded, such as the extended family, culture, society, and history (see Figure 1.1). To do this, one must ask the following questions. What is the family history of alcohol use? What family rules and interaction patterns are transmitted across generations? Similarly, what are the cultural mores surrounding the use of alcohol, and public and private sanctions related to alcohol abuse? Furthermore, what roles and interaction patterns are promoted within the culture? What are the societal values and norms regulating alcohol use, government intervention in families, the worth and rights of children, and promotion of personal and socially valued competencies? What is the historical evolution of these values and norms?

We must consider the level of consistency across contexts and the other systems beyond the family in which the child operates. Specifically, how consonant are the family values with those of the peer group, the school, and community? And are these value systems consonant with those of the society at large? Furthermore, the interactions among these systems

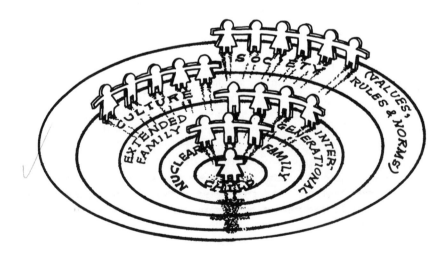

FIGURE 1.1. The ecological system of the child within the family context.

are important. For example, to what extent do families, schools, and community work together to promote the well-being of children?

We use an ecological perspective to examine the well-being and personal–social competence of COAs within multiple contexts throughout the life span. Next, we present a model of competence as a foundation for identifying the needs of this population and designing appropriate interventions.

Model of Personal–Social Competence

Common problems for COAs include those related to self-esteem (a sense that one is worthwhile and loveable), self-efficacy (a sense of control over one's environment), ability to establish and maintain intimate relationships, and the development of effective strategies for expressing feelings and solving problems (Nastasi & DeZolt, 1991). These areas of functioning represent important aspects of personal–social competence and coping ability, and provide important focal points for prevention and treatment (Elias & Branden, 1988; Strayhorn, 1988).

Definitions of personal–social competence are as numerous as the researchers and practitioners who work in this area. A review of the literature reveals a consistent set of characteristics or behaviors that are included in definitions of personal–social competence. These include (1) *social interaction skills* associated with establishing and maintaining interpersonal interactions and relationships; (2) *interpersonal problem-solving skills* necessary for solving interpersonal conflicts and problems in daily living; and (3) *self-efficacy*, self-perceptions, and intrinsic motives associated with initiating and maintaining efforts to adapt to life circumstances. Such competencies are likely to influence effective participation in society, academic and career success, social adjustment and peer acceptance, and adjustment to stress and change. Furthermore, this delineation of competence is consistent with other conceptualizations of personal–social competence and generalizable coping ability (Anthony & Cohler, 1987; Elias & Branden, 1988; Lazarus & Folkman, 1984; Parker, Cowen, Work, & Wyman, 1990; Rutter, 1979; Strayhorn, 1988).

Elias and Branden (1988) explain the incidence of mental health problems from person- and environment-centered perspectives. The person-centered model was originally proposed by the President's Commission on Mental Health in 1978 (Elias & Branden, 1988), based on a review of the literature on mental health and behavioral and emotional disorders. This model suggests that the occurrence of behavioral and emotional difficulties for the individual is determined by the amount of stress that is experienced and physical vulnerability to stress, in relationship to the individual's coping skills, availability and use of social support, and self-esteem. Thus, personal–social competencies can influence the level of adaptation, despite physical vulnerability and lack of control over stressors. Intervention focused on enhancement and use of these competencies by COAs might be particularly important, considering the genetic predisposition to alcoholism, the limited control over parental behavior, and the likelihood that experiences within the alcoholic family interfere with development of such competencies.

In contrast to the individual focus, Elias (1987; see also Elias & Branden, 1988) proposed an environment-centered model for explaining the incidence of behavioral–emotional disorders within the general population. From this perspective, the occurrence of such disorders within a community or culture is determined by the prevalence of stressors and risk factors, in relationship to the socialization practices, social resources, and opportunities for connectedness. This model, consistent with a systems orientation, relies on socialization practices and social support networks to buffer the impact of otherwise uncontrollable stressors that are internal or external to the system. Thus, schools might facilitate the adjustment of high-risk populations such as children of alcoholics by regulating the sociocultural milieu within the school system. Research on resilient children suggests that emotional support and opportunities for connectedness provided by teachers can be critical factors in successful adaptation to severe stressors experienced outside of school (Anthony & Cohler, 1987; Garbarino, Dubrow, Kostelny, & Pardo, 1992; Rutter, 1979).

As Figure 1.2 depicts, personal–social competence is a construction

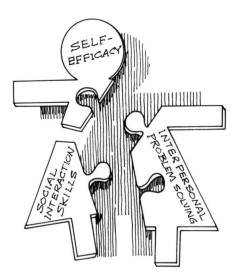

FIGURE 1.2. The puzzle metaphor of personal–social competence conveys the synergism of the three major components—self-efficacy, interpersonal problem solving, and social interaction skills.

(puzzle) that includes three major components (puzzle pieces)—self-efficacy, interpersonal problem solving, and social interaction skills. The puzzle metaphor conveys the synergism or complex interplay of these components in the development of personal–social competence. This synergism becomes explicit as we examine the theoretical and empirical bases of the three components of personal–social competence.

Self-Efficacy

Self-efficacy refers to perceived effectiveness in producing and regulating life events; that is, one's sense of competence and control (Bandura, 1977, 1982, 1986). Effectance or competence motivation refers to the intrinsic drive toward mastery, competence, and control of the environment (Harter, 1978; White, 1959). Perceived competence and effectance motivation are related, such that enhanced perceptions of competence or efficacy are associated with subsequent increases in intrinsic motivation (Harter, Whitesell, & Kowalski, 1992). The individual's perceptions of and motive toward competence are likely to influence initial attempts at coping or adaptation, the amount of effort expended, and the degree of persistence in the face of difficulty or failure (Bandura, 1977, 1982, 1986). Perceived competence is more important than actual ability in determining performance and effort (Schunk, 1990b). Success in attempts at mastery and social reinforcement of competence motivation further enhances one's sense of efficacy and motivation, and fosters internalization of a self-reward system and a set of mastery goals, which in turn influence future attempts at effecting or controlling the environment (Harter, 1978). Thus, individuals who perceive themselves as competent and are highly motivated to cope with life stresses are likely to meet such challenges with the confidence, effort, and persistence that is necessary for successful adaptation. Success and social feedback from significant others are likely to reinforce self-efficacy and motivation and facilitate future coping efforts.

Discrepancies between self-perceived competencies and socially valued (e.g., by parents and peers) competencies influence the development of self-esteem, which in turn influences mental health and social–behavioral adjustment (Harter, 1987, 1990a, 1990b, 1990c; Harter & Marold, 1991). For example, a low self-evaluation of academic competence coupled with perceptions of parental regard and support contingent on academic achievement is likely to lead to feelings of hopelessness, depression, and poor self-worth. Similarly, low self-perceptions of physical attractiveness coupled with expectations that peer acceptance and support are contingent on such attributes are likely to foster feelings of hopelessness, depression, poor self-worth, and suicidal ideation. Likewise, failure to meet normative expectations may contribute to poor self-esteem and delinquent behavior; engagement in delinquent behavior, in turn, may contribute to self-esteem enhancement as a function of social comparison with and acceptance by the delinquent peer group.

Harter portrays the self-concept as a social construction that involves the articulation and differentiation of perceptions of specific domains of competence across the life span, as a function of cognitive development and environmental influences (Harter, 1990a, 1990b, 1990c). That is, the increasing recognition of multiple aspects of the self and ultimate integration of seemingly contradictory self-perceptions are dependent on development of the capacity for abstract thinking and self-reflection (i.e., progression toward formal operations during adolescence and adulthood). Furthermore, the self-concept is influenced by the attitudes of significant others, the socially valued competencies within specific cultures, and the consistency of these attitudes and social values across contexts. In addition to the differentiation of self-perceptions about specific competencies, individuals develop an overall sense of worth or self-esteem. This global sense of worth is influenced in part by the discrepancy between perceived competencies and the value associated with those abilities. Personal value of specific competencies is influenced by the perceptions of value by significant others, particularly parents and peers. Furthermore, self-esteem is influenced by the level of perceived social support from parents and peers and the extent to which such support is dependent on meeting others' expectations or demands. Thus, relationships within both the public (e.g., classmates) and private (family) spheres are critical determinants of self-esteem and self-concept.

Similarly, self-efficacy and effectance motivation are influenced by external social and task-related factors. Social feedback about the quality of one's performance, comparison with more or less competent peers, and modeling of self-efficacy and motivation can alter an individual's sense of and motivation toward competence (Bandura, 1986; Harter, 1982, 1990c; Schunk, 1983, 1989b). Thus, a broad array of socialization agents may influence the development of self-efficacy; these include parents, siblings, peers, classmates, and teachers (Bandura, 1986). Collaborative learning activities provide particularly effective social contexts for enhancing self-efficacy and effectance motivation because of the continual availability of partners (Nastasi & Clements, 1991). In addition, task-related factors such as short-term goal setting, process-oriented goals, and performance-contingent feedback can enhance the self-efficacy of learners (Schunk & Rice, 1991). Furthermore, self-selection of goals and self-regulation of activity can foster self-efficacy (Schunk, 1990a).

Table 1.1 depicts the developmental progression of domain-specific aspects of perceived competence, as characterized by Harter and her colleagues. With increasing age, the number of domains increases and specific domains become more finely delineated. Even as young as 4 years of age, children are capable of making judgments about perceived com-

TABLE 1.1. Developmental Progression of Self-Perception, Interpersonal Problem Solving, and Social Interaction Skills

Self-perception[a]	Interpersonal problem solving[b]	Social interaction skills[c]
Early childhod (grades K–2)	Early childhood (ages 4–5 years)	Early childhood

General competence
  Cognitive competence
  Physical competence
Social acceptance
  Peer acceptance
  Maternal acceptance
	Alternative solution thinking	Comforting (primarily with family)
		Sharing & helping (especially with familiar peers)
		Interpret and respond to others' affective cues
		Differentiate affective state of self and others
		Prosocial reasoning:
		  Needs-oriented
		  Affectional-relationship
		  Approval-oriented
		  Reciprocity
		  Personal norms & preferences

Middle–late childhood (grades 3–8)	Middle childhood	Middle–late childhood

Scholastic competence
Athletic competence
Physical appearance
Social (peer) acceptance
Behavioral conduct
Global self-worth
	Alternative solution thinking
	Means-end thinking
		Sharing (with less familiar persons)
		Helping (based on self-perceived competence)
		Sensitivity to others' affective cues
		Role-taking ability reflects caring orientation
		Prosocial reasoning:
		  Approval-oriented
		  Social compliance
		  Reciprocity

Adolescence (grades 8–12)	Adolescence	Adolescence
Scholastic competence Job competence Athletic competence Physical appearance Social (peer) acceptance Close friendships	Alternative solution thinking Means-end thinking Perspective taking	Comforting to wider range of people Helping is conditional Perspective-taking and mutual role-taking ability

TABLE 1.1 *(continued)*

Self-perception[a]	Interpersonal problem solving[b]	Social interaction skills[c]
Adolescence (grades 8–12) *(cont.)*	Adolescence *(cont.)*	Adolescence *(cont.)*

Romantic appeal/relationships
Behavioral conduct/morality
Global self-worth
		Abstract, hypothetical thinking and self-reflection
		Compliance with social norms
		Internalized and co-constructed norms
		Prosocial reasoning:
		  Approval-oriented
		  Social recognition
		  Generalized reciprocity

College students (ages 17–23)	Adulthood (ages 25–35)	Adulthood	Adulthood
Intellectual ability Creativity Scholastic competence Job competence Athletic competence Physical appearance Social (peer) acceptance Close friendships Romantic relationships Parental relationships Morality Sense of humor Global self-worth	Intelligence Job competence Adequacy as a provider Household management Athletic competence Physical appearance Sociability Nurturance Intimate relationships Morality Sense of humor Global self-worth	Problem sensing Means–end thinking Consequential thinking Causal thinking	Recognize self in relation to others Contextual perspective Mutual role-taking ability Hypothetical reasoning Internalized values, norms, responsibilities Responsibility for self and others

[a]*Source*: Harter (1982, 1985a, 1988, 1990a); Harter and Pike (1984a, 1984b); Messer and Harter (1986); Neemann and Harter (1986).

[b]*Source*: Bernard and Joyce (1984); Spivack, Platt, and Shure (1976); Spivack and Shure (1974).

[c]*Source*: Berndt (1981); Berndt and Perry (1986); Colby and Damon (1992); Donenberg and Hoffman (1988); Eisenberg, Cameron, Tryon, and Dodez (1981); Eisenberg, Miller, Shell, McNalley, and Shea (1991); Eisenberg, Pasternak, Cameron, and Tryon (1984); Eisenberg and Shell (1986); Eisenberg-Berg (1979); Eisenberg-Berg and Hand (1979); Garrod, Beal, and Shin (1990); Gilligan (1982); Hoffman (1982); Ladd, Lange, and Stremmel (1983); Midlarsky and Hannah (1985); Peterson (1983); Radke-Yarrow, Zahn-Waxler, and Chapman (1983); Zahn-Waxler, Radke-Yarrow, Wagner, and Chapman (1992).

petence and social acceptance, using concrete behavioral descriptors. By 8 years of age, children also make reliable judgments about the value or importance of each dimension of perceived competence and about a general sense of personal worth (global self-worth or self-esteem).

In Harter's characterization of self-concept, sense of worth is a separate judgment or evaluation made by the individual, not the sum of multiple (separate) aspects of perceived competence. That is, evaluations of competence in specific domains are not necessarily related to each other or to global self-worth. Thus, a child can perceive himself as very competent regarding scholastic endeavors but minimally competent in interpersonal situations. Similarly, the individual can perceive herself as competent in academics, athletics, and peer interactions, but have a low overall sense of worth. Global self-worth is influenced by the discrepancies between perceived competencies and those valued by self or significant others. Thus, an individual with high levels of perceived competence may have poor self-esteem because personally or socially valued competencies are inconsistent with perceptions of actual competence. For example, a child who views herself as athletically competent but socially incompetent and who belongs to a peer group that values social but not athletic competence may have a poor sense of worth, in part because of this discrepancy.

The research of Harter and her colleagues suggests a developmental progression of self-definition (see Table 1.1). The self-concept of the young child (ages 4 to 7) includes perceptions of competence in cognitive and physical domains, and social acceptance by peers and parent (specifically, mother) (Harter, 1990a; Harter & Pike, 1984a, 1984b). At this developmental level, children do not make reliable judgments about the value or importance of these competence areas or about a global sense of worth (i.e., self-esteem, separate from domain-specific perceived competence). Harter suggested that self-esteem of the young child is best reflected in two categories of observed behavior (i.e., presented self-worth): (1) active displays of confidence, curiosity, initiative, and independence; and (2) reactive responses to change or stress (Harter, 1990a). In contrast, behavioral indices of competence, attention, persistence, activity level, friendships, or need for teacher encouragement failed to discriminate prototypic young children with high versus low self-esteem.

During middle childhood (ages 8 to 12), self-concept is characterized by five domain-specific areas of perceived competence—scholastic, athletic, physical appearance, social (peer) acceptance, behavioral conduct—and global self-worth (Harter, 1982, 1985a, 1990a). During adolescence (ages 13 to 18) three additional competence domains are delineated—job competence, close friendship, and romantic appeal—with the distinction between peer popularity and close friendship emerging in early adolescence (Harter, 1988, 1990b).

Harter distinguishes between the self-concepts of college-age (ages 17 to 23) and early adult (ages 25 to 35) populations (Harter, 1990a). The self-concept of college students includes global self-worth and 12 domains of perceived competence—intellectual, creativity, scholastic, job, athletic, physical appearance, social/peer acceptance, close friendships, romantic relationships, parent relationships, morality, and sense of humor (Neemann & Harter, 1986). Perceived scholastic competence (e.g., How successful am I in school work?) is distinguished from intellectual ability (How smart am I?) and creativity (How inventive or original are my ideas?). The adult self-concept includes global self-worth and 11 domains of perceived competence—intelligence, job, adequacy as provider, household management, athletic, physical appearance, sociability, nurturance, intimate relationships, morality, and sense of humor (Messer & Harter, 1986). In contrast to the greater differentiation of cognitive competence among college students, the self-concept of the young adult population reflects lack of differentiation in the cognitive area and greater distinction among domains related to work, home management, and family. Thus, self-concept differentiation in part reflects role differentiation.

Self-efficacy and effectance motivation are reflected in behavior and cognitions. Behavioral indicators include engagement in attempts at mastery such as self-directed problem solving or independent task completion, persistence in response to failed efforts, and displays of satisfaction or pleasure at mastery. Cognitive indicators of self-perceptions include self-evaluations of competencies and performance, self-confidence regarding ability, and attributions about success and failure. Cognitive indicators of effectance motivation include attitudes of optimism, curiosity, and enthusiasm. Thus, the individual with a high sense of academic competence and motivation is likely to attempt challenging academic tasks with minimal teacher direction and support, formulate rules to direct task performance, exert the necessary effort to succeed, persist despite failed attempts, and express satisfaction with the outcome of these efforts. This individual is also likely to express a positive view of self regarding academic abilities and to attribute successes to personal ability and effort. Furthermore, the self-efficacious, highly motivated person is likely to exhibit high levels of curiosity and enthusiasm regarding intellectual pursuits and to display self-confidence and optimism about the likely outcome of efforts.

In summary, self-efficacy is both influenced by and influences success in attempts to master the environment, control external events, solve personal and interpersonal problems, and cope with life's challenges. Furthermore, self-efficacy and self-identity are affected by and affect one's interpersonal relationships and interactions. This interaction of personal–social competence components becomes clearer as we examine interpersonal problem solving and social interaction skills.

Interpersonal Problem Solving

Interpersonal problem solving involves the application of cognitive problem-solving strategies to social or practical situations (Bernard & Joyce, 1984; Durlak, 1983; Lazarus & Folkman, 1984). Skillful social problem solvers are able to work and play cooperatively with others, resolve interpersonal conflicts, and solve everyday problems in a variety of situations. A wide repertoire of effective interpersonal problem-solving strategies provides individuals with flexibility in thinking and behavior, and thus enhances adaptability to environmental variation. Effective problem solvers are better equipped with the necessary strategies for coping with crisis and change, meeting personal goals, and satisfying personal needs. Furthermore, successful problem solving is likely to enhance self-efficacy, increasing the likelihood of future attempts to solve problems and resolve conflicts.

Problem solving refers to the process of problem definition and the selection, application, and evaluation of solution strategies. This process may be applied individually or in collaboration with others, as depicted in Figure 1.3. The interpersonal problem-solving process (Figure 1.3A) typically includes the following steps:

1. *Recognize feelings in self and others.* This step involves awareness and labeling of affective reactions, which are used as cues to problem identification. Affective reactions are defined by one's own internal physiological cues (i.e., my feelings) and others' external behavioral cues (i.e., others' feelings). This aspect of interpersonal problem solving may require intervention focused on identifying and labeling affective reactions.

2. *Identify and define the problem.* This step involves recognizing that a problem exists, defining the exact nature of the problem, and identifying the desired goal.

3. *Generate alternative solutions.* This step involves proposing possible solutions to the problem and is accomplished through brainstorming without evaluating the alternatives.

4. *Consider the consequences of each solution.* This step involves consideration of the possible outcomes of each solution identified in Step 3. Considerations include feasibility, positive and negative effects on self and others, short- and long-term consequences, and likelihood of solving the problem or reaching the goal defined in Step 2.

5. *Choose the "best" solution.* This step involves choosing one solution that is identified as most preferred, based on the considerations made in Step 4, and deciding an action plan.

6. *Implement the solution.* This step involves applying the solution chosen in Step 5. In contrast to the previous steps, which are conducted at a cognitive level, this aspect involves action toward problem resolution.

7. *Evaluate effectiveness of the solution.* This step involves reflection on the efficacy of the solution that was implemented in Step 6, as an ongoing process of monitoring or in retrospect. The obvious advantage of ongoing monitoring is that a change in strategy can be implemented immediately. The potential advantages of this reflective process are the understanding of the effects of one's actions and the identification of the conditions under

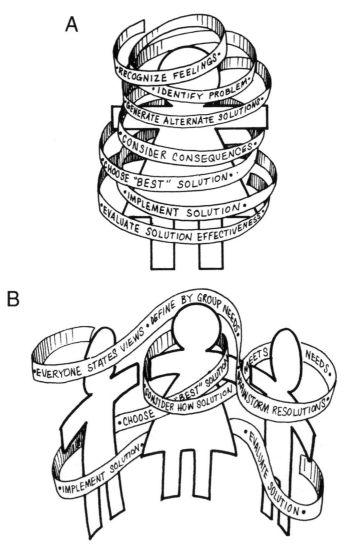

FIGURE 1.3. The interpersonal problem-solving process, applied individually (A) and collaboratively (B).

which certain solutions are likely to be successful. The ultimate goal is to develop a repertoire of effective solutions. It is critical at this step to emphasize that there is not always one best solution. In instances in which the selected solution fails, the preceding sequence of steps is repeated.

This model of interpersonal problem solving is consistent with the construct of problem-focused coping proposed by Lazarus and Folkman (1984). Problem-focused coping involves the application of cognitive and behavioral strategies for managing or altering the problem situation; that is, engaging in problem solving. In contrast, emotion-focused coping is directed toward modifying the level of emotional distress without addressing the source of distress. Emotion-focused coping is thus a more indirect process and includes such strategies as seeking social support, avoiding, self- or externalized blaming, distancing, or reappraising the situation to minimize the negative aspects and maximize the positive. Despite this distinction, the interpersonal problem-solving process may result in a decision to engage in emotion-focused coping. For example, a child living in an alcoholic family may seek the support of an extended family member in response to her fear over a parent's drinking binge. In such situations over which the child has limited control, emotion-focused coping is a more viable solution than attempting to control or change the parental drinking behavior. Such use of emotion-focused coping does not preclude the subsequent use of problem-focused coping. And, in such situations effective problem-focused coping might need to be collaborative. For example, the extended family member and the child discuss the situation with the non-drinking parent and decide on a strategy for protecting the child from potential harm.

Collaborative problem solving (Figure 1.3B) is the application of interpersonal problem solving in cooperation with others. Such collaboration requires that individuals communicate their feelings and ideas, engage in perspective taking, and negotiate an integration of ideas such that the goals of all parties are considered. The steps of collaborative problem-solving process are as follows:

1. *Each person states feelings.* This step requires that individuals explicitly communicate their feelings and listen to each other. Intervention is focused not only on helping individuals identify and label their affective reactions, but on facilitating the communication of those reactions.

2. *Define and clarify the problem in terms of needs and views of each person.* This step requires not only defining the problem from multiple perspectives, but clarifying the meaning of those definitions so that all individuals are operating from the same definition. From this discussion, goal setting can proceed.

3. *Brainstorm possible solutions.* This step requires that all parties par-

ticipate in proposing possible solutions to the problem, using a brainstorming approach.

4. *Consider how the solutions meet the needs or integrate the views of participants.* This step requires that participants discuss the possible outcomes of each solution identified in Step 3, consider the feasibility and consequences for each person, and attempt to integrate the views of all parties.

5. *Choose the "best" solution, seeking consensus or synthesis.* This step requires that individuals negotiate a single solution that best represents the views and needs of all parties. In addition, the action plan includes the roles and responsibilities for all participants. Optimally, the solution is a synthesis of discrepant views. Minimally, it should represent a consensus.

6. *Implement the solution.* This step may require specific actions on the part of some or all of the participants.

7. *Evaluate the solution process.* This final step requires reflection on the efficacy of the solution process at individual and group levels. This reflection includes consideration of both the collaborative process and the outcome (solution). When the process or the solution is deemed ineffective, the preceding sequence of steps is repeated.

A number of social skills training programs use the sequence of steps for teaching interpersonal cognitive problem solving to individuals (Bernard & Joyce, 1984; Camp & Bash, 1985; Shure, 1992; Urbain, 1982; Weissberg & Gesten, 1982; Weissberg, Gesten, Leibenstein, Doherty-Schmid, & Hutton, 1982). Conflict resolution and peer mediation training programs emphasize implementation in a collaborative or mediational mode, consistent with the collaborative process described above (Drew, 1987; D. W. Johnson, Johnson, & Dudley, 1991; D. W. Johnson, Johnson, Dudley, & Acikgoz, 1991; D. W. Johnson, Johnson, Dudley, & Burnett, 1991; Kreidler, 1984; Shrumpf, Crawford, & Usadel, 1991).

Table 1.1 presents a developmental progression of interpersonal cognitive problem solving, based on the relationship between these cognitive aspects and behavioral adjustment (Bernard & Joyce, 1984; Spivack, Platt, & Shure, 1976; Spivack & Shure, 1974). In early childhood (ages 4 to 5), the behaviorally well-adjusted child is one who is able to generate multiple solutions to problems (i.e., engage in alternative solution thinking). During middle childhood, the well-adjusted individual is able to engage in alternative solution thinking and devise steps to reach a goal (means–end thinking). The well-adjusted adolescent, in addition to effectively using alternative solution and means–end thinking strategies, is able to take the perspective of others (perspective taking). During adulthood a different set of strategies is associated with behavioral adjustment. These include awareness of a problem (problem sensing), means–end thinking, consideration of potential consequences (consequential thinking), and understanding cause–effect relationships (causal thinking). Figure 1.4 depicts the cognitive aspects of interpersonal problem solving at different developmental stages. Assessment of interpersonal cognitive problem solving should focus not only on developmentally relevant skills but also on those skills that are critical at earlier levels. Furthermore, interventions should include developmentally relevant skills and precursors of skills needed at subsequent levels.

Interpersonal problem solving incorporates cognitive, behavioral, and motivational components. The cognitive components include (1) social knowledge, or the understanding of social situations; (2) knowledge of cognitive problem-solving strategies such as those delineated above; (3) perceptions of competence with regard to solving interpersonal problems; and (4) cognitive strategies for self-control of behavior. The behavioral component encompasses the application of social knowledge and problem-solving strategies to real-life situations. The motivational component refers to the interest in solving problems or resolving conflicts. Because effective

FIGURE 1.4. Cognitive aspects of interpersonal problem solving at different developmental stages.

problem solving requires all three components, knowledge and cognitive planning are necessary but not sufficient. Failure to apply cognitive strategies may reflect a deficit in the behavioral repertoire (e.g., not knowing how to put a plan into action), in self-control (e.g., difficulty in inhibiting less adaptive behavior), or in motivation (e.g., having minimal interest in solving the problem). Furthermore, past experience may have reduced one's sense of efficacy with regard to specific situations. Thus, interventions directed toward interpersonal problem solving must embody all of the components. A closer examination of the category of social interaction skills provides additional understanding of the interplay of self-efficacy, interpersonal problem solving, and social interaction skills.

Social Interaction Skills

In this model, social interaction skills are defined as the communication patterns and behaviors necessary for interacting effectively within diverse social contexts (Lazarus & Folkman, 1984). These include skills that are important for initiating and maintaining social contacts; engaging in prosocial forms of behavior such as sharing, helping, and comforting; and exhibiting behaviors that are appropriate to contextual demands. Success in interpersonal relationships requires the affective capacity to experience the state of others (empathy), the cognitive ability to interpret physical and psychological states, and the behavioral competencies related to skillful prosocial interactions (Zahn-Waxler & Radke-Yarrow, 1990). Thus, the interpersonally skilled person is able to show care and concern for others and has a repertoire of verbal and nonverbal behaviors that facilitate cooperation and adaptation. Such adaptation requires that the individual also possesses the observational and cognitive skills necessary for determining what is appropriate to a given situation. For example, one must be sensitive to the nuances of social interactions that are cues for interpreting interpersonal dynamics and the implicit expectations of others. In addition, the ability to take the perspective of others enhances one's ability to interact with a wide variety of individuals and facilitates collaborative interactions in which negotiation of perspectives is necessary. Perspective taking is particularly important for effective collaborative problem solving, conflict resolution, and interactions with individuals from diverse backgrounds.

We use the construct of caring as the foundation for establishing and maintaining relationships. Caring is defined as a connection between human beings that reflects mutual receptivity and focuses on the interrelatedness of self and other. Care is motivated by concern for others and for establishing and maintaining relationships. The concept of care embodies the constructs of empathy and perspective taking. This definition is consistent with those of Gilligan (1982) and Noddings (1984). The ability to care for others is contingent on the capacity to care for oneself (Zahn-Waxler, 1991). The development of care proceeds from (1) caring for self, to ensure survival; to (2) caring for both self and others, thus valuing responsibility for others; to (3) recognition of interrelatedness of self and others, characterized by concern with relationships, response to others, and denunciation of exploitation and harm (Gilligan, 1982). Thus, the development of care involves an "increasing differentiation of self and other and a growing comprehension of the dynamics of social interaction" (Gilligan, 1982, p. 74). Facilitating the development of care requires four components—modeling, dialogue, practice, and confirmation (Noddings, 1984). For example, in an educational setting, students are provided with role models of individuals engaged in caring, are encouraged to communicate their ideas and personal experiences, are given opportunities to engage in caring actions, and are provided with informational feedback and social reinforcement regarding these actions.

Caring by definition requires responsiveness from both the carer (the caregiver) and the caree (the one cared for) (Noddings, 1984). That is, the carer must be open and responsive to the needs of others. The caree must be receptive to, recognize, and respond to caring actions. Consider, for example, the following caring interaction between two kindergarten students. The teacher had introduced facial depictions of feelings as a way of helping children to recognize and interpret others' affective reactions, and provided students with "feelings tags" (yarn necklaces with cardboard faces depicting various emotions; see Chapter 4). One morning, Kevin was sitting alone crying. Jamar picked up a sad-face feelings tag, walked over to Kevin, and said, "You must be feeling sad. Put this on. What happened?" Kevin told Jamar about an argument he just had with another classmate. As the conversation progressed and Kevin began to smile, Jamar returned to the feelings tags and picked up a happy face. He handed it to Kevin and said, "Now you are feeling better. Put this one on." Kevin responded with an even bigger smile and said, "Let's play."

In addition to enhancing interpersonal relationships and collaborative interactions, effective social interaction skills can facilitate coping with social stressors and academic challenges (Harter, 1987, 1990a; Lazarus & Folkman, 1984; McGinnis & Goldstein, 1990; Nelson-Le Gall, 1992; Oden, 1986). Enlisting social support and seeking help are dependent on one's ability to maintain supportive relationships and initiate social contact when needed, in addition to the capacity to recognize when such assistance is warranted. Social interaction skills also influence the extent to which one is able to solve problems and resolve conflicts collaboratively. Furthermore, successful social interactions and interpersonal relationships are likely to enhance one's perceptions of social acceptance, sense of social competence, and self-esteem, which in turn influence engagement in future interactions and relationships. To the extent that social interaction skills influence engagement in cooperative learning activities and facilitate seeking help with academic tasks, an individual's sense of competence in the academic domain also is likely to be enhanced; in turn, motivation and effort in meeting academic challenges are likely to be strengthened. Thus effective social interaction skills may have widespread influence on adaptation.

Table 1.1 presents the developmental progression of the emotional, cognitive, and behavioral aspects of caring and prosocial interaction. Even in early childhood, children demonstrate a range of prosocial and caring behaviors. Comforting is demonstrated through acts such as hugs, pats, and verbal sympathy, especially with family members and to a lesser extent with peers (Eisenberg-Berg & Hand, 1979; Zahn-Waxler, Radke-Yarrow, Wagner, & Chapman, 1992). Preschoolers help and share (Hoffman, 1982; Zahn-Waxler et al., 1992), especially with consistent playmates or with peers who share with them (Eisenberg, Cameron, Tryon, & Dodez, 1981). Young children possess the cognitive and emotional capacities to interpret affective states of others. They recognize that their feelings may differ from others and are responsive to others' affective cues (Hoffman, 1982). For example, a preschooler who encounters a tearful child is able to recognize that the child is upset and to provide solace.

Justification of prosocial moral reasoning follows a developmental progression (Eisenberg & Shell, 1986). Preschoolers and young school-age children may operate from a hedonistic, self-focused orientation. Young children, when asked why they help or share with others, justify their behaviors based on the needs of others and on the affective relationship with the helpee. For example, at a recent birthday party, when 4-year-old Trevor was asked why he helped his friend distribute party favors, he responded, "Billy's my best friend. He'll give me two toys instead of just one." Trevor spoke about both his relationship with his friend and his potential gain as a result of his helping behavior. Such responses reflect the concept of reciprocity. In addition, young children are responsive to the needs of others (needs-oriented) even when those needs conflict with their own, and they express concern for others' approval (Eisenberg, Pasternack, Cameron, & Tryon, 1984; Eisenberg-Berg, 1979). Young school-age children's intentions to help and share also are justified by their personal norms or preferences (what they should do or wanted to do) rather than perceived social norms (perceived expectations of other partner) (Berndt, 1981).

School-age children, compared to preschoolers, extend their helping and sharing to others who are less familiar and help others in a wider range of situations (Ladd, Lange, & Stremmel, 1983; Radke-Yarrow, Zahn-Waxler, & Chapman, 1983; Zahn-Waxler et al., 1992). In addition, their willingness to help seems to be related to self-perceived ability to help (Midlarsky & Hannah, 1985; Peterson, 1983). That is, a child who perceives him/herself as capable in mathematics is likely to help a peer who is having difficulty. With increased perspective taking, school-age children are more empathic and sensitive to others' needs (Berndt & Perry, 1986). Furthermore, school-age children employ caring resolutions to hypothetical and real-life moral concerns (Donenberg & Hoffman, 1988; Garrod, Beal, & Shin, 1990).

Adolescents, compared to younger children, provide comfort to a wider range of people. Helping, however, may be more restricted (Midlarsky & Hannah, 1985). For adolescents, helping is contingent on if they perceive helping to constitute interference with others, and on how congruent their helping actions are with personal values. Thus, an adolescent may not assist a peer because doing so might constitute meddling. Alternatively, a student who is a recovering alcoholic may refuse to loan money to a friend to buy beer. Despite the apparent egocentric quality of this thinking, adolescents are better able than younger children to take others' perspectives, engage in mutual role-taking, and to think and view situations abstractly. Thus, they are better able to co-construct normative standards regarding social conduct and interpersonal relationships.

Older elementary and high school students justify their prosocial behavior on the basis of approval seeking, social compliance, and social recognition and acceptance (Eisenberg & Shell, 1986; Eisenberg, Miller, Shell, McNalley, & Shea, 1991). They emphasize compliance with stereotypic (normative) behavior, although norms do not necessarily reflect authority-based rules. Instead, adolescents are able to operate from internalized norms. Furthermore, their reasoning involves self-reflection about whether they demonstrate care and concern for others and about the consequences of their actions in relation to others. The concept of reciprocity extends beyond the consideration of specific interactions to the consideration of reciprocity on a more abstract level. Older adolescents and adults appear to operate from a more internalized set of justifications based on values, norms, and responsibilities (Eisenberg & Shell, 1986).

The prosocial and caring behaviors of adults reflect the recognition of interrelatedness between and among individuals as well as with the global community (Gilligan, 1982). This emergence of care reflects the progressive differentiation of self and other and the dialectical nature of development through social interactions. In addition to mutual role-taking and hypothetical thinking, adult reasoning reflects the contextual nature of decision making.

An examination of the lives of moral exemplars, individuals who exhibit the highest level of caring, revealed the following four characteristics related to exemplary behavior (Colby & Damon, 1992): (1) certainty about the validity of personal action; (2) sense of self-efficacy and optimistic thinking; (3) sense of responsibility for personal behavior and others' welfare, and recognition of their interrelatedness; and (4) openness to moral growth. Of particular relevance to prosocial development is the responsibility for self and others. These moral exemplars were able to translate their personal, individualistic commitment to moral ideals into action on behalf of others, reflecting the ability to apply problem solving or coping skills to their personal lives and to enhance the welfare of others. Thus, the lives of these individuals reflected the interconnectedness of self-efficacy, interpersonal/collaborative problem solving, and social interaction (caring) skills. In the next section, we address the synergistic relationships among these components of personal–social competence and the multiple environments in which individuals develop.

The Synergism of Personal–Social Competence and the Environment

Across the life span, the development of personal–social competence involves a complex interplay of the three components—self-efficacy, interpersonal problem solving, and social interactions—with the multiple contexts in the individual's ecology (e.g., family, peer group, school, community). That is, self-efficacy is influenced by success in attempts to master the environment, control external events, solve problems, and cope with life's challenges. In addition, self-efficacy and global self-worth are affected by the values and conditions of acceptance from significant others, including adults and peers. These self-perceptions in turn influence concurrent and subsequent attempts to solve problems, cope with difficult situations, and establish and maintain interpersonal relationships in multiple contexts. Thus, the interplay of self-efficacy, interpersonal problem solving, and social interaction is reciprocal and complex. Furthermore, an ecological–developmental perspective suggests that these aspects of personal–social competence interact with contextual variables in a reciprocal manner across the life span. That is, early experiences in family, school, and peer group contexts influence development of personal–social competencies, which in turn influence interactions with subsequent similar environmental contexts. For example, a child growing up in an alcoholic family develops certain personal–social competencies which are adaptive to the norms of his/her family. The child's sense of efficacy, interpersonal problem solving, and social interaction skills learned within the family subsequently influence his/her interactions within other intimate relationships. Despite the critical role of the family in early development of self-concept and global self-worth, the values and behavioral standards of the peer group become increasingly important as individuals approach adolescence and adulthood. Thus, school and community contexts also provide important environments for development of personal–social competence.

Ultimately, the internalization of these experiences and the resolution of discrepancies across contexts influence the development of an integrated sense of self (Harter, 1990b, 1990c). According to Harter the extent to which social feedback across multiple contexts is distorted or in conflict may hinder the construction of a generalized other (e.g., consistent expectations and norms) and realistic self-appraisal. Failure to reconcile such discrepancies may inhibit the internalization of a coherent self-identity. Although the developmental progression of self-concept requires increasing differentiation of the self through adolescence and early adulthood, one's multiple attributes must be integrated into a coherent, unified whole during adulthood. Failure to do so may result in self-definitions characterized by continual, uncritical reliance on external standards of behavior and acceptance, which puts the individual at risk for emotional and behavioral disorders. An integrated, positive self-identity, in contrast, provides a buffer against stress and is associated with a wide range of productive coping strategies, effectance motivation, and positive emotional states. Healthy identity formation requires the development of relationships that provide opportunities for connectedness and separateness, such that the individual has a secure base of social support and acceptance but is permitted to develop personal values and beliefs. Such relationships are developed within contexts in which multiple perspectives are valued, and knowledge, beliefs, and behavioral norms are co-constructed.

Social Construction Perspective

We view socialization and learning from a social construction perspective, which is based on the premise that values, knowledge, and behavioral norms are co-constructed by the individuals within a given sociocultural context (Bearison, 1982; Berger & Luckman, 1966; Damon, 1983; Rogoff, 1990; Vygotsky 1978; Wertsch, 1991). From this perspective, social interaction and the coordination of perspectives are essential to the development of individual cognitions and behaviors and to the formation of group norms of behavior. Vygotsky (1978) suggested that development of new forms of knowledge and behavior first occurs on the social (interpsychological) plane during social exchanges. Through repeated interchange within a sociocultural context, these cognitions and behaviors are internalized; that is, transformed to the individual (intrapsychological) plane. This process has been used to explain socialization of children regarding the knowledge, values, and behavioral norms of a given culture (e.g., Rogoff, 1990). That is, children learn accepted social practices in their families and communities through interactions with adults and older children, as if through an apprenticeship in daily living. Individuals within social contexts can serve as both co-participants within and mediators of a given culture. Thus, adults and peers are important agents in the socialization process. During adolescence especially, the peer group plays a critical role as individuals explore alternatives and consolidate standards of behavior that have been transmitted through earlier exchanges with adults and older peers.

Ideally, the co-constructive process involves dialectical exchanges in which "individuals face others who contradict their own intuitively derived concepts and points of view, and thereby create cognitive conflicts whose resolutions result in the construction of higher forms of reasoning" (Bearison, 1982, p. 203). The dialectical process requires that individuals communicate their ideas, consider alternative perspectives, and negotiate the integration of perspectives. Thus, social interaction skills, perspective taking, and negotiation of perspectives are critical for knowledge acquisition and socialization. These skills are especially important in contexts in which diverse perspectives are represented. The creation of contexts in which individuals have opportunities to express discrepant ideas and negotiate perspectives both requires and facilitates the development of social interactions skills. Guided participation in such interactions provides important learning contexts. In the program we subsequently describe, adults serve as facilitators or mediators of students' social exchanges in collaborative learning contexts designed to foster both cognitive–academic and personal–social competence. Furthermore, both adults and students participate in the co-construction of a culture that fosters the development of personal–social competence of all members. In Chapter 2, we provide empirical evidence that collaborative learning is effective in enhancing cognitive, academic, social and personal competencies and in fostering appreciation of diversity.

CHILDREN OF ALCOHOLICS

In this section, we define alcoholism and briefly describe the characteristics of families affected by alcohol. In Chapter 2, we provide a more comprehensive review of research on the personal and family environment characteristics of COAs.

Alcoholism: Incidence and Definition

Despite the reported decline in drug use by youth and adults, incidence figures suggest that the war on drugs in the United States is not over (Drugs and Drug Abuse Education, 1990b). With regard to reported alcohol use (based on a national household survey), the National Institute on Drug Abuse revealed the following figures for 1990: ages 12 to 17, 24.5% (cf. 25.2% in 1988); ages 18 to 25, 63.3% (65.3%, 1988); and adults ages 26 and older, 52.3% (54.8%, 1988) (Drugs and Drug Abuse Education, 1990b).

The National Association of State Alcohol and Drug Abuse Directors reports that alcohol is still rated as the number one drug problem in the United States (Drugs and Drug Abuse Education, 1990a). Among adolescents, alcohol is the most widely used drug (National Education Goals Panel, 1992; National Institute on Alcohol Abuse and Alcoholism, 1990a). In a 1991 national survey, 54% of high school seniors reported using alcohol within the past 30 days (43%, grade 10; 25%, grade 8) (National Education Goals Panel, 1992). Incidence figures confirm the prevalence of the familial nature of alcoholism. It is estimated that 38% of the U. S. adult population has a family history of alcoholism (i.e., among biological first-, second-, and/or third-degree relatives; Harford, 1992).

Ask any 20 people to define alcoholism and you will likely find 20 definitions. Similarly, many definitions of alcoholism have been proposed by professional and lay groups. The common criteria found across definitions include the following: (1) interference with life functioning, including personal, work, or family; (2) continued use despite adverse consequences; (3) psychological or physical dependence; (4) loss of control over drinking; and (5) withdrawal symptoms upon discontinuation of drinking. Some definitions also include criteria such as marked or increasing tolerance for alcohol, drinking to feel normal, and blackouts (Brown, 1985; Goode, 1992; V. E. Johnson, 1980; Kinney & Leaton, 1987; Steinglass, Bennett, Wolin, & Reiss, 1987).

In the early 1990s, a 23-member multidisciplinary committee convened to establish a definition of alcoholism that was scientifically valid, clinically useful, and understandable for the general public (Morse & Falvin, 1992). This two-year study by the joint committee of the National Council on Alcoholism and Drug Dependence and the American Society of Addiction Medicine yielded the following definition:

> Alcoholism is a primary, chronic disease with genetic, psychosocial, and environmental factors influencing its development and manifestations. The disease is often progressive and fatal. It is characterized by impaired control over drinking, preoccupation with the drug alcohol, use of alcohol despite adverse consequences, and distortions in thinking, most notably denial. Each of these symptoms may be continuous or periodic. (p. 1013)

Although Alcoholics Anonymous (AA) offers no specific definition, it recognizes alcoholism as a progressive illness with spiritual, emotional, and physical dimensions. A salient criterion is the loss of control over drinking; that is, the alcoholic cannot predict what will happen when he/she takes the first drink. In the revised third edition of *The Diagnostic and Statistical Manual of Mental Disorders,* (DSM-III-R) (American Psychiatric Association, 1987), alcoholism is subsumed under the diagnosis of psychoactive substance dependence. This classification is characterized by "a cluster of cognitive, behavioral, and physiological symptoms that indicate that the person has impaired control of psychoactive substance use and continues use of the substance despite adverse consequences" (p. 166).

Contributing to the difficulty in defining alcoholism is the controversy about etiology. This controversy involves the alternative conceptualizations of alcoholism from medical, psychological, and sociocultural perspectives. The medical model characterizes alcoholism as a disease. From this perspective, alcoholism is a primary condition, not a secondary symptom; has a recognizable set of symptoms; has a predictable and progressive course; is chronic; and if untreated, is fatal (Jellinek, 1960; Kinney & Leaton, 1987). Consistent with the disease concept is the notion of a genetic predisposition to alcoholism, exemplified by familial alcoholism (Goodwin, 1988). According to Goodwin, this type of alcoholism is primary and characterized by a family history of alcoholism, early onset, and more severe symptomatology requiring early intervention. Support for this perspective comes from twin and adoption studies (Anthenelli & Schuckit, 1990–91; Goodwin, 1988). Such research suggests that children of alcoholics have rates of alcoholism three to five times greater than what is expected in the general population.

Psychological explanations tend to focus on "the alcoholic personality" and its behavioral correlates. These explanations vary according to different theoretical perspectives. For example, Johnson emphasizes the importance of learning in explaining the progression from "drinking to feel good" to "drinking to feel normal" (V. E. Johnson, 1980). This progression involves initially learning the relationship between alcohol use and mood alteration, then seeking mood alteration through alcohol use. This is followed by a stage of harmful dependency and ultimately use of alcohol to feel normal (i.e., mood characterized by intoxication feels normal for the individual). From a sociocultural perspective, alcohol use is influenced by values and norms inherent in the culture. This view is consistent with temperance movements, which emphasize the importance of social control (Room, 1992).

Current thinking combines elements of psychological and sociocultural perspectives, resulting in an adaptive or lifestyle model of alcohol use (Alexander, 1990; Walters, 1992). From this orientation, alcoholism is characterized as a means of coping with psychosocial stressors and incorporates the notion of choice. For example, when faced with a major life stressor the individual *chooses* drinking as a coping strategy. Subsequent addiction to alcohol results from a cycle of drinking to cope with routine life stressors and with alcohol-related problems. That is, alcohol is used to cope with problems created by its abuse.

Researchers have provided support for each of these views. No single view, however, has sufficiently addressed the complexity of alcoholism or its impact on the family. The ecological–developmental perspective provides a means for integrating the various definitions of alcoholism and for understanding its potential influence on the family system and child adjustment.

Alcoholism and the Family

Alcoholism has been characterized as a family disease in that family members participate in the dysfunctional behavior of the alcoholic by assuming individual, and complementary, dysfunctional behaviors (Brown, 1988; Jackson, 1954; Steinglass et al., 1987). The family's attempts to cope with the alcoholic follow a progressive course, paralleling the progression of alcoholism (Jackson, 1954). Thus, as the alcoholism worsens the family takes more extreme measures in order to adjust. The initial coping mechanism, a frequently identified characteristic of the family affected by alcohol, is denial. Family members, for example, deny that a problem exists by not talking about it or by adjusting family responsibilities so that the alcoholic's neglect of routine tasks is not apparent. The next stage involves attempts to eliminate the problem; for example, discarding the alcohol or encouraging the alcoholic to get help. When such efforts fail, the family system may become more disorganized. Family members are then likely to initiate efforts to reorganize in order to create a sense of normality; these attempts may resemble the early efforts of denial. When these efforts fail (and as the alcoholic's condition worsens), one or more family members may try to escape (e.g., through divorce, running away). Finally, part of the family may try to reorganize itself, in order to meet the needs of some of the members. This may involve one or more of the members seeking professional help. Assuming the entire family seeks help, the family may enter a stage of recovery and reorganization directed toward establishing a healthy system.

In the absence of intervention, the family affected by alcohol develops rules that serve to maintain the system. Figure 1.5 depicts the primary rules of the alcoholic family, as portrayed in the clinical literature (Black, 1981; Wegscheider, 1981): DON'T TALK! DON'T TRUST! DON'T FEEL! These rules, which may or may not be explicit, are assumed to maintain the dysfunctional nature of the family and to perpetuate the system of denial described earlier. In addition, such rules can interfere with the development of personal–social competence. That is, the "don't talk" rule is likely to discourage children from communicating their concerns. The "don't trust" rule implies lack of trust in other people as well as lack of trust in personal judgment; thus, it can interfere with development and maintenance of relationships and with self-efficacy. Finally, the "don't feel" rule inhibits awareness and thus appropriate expression of feelings. Furthermore, such rules preclude identification of and intervention with COAs. That is, difficulties in communicating concerns, distrust of others, diminished sense of efficacy, and denial of feel-

FIGURE 1.5. The rules of the alcoholic family—Don't talk, Don't trust, Don't feel.

ings may prevent self-identification and inhibit participation in therapeutic interventions.

Each individual's role in the family reflects the changing nature of the addicted person, typically becoming more rigid in the absence of intervention. The clinical literature portrays the rigid, maladaptive patterns as roles that individuals initially assume to stabilize the family system. Table 1.2 presents delineations of roles as depicted by several authors. These roles not only serve to maintain the alcoholic family, but help to re-create dysfunctional systems in other contexts (as suggested by the ecological model described earlier). Roles assumed in childhood can persist into adulthood and limit the flexibility of the individual in adapting to a wider range of contexts.

The cognitions and behaviors that are adaptive within the alcoholic family may interfere with development of personal–social competencies. For example, whereas the placater is seemingly independent and adapts to the needs of others, this person also is detached in social relationships and has a poor sense of control over the environment. As suggested by Figure 1.6 and Table 1.2, the external appearance may not match, and perhaps even masks, personal–social difficulties. For some children, the rigidity of role-related functioning presents a semblance of stability and coping, and thus precludes the identification of adjustment difficulties. For example, Maggie, who would be characterized as a family hero, gave the appearance of being well-adjusted. Her successes helped to maintain an image of a well-functioning family, but prevented recognition of emotional difficulties related to her low self-esteem and depression. Indeed, others dismissed her requests for help because of the external appearance of healthy adjustment.

Clinical study of individuals, primarily adults, from families affected by alcohol provides consistent documentation of the rules and roles de-

TABLE 1.2 Roles and Functions of Individuals in Families Affected by Alcohol

Black (1981)	Wegscheider (1981)	Brenner (1984)
Responsible one	**Hero**	**Superkid (responsible one)**
Provides structure and consistency Self-reliant, mature, dependable Responsible for the entire family	Often the oldest child Success in school, sports, community, clubs brings recognition to family Self-critical Poor self-esteem Sense of inadequacy Lonely	Responsible Cares for others at expense of own needs Manipulates/controls behavior of family members Socially and academically competent Home management skills Difficulty being childlike (e.g., dependent, spontaneous)
Adjuster	**Lost child**	**Adjuster**
Rolls with the punches Detached, acts without thinking or feeling Rather nondescript	Often the third/middle child Quiet, withdrawn emotionally and physically Undemanding so as not to add to family stress Appears independent Lonely, hurt Feelings of inadequacy Extended fantasy life	Flexible, adapts to others at expense of own needs Poor self-esteem and self-efficacy
Placater	**Mascot**	**Placater**
Sensitive Skilled listener Family comforter	Usually youngest Provides fun and laughter (comic relief) Diverts attention from alcoholic Hyperactive Fearful of losing contact with reality Anxious, insecure, frightened, lonely	Sensitive to and monitors moods of others Socially competent People pleaser Good listener Poor self-esteem
Acting-out child	**Scapegoat**	**Allykid**
Draws attention to self (and away from alcoholic) Often delinquent Focus of family problems	Often middle/second child Acts out to draw attention away from alcoholic Defiant Abuses drugs Angry, hurt, guilty, lonely	Manipulates others to get own needs met Demanding, dependent Poor self-control Low tolerance for frustration Poor self-esteem Academic problems Expresses anger and evokes anger from others

FIGURE 1.6. The roles of children within the alcoholic family (from left to right)—scapegoat, placater, mascot, hero, lost child.

scribed above (Black, 1981; Brenner, 1984; Wegscheider, 1981). Cross-sectional and longitudinal studies (reviewed in Chapter 2) provide evidence of differences in the characteristics and adjustment of COAs and non-COAs, but have not adequately addressed rules and role-related variables. Despite the insufficient empirical support for delineation of roles, these behavioral patterns are recommended as targets for school-based intervention (Robinson, 1989). Particularly because of the potential implications of rules and role-related variables for identification and treatment, it is imperative that systematic comparisons of COAs and non-COAs be conducted regarding these variables.

Research with children, adolescents, and adults indicates that COAs are at risk for developing mental health problems such as depression, anxiety, aggressive and delinquent behaviors, somatic disorders, academic and work-related adjustment difficulties, and alcoholism (see review of studies in Chapter 2). Furthermore, there is evidence that their personal–social competencies are less well developed. COAs, compared to non-COAs, are more likely to have low self-esteem and poor self-efficacy, difficulty establishing and maintaining intimate relationships, and less effective interpersonal problem-solving skills. These variables represent critical components of generalizable coping ability. Families affected by alcohol are less likely to provide environmental supports (e.g., through parenting practices and family relationships) and more likely to experience stressors (e.g., spousal conflict, family disruption, and physical and emotional abuse). Furthermore, these environmental stressors have been associated with maladjustment among COAs. As suggested by the aforementioned person- and environment-centered models (Elias & Branden, 1988), this combination of underdeveloped personal–social competencies and negative environmental factors increases the likelihood of adjustment problems amongst COAs. In the next chapter we review research regarding the characteristics of COAs and their family environments.

THE ROLE OF SCHOOLS

In 1986, the National Mental Health Association Commission on Prevention of Mental–Emotional Disabilities called for the development of school-based primary prevention programs (across grades kindergarten (K) through 12), claiming that personal–social competence was as critical as academic competence and suggesting the integration of personal–social and academic goals into the school curriculum (Elias & Branden, 1988). This call for school-based primary prevention parallels the rising concern about the social–behavioral and academic adjustment of several groups of at-risk children, including those from single-parent families, those living with alcoholic or mentally ill parents, or those living in poverty. Furthermore, the integration of mental health goals into academic curricula is consonant with the inclusion of drug education and prevention programs as a routine part of the school health curricula (National Education Goals Panel, 1992). Such programs, however, are not necessarily integrated across existing academic curricula and are often implemented by classroom teachers without the assistance of school-based mental health professionals.

Drug education and prevention programs provide an excellent forum for discussing alcoholism as a family phenomenon, identifying COAs, and delivering primary prevention to this population of students who are at greater risk for substance abuse than their peers from nonalcoholic families. School-based mental health professionals with the appropriate education and experience can provide valuable assistance to teachers and administrators in extending the focus of extant drug education and prevention programs (Severson & Zoref, 1991). Additionally, a comprehensive school-based drug prevention program would include intervention at a secondary level for identified COAs, treatment at a tertiary level for those students experiencing adjustment problems related to personal alcohol use or use by a family member, and parent education regarding family alcoholism and related family-based interventions. Furthermore, school–family–community partnerships are imperative. In one survey, 176 high school administrators and support personnel rated a substance abuse prevention/intervention program with a multilevel, multidisciplinary systems approach and community involvement as more effective than more narrowly focused approaches (Caudill, Kantor, & Ungerleider, 1990). In

Chapter 2, we review research relevant to the development of school-based programs. In Chapter 3, we provide guidelines for design, implementation, and evaluation of such programs. In Chapter 4, we present ESCAPE, a curriculum-based prevention program for COAs that integrates personal–social competence goals into existing academic curricula.

2

Review of Research on Children of Alcoholics and Effective Interventions

In this chapter we review research relevant to the development, implementation, and evaluation of school-based interventions for COAs. First, we review research on the characteristics of COAs regarding their personal–social competence and their behavioral, academic–occupational, and health-related adjustment. We also examine environmental variables that characterize the family system affected by alcohol and that contribute to children's adjustment within these families. Secondly, we review the literature on substance abuse (alcohol and other drugs) prevention programs, with a specific focus on outcome variables relevant to the needs of COAs. Third, we provide an empirical basis for the essential components of the curriculum-based program presented in subsequent chapters.

CHARACTERISTICS OF CHILDREN OF ALCOHOLICS

Appendix 2A presents the methodology and findings of selected studies that compare the personal–social characteristics; behavioral, academic–occupational, and health-related adjustment; and family environments of individuals in families affected by alcohol (COAs) and/or other substance abuse (COSAs) with their counterparts (i.e., non-COAs or non-COSAs, respectively). Most of the studies focus on a specific age group (children, adolescents, college students, adults); however, a few are longitudinal (e.g., following subjects from adolescence to adulthood). Some of the studies compare subgroups of COAs/COSAs; for example, those receiving treatment versus those untreated, or those with parents diagnosed versus un-diagnosed for substance abuse. Our discussion is focused on the criterion variables most relevant to the theoretical model presented in Chapter 1.

Personal–Social Competence

Within the ecological–developmental model presented in the previous chapter, personal–social competence variables are important mediators of the effects of environmental stressors on the adjustment of COAs. Furthermore, the development of such competencies among COAs is an important focal point of intervention. Only a limited amount of research regarding the characteristics of COAs has addressed personal–social competence, with the majority of this work focused on indices of adjustment that theoretically are influenced by competence. We first examine the existing research for each of the major components of personal–social competence—self-efficacy, interpersonal problem solving, and social interaction skills.

Self-Efficacy

Research findings provide some support for the clinical data suggesting that COAs have poorer self-efficacy, -concept, or -esteem, at least among older populations. Studies of college-age and other adult populations revealed lower levels of positive self-appraisal, -regard, and -acceptance; higher levels of self-criticism and -deprecation; greater need to control internal (e.g., emotions) and external events; and lower sense of personal power (Berkowitz & Perkins, 1988; Fisher, Jenkins, Harrison, & Jesch, 1992; Jarmas & Kazak, 1992; Jones & Houts, 1992; Knoblauch & Bowers, 1989; Slavkin, Heimberg, Winning, & McCaffrey, 1992; Velleman, 1992). Examination of subgroups of adult COAs suggests that this population is not homogeneous. For example, greater self-criticism was found only for female COAs (Berkowitz & Perkins, 1988). Less positive self-appraisal of personal problem solving was evident only for alcohol-abusing children of problem drinkers (COPDs) compared to alcohol-abusing non-COPDs (Slavkin et al., 1992). College-age COAs seeking treatment reported lower levels of self-regard and -acceptance, and lower sense of personal power, compared to those not seeking treatment and to non-COAs; self-reports from the latter two groups failed to show significant differences (Barnard & Spoentgen, 1986).

Only a few studies of school-age populations included variables relevant to self-efficacy, self-concept, or self-esteem. Results of one study suggest that school-age COAs and their parents underestimate the academic competence of these children (J. L. Johnson & Rolf, 1988). In another study, high school-age COAs, self-identified using the Children of Alcoholics Screening Test (CAST; Jones, 1981), reported poorer self-esteem than non-COAs (Roosa, Sandler, Beals, & Short, 1988). A study of a high-risk, urban, predominantly Black* adolescent population failed to provide support for differences in self-concepts of COSAs and non-COSAs (Gross & McCaul, 1990–91).

Interpersonal Problem Solving

Researchers have devoted insufficient attention to the study of interpersonal problem-solving skills of COAs. The only direct evidence regarding specific problem-solving skills of COAs comes from a study of college-age students, self-identified as COPDs or non-COPDs (Slavkin et al., 1992). Subjects were asked to generate all possible solutions to hypothetical interpersonal and noninterpersonal problems within an analogue context, and solutions were then rated for effectiveness (by trained raters). An effective solution is one that eliminates the problem with maximum positive and minimum negative short- and long-term personal and social consequences. In response to specific hypothetical problems, individuals in general generated more effective "first" solutions than second or third. COPDs generated more effective solutions than non-COPDS, for the first solution only. Later-born COPDs generated the most effective first solutions. These findings suggest that COA/COPDs might possess a repertoire of highly effective solutions, yet be limited in the number of effective alternatives they can generate at any given time. The performance of later-born COA/COPDs may reflect the modeling of effective solutions by older siblings.

Indirect evidence about problem solving comes from a study of school-age COAs and non-COAs (ages 5 to 17), which included measures of Type A personality—impatience/aggression, competition, energy, leadership, and alienation (Manning, Balson, & Xenakis, 1986). The Type A behavior pattern was defined as "a relatively chronic struggle to achieve a series of poorly defined goals in the shortest period of time possible" (p. 184). From our perspective, this pattern of behaviors reflects poor problem-solving skills related to goal setting, thus providing an indirect measure of problem solving. Results revealed higher levels of impatience/aggression for COAs than non-COAs, based on mothers' ratings. Findings also indicated differences within the COA population. Specifically, fathers rated first-born COAs as more competitive than their siblings. Youth self-reports failed to provide evidence of between or within group differences.

Interpersonal problem-solving skills are reflected not only in specific cognitive and behavioral responses to problematic or stressful situations,

*Terms denoting race reflect the terminology of the original authors (e.g., African American, Anglo, Black, White, Causcasian).

but also in an individual's emotional responsiveness and attempts to cope with the emotional expression of others. Because of the relatively high level of conflict in alcoholic homes and the relationship of conflict to child adjustment (discussed in a subsequent section), the response of children to anger and conflict among adults is of particular importance. The results of one study failed to document differences between COAs and non-COAs in children's (ages 6 to 10) responsiveness to videotaped depictions of adults' anger (Ballard & Cummings, 1990). Children in both groups perceived angry expressions as more negative than friendly expressions, perceived adults who appeared angry to have more negative feelings toward children, and expressed more anger and distress in response to adults' angry expressions. Gender differences in response to adults' angry expressions varied as a function of family alcoholism. That is, male COAs responded to adults' angry expressions with less anger than female COAs; whereas male non-COAs responded with more anger than their female counterparts. COAs and non-COAs differed in their proposed solutions to the videotaped adult interactions. COAs proposed more solutions, particularly with regard to using indirect strategies (e.g., attempting to make the adults feel better vs. intervening directly to resolve the conflict).

A retrospective study of the self-reported coping strategies of young adults (ages 18 to 23) indicated that COAs, compared to non-COAs, were more likely to appraise real-life disruptive family situations as unchangeable and to use specific emotion-focused coping strategies characterized by wishful thinking, seeking help, and/or avoidance (e.g., sleeping, eating, smoking, or drinking; Clair & Genest, 1987). COAs reported greater differential use of emotion-focused (attempts to alter one's emotional response) than problem-focused (attempts to alter the problem situation) coping; non-COAs did not differ significantly in the preference for emotion- versus problem-focused coping. The results of these two studies (Ballard & Cummings, 1990; Clair & Genest, 1987) support the notion that COAs may not be well prepared for coping with interpersonal problems. That is, they may use indirect or emotion-focused strategies that help them cope emotionally with the problem situation without eliminating the source of distress. Furthermore, the study by Slavkin et al. (1992) suggests that COAs may rely on a restricted range of highly effective solutions, thus limiting flexibility of adaptation. Such findings have implications for intervention, and they warrant replication.

The dearth of studies that have examined the characteristic interpersonal problem-solving skills of COAs is especially noteworthy for several reasons. First, as we discussed in Chapter 1, good problem solvers are better equipped to cope with crisis and change, set and meet personal goals, and adapt to environmental variation. These skills might be especially critical for coping with the environmental stressors common to the COA population (as described in a later section). In addition, the available evidence suggests that COAs may be ill equipped to cope with such inter-personal problem situations. Furthermore, interpersonal problem-solving skills are among the predominant cognitive–behavioral targets of existing school-based intervention programs available to COAs (i.e., through sub-stance abuse prevention programs). (We review specific intervention stud-ies in a later section of this chapter.)

Social Interaction Skills

None of the research on the characteristics of elementary and secondary school-age COAs included specific social interaction variables. One study of 62 COAs, ages 6 to 16 (Calder & Kostyniuk, 1989), included a measure of social acceptance and social competence (the Social Skills subscale of the Personality Inventory for Children, PIC; Wirt, Lachar, Klainedinst, & Seat, 1984). Parent ratings indicated significantly poorer social skills for COAs compared to the norm population, with 5% of the COA sample scoring in the clinical range (i.e., two standard deviations above the mean). Results suggest that school-age COAs are less socially competent and less successful in peer relationships than the general population of same-age peers. Such findings warrant replication.

The few studies that have examined specific social interaction skills of COAs used college-age samples and yielded equivocal findings. One study revealed differences between college-age COAs and non-COAs in self-reported interpersonal orientation. Specifically, male COAs reported a stronger orientation toward independence/autonomy compared to their non-COA counterparts; this comparison was nonsignificant for females (Berkowitz & Perkins, 1988). In another study, the self-reports of college-age COAs seeking treatment (i.e., participation in an educational support group for COAs on a college campus) indicated a lower ability for forming meaningful intimate contacts, compared to both COAs not seeking treat-ment and non-COAs (Barnard & Spoentgen, 1986). In comparison to the other groups, the COAs not seeking treatment viewed themselves as the most able to form intimate relationships. These findings suggest that the self-perceived capacity to form supportive relationships may be a deter-mining factor in the self-perceived well-being of adult COAs. Alternatively, perceived inability to form such relationships may motivate COAs to seek support within a therapeutic or self-help context. The findings of these two studies further emphasize the heterogeneity of the COA population and the need to examine both group and individual differences.

The reason for the scarcity of research on specific social interaction skills of COAs might be the overemphasis on this group as a clinical popula-tion and the concomitant inclusion of indicators of pathology, rather than competence (Barnard & Spoentgen, 1986). This emphasis is evident in the next section on behavioral and academic–occupational adjustment.

Behavioral, Academic–Occupational, and Health-Related Adjustment

A number of studies comparing COAs and non-COAs have included indices of psychological adjustment, reflecting successful adaptation to social, academic, or work contexts, or coping with stress; and health-related adjustment variables such as somatic disorders and substance abuse (see Appendix 2A). Examination of longitudinal and *ex post facto* research provides consistent evidence that COAs are at greater risk for psychological and health-related difficulties from childhood through adulthood, compared to their non-COA counterparts. In general, COAs score higher on measures of depression, anxiety, delinquency, somatic disorders, and substance abuse, and lower on indices of academic or work/job adjustment. They are also more likely to receive psychiatric diagnoses (e.g., DSM-III behavioral and substance abuse diagnoses; American Psychiatric Association, 1982), though not necessarily more likely to receive special education for learning or behavioral problems. We examine findings by developmental level.

Elementary and secondary school-age COAs, compared to their non-COA counterparts, experience more behavioral and academic difficulties. Parent and self-reports indicate a higher prevalence of depression, anxiety, delinquency, behavioral maladjustment, somatic complaints, and alcohol and other drug use (Ballard & Cummings, 1990; Gross & McCaul, 1990–91; J. L. Johnson, Boney, & Brown, 1990–91; Roosa, Beals, Sandler, & Pillow, 1990; Roosa, Gensheimer, Ayers, & Short, 1990; Roosa et al., 1988; Weintraub, 1990–91). Parent ratings of their children's behavioral adjustment on the Child Behavior Checklist (CBCL; Achenbach, 1991b) indicated a higher frequency of total behavior problems for elementary-age (6 to 10 years) COAs than non-COAs (Ballard & Cummings, 1990). Adolescent, self-identified COAs report higher levels of anxiety and depression (Roosa, Beals, Sandler, & Pillow, 1990). Comparison of COAs to the norm population of the PIC (Wirt et al., 1984) indicated higher mean scores on 11 of the 12 clinical scales (excluding Intellectual), with scores on Delinquency, Depression, and Withdrawal scales greater than 1 standard deviation above the mean (Calder & Kostyniuk, 1989). Examination of individual profiles revealed overrepresentation of COAs in the clinical range (4:1). Specifically, 21%, 15%, and 13% of the sample scored within the clinical range on Delinquency, Depression, and Withdrawal scales, respectively. Despite these findings, the majority of the sample scored within the normal range and a specific clinical profile for COAs was not evident. Indeed, the variability in individual profiles reflected the heterogeneity of the COA population.

Teacher reports and standardized test performance indicate more academic difficulties (e.g., in reading and mathematics) among COAs compared to non-COAs (J. L. Johnson et al., 1990–91; Weintraub, 1990–91).

In addition, the rates of school dropout, grade retention, and referrals to school psychologists are higher for COAs (National Institute on Alcohol Abuse and Alcoholism, 1990b). Research on Fetal Alcohol Syndrome (FAS) and Fetal Alcohol Effects (FAE) suggests that children born to alcoholic and alcohol-abusing mothers are at risk for mental disabilities, hyperactivity, learning difficulties, and psychosocial problems (Coles & Platzman, 1992; National Institute on Alcohol Abuse and Alcoholism, 1991a; Phelps & Grabowski, 1992; Streissguth et al., 1991; Streissguth, Sampson, & Barr, 1989). Specifically, children with FAS/FAE are more likely than non-FAS/FAE peers to exhibit impulsiveness, social withdrawal, dependency, antisocial behavior, speech and hearing impairments, poor motor coordination, and cognitive difficulties related to memory, problem solving, and attention. Furthermore, many of these difficulties persist into adulthood.

Despite the higher prevalence of behavioral and academic difficulties among COAs and the risk associated with FAS, at least one study suggests that COAs do not necessarily receive special education services (Stern, Kendall, & Eberhard, 1991). Stern and colleagues failed to find differences among COAs with regard to educational placement (i.e., regular education vs. special education for students with learning disabilities or emotional disturbance). Experts on children born to alcoholic and other drug-addicted mothers have cautioned practitioners against considering these children as a homogeneous group with a clearly identifiable profile of functioning (Delapenha, 1992; Griffith, 1992; Horgan, Rosenbach, Ostby, & Butrica, 1991; D. J. Johnson & Cole, 1992; Lecca & Watts, 1993; National Institute on Alcohol Abuse and Alcoholism, 1991a; Office of Substance Abuse Prevention, 1992; Welch & Sokol, 1992). Instead, assessment and intervention should address specific needs of the individual child. Furthermore, they recommend (1) an inclusive educational approach with school-age drug-exposed children (i.e., integration into regular education programs); (2) early intervention with these at-risk children and their families (e.g., preschool programming consistent with Public Law 99-457); (3) primary prevention with women of child-bearing age (e.g., through wide-scale drug education); and (4) early identification and treatment of substance-abusing pregnant women (i.e., in lieu of prosecution). (The National Association for Perinatal Addiction Research and Education, NAPARE, is an excellent resource for information regarding research, prevention, and intervention with drug-exposed infants and children, including those exposed to fetal alcohol; see the resource list in Chapter 6).

Longitudinal studies provide support for the concern about long-term effects of family alcoholism on child adjustment. One 33-year study of adolescent males revealed poorer overall adjustment during adolescence and higher incidence of personality and alcohol dependence disorders in adulthood among COAs compared to non-COAs (Drake & Vaillant, 1988). Of these adult COAs, 28% received a diagnosis of alcohol dependence, and 25% were diagnosed with personality disorder. Furthermore, specific adjustment problems in adolescence predicted specific psychiatric difficulties in adulthood. For example, school behavior problems during adolescence predicted alcohol dependence in adulthood, and feelings of inadequacy during adolescence predicted adult personality disorder. A retrospective study of adult COAs suggested that use of emotion-focused coping during adolescence predicts a tendency toward depression and poor self-esteem in early adulthood (Clair & Genest, 1987). In particular, coping through self-blame was related to depressive tendencies.

A study of children (ages 7 to 16) whose parents were diagnosed with psychiatric disorders, with and without substance abuse (comorbid and psychiatric diagnosis groups, respectively) confirmed the at-risk status of both groups, compared to children whose parents were diagnosis free (Weintraub, 1990–91). Individuals in both at-risk groups were more likely to experience difficulties related to social–emotional and academic–occupational competence and substance abuse, from childhood through adulthood. The comorbid group showed the highest levels of maladjustment. Specifically, children in the two at-risk groups exhibited more externalizing and conduct problems, academic difficulties, school dropout, and alcohol and drug abuse than their counterparts in the diagnosis-free group; the comorbid group exhibited the highest levels. In adulthood, the incidence of psychiatric diagnoses was higher among the at-risk groups (30–40%, compared to 9% for the diagnosis-free group). Those in the comorbid group (i.e., having a parent with both alcoholism and psychiatric disorder) were most likely to receive diagnoses of depression, antisocial personality, and substance abuse disorder, and to rate themselves as less socially and occupationally competent. The combined risk for substance abuse and psychiatric disorders in this sample is consistent with research findings for adult alcoholics. That is, alcoholics are 21 times more likely than nonalcoholics to receive a diagnosis of antisocial personality and approximately 2 times more likely to receive a diagnosis of major depressive disorder (National Institute on Alcohol Abuse and Alcoholism, 1991b).

Family Environment

Researchers have examined family environment variables both as characteristics of families affected by alcohol and as moderators of the adjustment of COAs. Comparisons of family environment variables suggest that families affected by alcoholism and other drug abuse, compared with those unaffected by substance abuse, are more likely to be characterized by spousal and parent–child conflict, physical and emotional abuse, poor parental functioning, family disorganization, family disruption (e.g., through separation and divorce), and related environmental stressors.

These findings apply to children, adolescents, and adults affected by family alcoholism.

Information about family environments of children and adolescent COAs comes from a number of sources. Structured interviews with family members (parents and school-age children) reveal alcoholic family environments characterized by higher levels of marital and parent–child conflict, physical and emotional abuse, and poorer parental functioning compared to nonalcoholic family environments (Reich, Earls, & Powell, 1988). Parents of school-age COAs (ages 6 to 16) rate their family functioning (on the Family Relations scale of the PIC) as significantly more problematic than the general population, with 30% of the parents reporting difficulties at a clinical level (Calder & Kostyniuk, 1989). Self-reports by parents of elementary-age children (ages 6 to 10) indicate higher levels of marital distress and verbal and physical conflict in families with a diagnosed or self-identified alcoholic parent (Ballard & Cummings, 1990). Data from social service records and interviews with family members of adolescent COAs suggest a similar pattern of family environment stressors, characterized by poor parent–child relationships, physical abuse, and family disruption (e.g., separation from parents) (Drake & Vaillant, 1988). Self-identified adolescent COAs report a higher incidence of negative life events and lower incidence of positive life events compared to their non-COA counterparts (Roosa, Beals, Sandler, & Pillow, 1990). In particular, COAs report higher levels of negative stressors characterized by family conflict (Roosa, Gensheimer, Ayers, & Short, 1990).

Adult COAs, compared to non-COAs, characterize their family-of-origin systems as less consistent, organized, and cohesive, with family interactions characterized by lower intellectual orientation, poorer communication, less positive regard and emotional expressiveness, and greater conflict and physical and sexual abuse (Clair & Genest, 1987; Jarmas & Kazak, 1992; Jones & Houts, 1992). Fewer adolescent COAs and COSAs live in intact, nuclear (two-parent) families (Drake & Vaillant, 1988; Gross & McCaul, 1990–91). That is, they are more likely to be living with one parent due to separation, divorce, or death, or to be living with relatives or in foster care. COAs also report a greater number of alcoholic relatives in addition to the alcoholic parent than do non-COAs (Drake & Vaillant, 1988), suggesting that the family environment related to alcoholism may encompass and be influenced by the extended family. Drinking problems amongst adult COAs are greater for individuals with both an alcoholic parent and grandparent (Perkins & Berkowitz, 1991). From an ecological viewpoint, such findings suggest that the impact of family alcoholism is potentially both direct (through nuclear family dynamics) and indirect (through interactions of the extended and nuclear family). Alternatively, genetic transmission is a viable explanation for the consistency of alcoholism among biological relatives.

Differences in family environment variables may reflect the impact of the alcoholic parent's personal–social functioning. As we discussed previously, adjustment (psychiatric) difficulties may co-occur with alcoholism. The findings from one study suggest that family disorganization may be related more to the psychiatric status of the alcoholic parent than to alcoholism alone (Weintraub, 1990–91). Family disorganization was defined by high levels of conflict, poor marital adjustment, and low levels of cohesiveness, warmth, and stability. Families in which one parent was diagnosed for both alcohol abuse and psychiatric disorder, or for psychiatric disorder alone, exhibited more disorganization than those in which parents were diagnosis free. In another study, adult male alcoholic military veterans (in treatment), compared to nonalcoholic male veterans, reported attitudes that were less supportive of child-rearing practices such as encouraging verbalization and emotional expression and avoiding harsh punishment, and they were more tolerant of aggression in children, irresponsibility of father, and inconsiderateness toward spouse (Pease & Hurlbert, 1988). Differences were not found to correlate with age, race, social class, or fatherhood status. The extent to which such attitudes were reflected in actual child-rearing practices was not assessed. Nevertheless, these studies suggest the importance of examining the influence of the alcoholic parent's personal functioning on the family environment. From an ecological perspective, each member (and thus each individual's behavior) contributes to the functioning of the system. Examination of the role of each family member in creating and maintaining the family ecology is critical to understanding the impact of alcoholism and designing effective interventions.

In addition to documenting differences between the family environments of COAs and non-COAs, research suggests that variations of these environmental factors account for variations in adjustment within the COA population. In particular, family disharmony and disorganization, poor parent–child relationships, poor parenting practices, and environmental stressors have been associated with adjustment difficulties among children, adolescents, and adults with an alcoholic parent. The results of one study suggest that the higher frequency of behavior problems among elementary-age COAs (ages 6 to 10) is mediated by marital distress and parental conflict (Ballard & Cummings, 1990). Among one group of school-age COAs (ages 6 to 17), psychiatric diagnoses related to behavioral maladjustment were associated with greater exposure to the effects of parental drinking (e.g., seeing a parent drunk, fear of embarrassment due to parental intoxication), more parent–child conflict, and less parent–child interaction (Reich et al., 1988).

Studies of adolescents also support the contention that environmental variables related to family alcoholism mediate the relationship between parental alcoholism and child adjustment difficulties. Stressful life events, for example, may mediate the relationship between family alcoholism and mental health status of COAs (Roosa, Beals, Sandler, & Pillow, 1990; Roosa, Gensheimer, Ayers, & Short, 1990). COAs are more likely than their non-COA peers to experience negative life events and less likely to experience positive events. High levels of negative events and low levels of positive events in turn are correlated with symptoms of depression and anxiety, which are experienced more frequently by COAs. In particular, family conflict rather than drinking behavior of the alcoholic parent accounted for the relationships between negative life events and symptomatology. Furthermore, adjustment difficulties of male COAs in adolescence and adulthood may be mediated by the quality of parent–child relationships in adolescence (Drake & Vaillant, 1988). In particular, a poor maternal relationship was related to adjustment difficulties in adolescence and diagnosis of personality disorder in adulthood. These longitudinal findings are consistent with those of retrospective studies of adult COAs. For example, adult COAs' reports of adjustment difficulties in childhood (e.g., symptomatology, friendship problems, conflict between home–peer environments) and adulthood (e.g., low self-esteem, dissatisfaction, negative self-perception, anxiety, depression) were explained by parental disharmony rather than parental drinking. When disharmony was not reported, COAs did not differ significantly from non-COAs on adjustment variables (Velleman & Orford; cited in Velleman, 1992).

Research with the general population provides additional support for the association of family disharmony (e.g., marital conflict, parent–child relationship difficulties) and adjustment difficulties that persist into adulthood (Velleman, 1992). Velleman's review of research in the United States and other countries suggests that marital conflict is the most powerful predictor among family environment variables (e.g., divorce, poverty, mental health problems of parents) of child and adolescent antisocial and delinquent behavior. In addition, existing research suggests that marital disharmony mediates the relationship between parental mental illness and child conduct disorders. Furthermore, findings of marital disharmony, divorce, and poor parent–child relationships among grandparents of delinquent boys lend support to the concept of intergenerational transmission of family dynamics. Both retrospective and prospective studies of adults in the general population support the relationship of family disharmony and adjustment difficulties. For example, findings from retrospective studies suggest that family disharmony is a critical predictor of adult maladjustment (e.g., suicide, substance abuse, marital problems). In addition, prospective studies of families with high levels of discord document a relationship between the quality of family and parent–child relationships and adult adjustment, particularly with regard to antisocial disorders. Furthermore, prospective studies of presumably healthy individuals indicate that adult difficulties are associated with parental and familial relationship difficulties. This body of research suggests that family discord, reflected in parental or parent–child relationships, increases the risk of childhood and adulthood adjustment problems. Although much of this work has focused on male populations and the incidence of conduct disorders, there is evidence of a link between family disharmony and adjustment difficulties of females, particularly with regard to internalized disorders.

One caveat warrants consideration. Much of the work regarding the influence of parental alcoholism during childhood on the adjustment of adult COAs is based on retrospective reports by young adults, particularly within college populations. In many of these studies, COAs are self-identified based on their perceptions of parental alcohol use, and their reports of adolescent and childhood experiences are retrospective. In addition, subjects are often self-selected. These adult studies generally confirm correlational and longitudinal studies of children and adolescents, regarding the role of family environment variables as mediators between parental alcoholism and adjustment. The consistency of findings with regard to family environment, adjustment of COAs, and the relationship between these sets of variables suggests that the impact of these childhood experiences persists into adulthood. However, well-designed prospective longitudinal research is needed to confirm the available evidence.

In conclusion, research supports clinical evidence of adjustment difficulties and family dysfunction related to family alcoholism. Furthermore, family disharmony related to parental alcoholism may mediate both short- and long-term connections between parental alcoholism and child adjustment. Such research confirms the need to intervene with families affected by alcohol and points to both child and family variables as foci of intervention.

Our school-based approach to intervention uses the classroom as the context for development of the personal–social competence of COAs to prepare them better to cope with the environmental stressors related to family alcoholism. We also recommend direct intervention with identified COAs who are at-risk for or are currently experiencing adjustment difficulties. The primary focus on the child does not preclude the need for direct intervention with families. In the next chapter, we address the role of the school psychologist and other school personnel with regard to procuring such services for identified COAs.

SUBSTANCE ABUSE PREVENTION PROGRAMS

In this section, we review research on the effectiveness of school-based intervention programs that are designed to prevent the abuse of alcohol and other drugs. These programs typically include components related to education about alcohol and other drugs and enhancement of personal–social competencies for resisting drugs. The personal–social competencies that are integral to many of the programs are consistent with the model of personal–social competence that we propose. Existing drug education and prevention programs address, at least indirectly, the needs of COAs; for example, through drug education and resistance skill enhancement. These programs also provide potential contexts for addressing more directly the needs of COAs; for example, through education about family alcoholism and skill enhancement related to coping with family crisis. Because of the high-risk status of COAs for substance abuse in adolescence and adulthood, drug education and prevention programs are of particular importance for this population. Thus, examination of the extent to which they address the needs of COAs is critical in the evaluation of such programs.

Risk and Protective Factors for Adolescent and Early Adult Substance Abuse

Substance abuse prevention programming is predicated on the assumption that education about drugs and their effects and the development of certain personal–social competencies will prevent individuals from abusing alcohol and other drugs. In particular, such programs target the middle school years and early adolescence as critical periods for prevention efforts, in order to prevent the onset of substance abuse in adolescence and early adulthood. Selection of content and target skills should thus be guided by scientific knowledge about the risk and protective factors related to substance abuse by adolescents and young adults. Hawkins and his colleagues (Hawkins, Catalano, & Miller, 1992) provide a comprehensive review of research regarding individual, interpersonal, and contextual factors that contribute to the risk of substance abuse among adolescents and young adults, and they discuss protective factors that may serve to reduce the level of risk. Their framework is consistent with the person- and environment-centered perspective proposed by Elias and Branden (1988) to explain the incidence of mental health problems, which we use as a framework for discussing personal–social competence (this perspective is described in detail in Chapter 1).

Despite attempts to change societal norms regarding substance use, the risk factors identified by Hawkins and colleagues (Hawkins et al., 1992) have shown stable relationships with substance abuse (e.g., over the past two decades). The presence of multiple risk factors increases the risk for substance abuse; that is, the more factors present, the greater the risk. The risk factors identified by Hawkins et al. are related to both substance abuse and poor social competence (e.g., as reflected in adjustment or mental health problems). In addition, the protective factors correspond to the components of our personal–social competence model (presented in Chapter 1). Therefore, information about risk and protective factors is critical to development of prevention programming focused on enhancing personal–social competence and preventing substance abuse. We use the Hawkins et al. review as a basis for discussing these factors and for examining the research on substance abuse prevention programming.

Contextual or environmental factors include (1) norms and laws that promote drug use and availability, (2) extreme economic deprivation, and (3) neighborhood disorganization indicated by factors such as high density, physical deterioration, high crime rates, and illegal drug trafficking (Hawkins et al., 1992). These environmental variables are most appropriately targets for intervention at a societal or community level. Individual and interpersonal variables are more suitable targets for school-based interventions.

Physiological, cognitive, emotional, and behavioral variables comprise individual risk factors (Hawkins et al., 1992). Physiological variables related to abuse of alcohol and other drugs include biochemical (e.g., platelet monoamine oxidase activity and the enzyme aldehyde dehydrogenase) and genetic (e.g., genetic predisposition to alcoholism for male COAs) factors. The cognitive variables are attitudes and beliefs that favor drug abuse and that reflect a low degree of commitment to school (e.g., perceived relevance of course work, attitude toward school). Behavioral and emotional factors that predict substance abuse in adolescence include early and persistent adjustment problems, such as frequent negative mood states, withdrawal, difficult temperament, emotional distress, antisocial behavior, hyperactivity, attention deficit disorder, and aggression (particularly in males). Those indicators specifically related to school functioning include misconduct, truancy, poor academic performance, school failure, early dropout, and special education placement. During the early elementary years, those variables related to social rather than academic school adjustment appear to be more important indices of risk for later drug abuse. In addition, early onset of drug use (e.g., before age 15) predicts subsequent drug misuse. For example, early onset is related to greater frequency of substance use, use of more dangerous drugs, and greater involvement in use of other drugs, crime, and drug dealing.

Interpersonal risk factors include family and peer environments, peer relationships, and alienation and rebelliousness (Hawkins et al., 1992). Family environment variables that predict substance abuse in adolescence and early adulthood correspond to those variables that are associated with family alcoholism and that mediate the impact of alcoholism on COAs. That is, family conflict, quality of parenting and of parent–child relationships, inconsistency of parenting and family management, and excessively severe and inconsistent punishment are all related to substance abuse. In addition, substance abuse is predicted by the family norms regarding use of alcohol and other drugs. These norms are reflected in attitudes of family members about alcohol and other drugs, number of household drug users, siblings' substance use, and the modeling of substance abuse within the family. Peer norms are also important predictors of an individual's substance abuse, such that association with peers who use drugs is consistently among the strongest predictors across diverse ethnic groups (Caucasian, African-, Asian-, Hispanic-American) and is a stronger predictor than parental use. Peer relationships, however, can have a positive influence. Peer rejection in the elementary grades, for example, has an indirect relationship to adolescent substance abuse. That is, early rejection predicts adolescent school problems and criminality, which predict adolescent drug abuse. Finally, alienation and rebelliousness, reflecting disconnection from the norms of society, are related to adolescent substance abuse and delinquency. Indicators of such disconnection include alienation from the dominant values of society, high tolerance for deviance, low religiosity, normlessness, and strong need for independence.

In conclusion, the individual and interpersonal risk factors related to substance abuse in adolescence and early adulthood correspond to the personal and environmental variables that characterize the personal–social adjustment and family environment of COAs. This parallel substantiates the at-risk status of COAs and the particular relevance of substance abuse education and prevention programs for this population. Furthermore, drawing from their own work and from research on resiliency by Garmezy and Rutter, Hawkins and his colleagues (Hawkins et al., 1992) identified as protective factors (1) certain personal–social competencies, namely self-efficacy, social problem solving, interpersonal relationships; and (2) social environments that support coping efforts and have norms that are antithetical to drug abuse. These protective factors are consistent with the personal–social competence and environmental variables (described in Chapter 1) that underlie our model of intervention. In the next section, we review research on the efficacy of school-based substance abuse prevention programs, with specific attention to their focus on critical risk and protective factors.

Efficacy of School-Based Substance Abuse Prevention Programs

The effectiveness of school-based substance abuse education and prevention has become particularly important in light of the National Education Goals adopted in 1989 (National Education Goals Panel, 1992). Goal 6 calls for the provision of safe, disciplined, and drug-free schools. The objectives include developing comprehensive K–12 drug and alcohol preventive education programs to be integrated into health curricula. In addition, the Drug-Free Schools and Communities Act (PL 99-570, 1986) provides federal funding to states for the development and improvement of school-based drug education and prevention programs.

In this section we review research on the efficacy of school-based substance abuse education and prevention programs. We discuss this research with regard to specific substances, domains, goals, and outcomes. Substance abuse prevention efforts have been directed toward a number of substances, most frequently, tobacco, alcohol, and marijuana. Target domains of functioning include affective, cognitive, and behavioral. In addition to the primary goal of prevention of substance use and abuse, program goals include information dissemination (e.g., designed to influence knowledge and attitudes about drugs), affective education (e.g., focused on self-esteem enhancement), provision of alternative activities (e.g., recreational, vocational), and enhancement of personal–social competence (e.g., social and resistance skills training). Program outcomes consist of *knowledge* about drugs and their effects, *attitudes* that influence drug use (e.g., beliefs, norms, self-efficacy), and *behaviors* reflecting frequency and severity of substance use and personal–social competence (e.g., resistance skills, assertiveness).

First we present the results of two meta-analytic studies, which provide an overview of this area of research (Bangert-Drowns, 1988; Tobler, 1986). Tobler reviewed 98 studies of secondary school (Grades 6–12) drug prevention programs, conducted between 1972 and 1984; all studies employed either control or comparison groups. Bangert-Drowns reviewed 33 studies of school-based drug and alcohol education programs, conducted between 1968 and 1982 with elementary school through college-age samples; all studies employed control groups.

Tobler's study of secondary school drug prevention programs (Tobler, 1986) provides information about the relative effectiveness of programs with different foci; that is, affective education, knowledge acquisition, personal–social competence (protective skills), and alternative activities (which included a skill-based component). The meta-analysis supports the following conclusions. The least effective types of prevention programming are those focused on affective education and knowledge acquisition, without a skill-based component. *The most effective programs are those designed to enhance personal–social competencies that serve as protective factors against drug abuse (e.g., resistance or interpersonal skills), followed by programs that provide alternative activities in addition to a skill-based focus.*

Knowledge-based programs are effective only for knowledge outcomes (e.g., knowledge about drugs and their physical and psychological effects). Affective education programs have negligible effects on all outcome variables (knowledge, attitudes, behaviors). Alternative activities are most effective for fostering general behavioral and academic adjustment (e.g., based on parent and teacher ratings; most likely reflecting transfer effects), but they also enhance specific personal–social competence skills, and, to a lesser degree, are effective for preventing or reducing drug use. Providing alternative activities has minimal effects on drug-related knowledge and attitudes. Skill-based programs (focused on enhancing personal–social competencies related to resisting drug use/abuse) have substantial effects on all target outcomes including specific personal–social competencies and drug-related knowledge, attitudes, and behavior (self-reported drug use), with the strongest effects on knowledge and competencies. These skill-based programs have negligible effects on general measures of behavioral and academic functioning (the measures most likely reflect transfer). *Tobler's (1986) results suggest that skill-based programs provide the most effective form of short-term intervention.* Of these programs, 50% achieved maximum effects within 9 hours or less, with 30% achieving slightly lower but still significant effects in 10–20 hours. Alternative programs, in contrast, showed increasing effects with longer duration, achieving maximum effects (consistent with skill-based) after an average of 182 hours. Thus, as much as 180 hours of alternative programming may be required to achieve effects equivalent to the maximum effects of skill-based programs. The one advantage of alternative activities, however, is the impact on more general measures of behavioral and academic adjustment, which are more likely to reflect generalization of program effects. Furthermore, alternative activities (of greater than 20 hours) were the most effective program type for adolescents exhibiting problems related to drug abuse, delinquency, or poor school performance. In conclusion, Tobler's study suggests that program outcome varies as a function of program focus.

Bangert-Drowns (1988) meta-analytic study of school-based drug (50% specifically focused on alcohol) education programs examined differential efficacy with regard to traditional outcome variables (knowledge, attitudes, behavior) and specific program features (e.g., mode of delivery, peer vs. adult facilitators, methods for selecting participants). The majority (58%) of the programs were focused on knowledge acquisition and affective education. These drug education programs were found to be most effective for changing drug-related knowledge, less but still significantly effective for changing drug-related attitudes, and ineffective for changing or preventing drug use (behavior). Voluntary participation was more effective than mandatory with regard to behavioral (drug use) outcomes, with mandatory programs showing negligible effects. Peer-led programs were more effective for influencing drug use and drug-related attitudes than teacher-led programs, with teacher-led programs showing negligible drug-use effects. Lecture-only delivery was ineffective for promoting attitude change, in contrast to programs that used discussion alone or in combination with lecture. Discussion-only programs without information, however, were ineffective for promoting knowledge acquisition. Thus, voluntary participation in peer-led drug education programs that use information-based discussion formats may be the most effective method for promoting drug-related knowledge, attitude, and behavioral change. Furthermore, drug education programs (with a predominant focus on knowledge acquisition and affective change) may be most effective for changing drug-related knowledge, effective to a lesser degree for changing drug-related attitudes, and ineffective for changing drug use. The knowledge and affective focus of the majority of these programs might explain the relative ineffectiveness on behavioral outcomes; program effectiveness was not examined separately with regard to primary program focus. *The features most strongly associated with behavioral change (e.g., reduction in drug use) were voluntary participation and use of peer facilitators.* In addition, studies published after 1979 reported stronger behavioral effects; those prior to 1979 reported negligible effects.

The findings of these two meta-analytic studies might best be understood in the context of a historical perspective of drug education and prevention programming (Schinke, Botvin, & Orlandi, 1991). Early drug education programming in the 1960s and 1970s focused on disseminating information to facilitate knowledge acquisition and attitude change related to use of alcohol and other drugs (e.g., tobacco, marijuana). The assumption was that knowledge and attitude change leads to behavioral change. Such approaches proved ineffective for changing drug use behavior. As suggested by the meta-analytic studies (Bangert-Drowns, 1988; Tobler, 1986), program effects on knowledge and attitudes are not necessarily reflected in behavioral change. This discrepancy between attitudes and behavior is exemplified by recent national statistics on U. S. high school students (National Education Goals Panel, 1992). Although 67% of twelfth graders disapproved of adults having five or more drinks in a row once or twice each weekend (Grade 8, 85%; Grade 10, 77%), 30% of these students reported having had five or more drinks in a row during the past 2 weeks (Grade 8, 13%; Grade 10, 23%).

In the 1980s and early 1990s, drug education and prevention programming promoted the development of personal–social competence, primarily through cognitive–behavioral approaches (Schinke et al., 1991). Based on social learning theory, these approaches employ instruction, demonstration, behavioral rehearsal, feedback, reinforcement, and extended practice through homework activities. In some instances, booster sessions are used to promote maintenance. The goal of programming is to enhance specific skills related to developing personal–social competence and resisting peer and media pressure to use drugs. These skills include interpersonal and coping skills such as problem solving, decision making, communication, assertiveness, and anxiety reduction. Interventions emphasize both cognitive and behavioral components of relevant skills. Furthermore, skill-based training typically is combined with knowledge-based education to enhance the informational basis for decision making about drug use and abuse. Some of the earliest work focused solely on cigarette smoking (e.g., the work of Botvin and Schinke, cited in Schinke et al., 1991). Efficacy studies revealed consistent effects on targeted behavioral outcomes, particularly initiation and reduction of drug use, in addition to drug-related knowledge and attitude change. When focused on teaching more generic personal–social skills in addition to specific drug-resistance skills, programs showed general (personal–social) as well as specific (drug use) skill outcomes (see Botvin & Wills, 1985; Dusenbury, Botvin, & James-Ortiz, 1990; Rhodes & Jason, 1988; Schinke et al., 1991). In general, the examination of drug education and prevention from a historical perspective suggests that early efforts through disseminating information were successful for effecting knowledge and, to some extent, attitude change, but were ineffective with regard to behavioral change. The inclusion of cognitive–behavioral methods to teach specific resistance skills and generic personal–social competence resulted in more comprehensive program effects, including changes in drug-related knowledge, attitudes, and behavior, as well as in personal–social competencies. The goals of contemporary drug prevention programs are consistent with the protective-skills approach to prevention of maladjustment discussed earlier. Next, we examine the results of selected drug education/prevention efficacy studies published since 1980, which focus on protective- or resistance-skill enhancement.

Appendix 2B presents the goals, methodology, and results of selected program efficacy studies with particular focus on prevention through enhancement of two types of protective skills—specific resistance (to social influences to use drugs) skills and general personal–social competence. These programs were implemented with the general population in school classrooms; two were implemented in a classroom format on Native American reservations. All studies employed experimental or quasi-experimental designs. Some included booster sessions and/or follow-up evaluation components. Program variations included the following: (1) implementors (teacher, professional/paraprofessional, and/or peers); (2) number and length of intervention sessions; (3) inclusion of knowledge-based component; (4) size of the group (ranging from small group to whole class); (5) activities, content, and target skills; and (6) inclusion of program evaluation activities. These variations are reflected in the program descriptions in Appendix 2B. In general, these studies confirm the positive outcomes of skill-based programs. We examine program efficacy separately, with differential focus on resistance skills and personal social–competence.

The primary goal of several programs was the promotion of resistance skills (i.e., to resist peer and media influences) through knowledge acquisition and specific skill training (Baer, McLaughlin, Burnside, & Pokorny, 1988; Dielman, Shope, Butchart, & Campanelli, 1986; Duryea, 1983, 1985; Duryea, Mohr, Newman, Martin, & Egwaoje, 1984; Duryea & Okwumabua, 1988; Ellickson & Bell, 1990; Gilchrist, Schinke, Trimble, &

Cvetkovich, 1987; Hansen, Graham, et al., 1988; Hansen, Johnson, Flay, Graham, & Sobel, 1988; Hansen, Malotte, & Fielding, 1988; Newman, Anderson, & Farrell, 1992; Schinke, Botvin, Trimble, Orlandi, Gilchrist, & Locklear, 1988; see Appendix 2B). Typical outcome measures for such programs included knowledge about target substances (i.e., alcohol and other drugs) and self-reported substance use. In addition, some studies employed outcome variables related to self-efficacy or confidence in resisting social and media influences, and to specific resistance skills such as resisting peer pressure to drink, drink and drive, or ride with a drinking driver. Optimally, outcome measures reflect specific program content. For example, two studies (Gilchrist et al., 1987; Schinke et al., 1988) used analogue measures of interpersonal skills (i.e., responses to hypothetical situations that involved resisting peer pressure to use drugs) that were directly relevant to program content. Overall, these studies document the efficacy of resistance skills programs for preventing the initiation of drug use, reducing actual use, and preparing youth to resist dangerous drug-related situations (e.g., riding with drinking drivers). Some studies also documented enhancement of knowledge, self-efficacy regarding ability to resist, and interpersonal skills (e.g., communication, assertiveness) related to resistance. Variations in results may be attributed to the relative emphasis on specific foci and the link between content and outcome measures. For example, Hansen and colleagues (1988) found differential effects as a function of program content. Furthermore, the timing of postintervention evaluations may affect results. Newman et al. (1984), for example, found immediate effects on knowledge and self-efficacy, but did not document behavioral outcomes (resisting riding with drinking drivers) until one year later.

At least one study suggests that program effects vary as a function of participant beliefs or attitudes. Baer and colleagues (1988) found resistance training to be more effective with adolescents who perceived peer or parent modeling influences to be high; whereas intervention focused on attitude change and decision making was more effective when modeling influences were perceived to be low. These perceptions of modeling influences were defined as perceived level of approval of and actual drug use by peers or parents. There is some support for differential levels of influenceability based on sociocultural, historical, and possibly biological factors. In one experimental study (Chipperfield & Vogel-Sprott, 1988), male adults with self-reported histories of family alcoholism changed their drinking behavior to conform to that of a live model (confederate in cocktail-testing task). This pattern was nonsignificant for individuals without a history of family alcoholism. Such results emphasize the need to consider the sociocultural experiences of prevention program participants when determining program goals and evaluating outcomes. In addition, one cannot ignore the potential role of biological/genetic factors in determining intervention needs for COAs (e.g., the relatively higher risk status for alcoholism and drug dependence, compared to the general population).

Several programs were designed to prevent substance use through enhancement of personal–social competence (Botvin, Baker, Botvin, Filazzola, & Millman, 1984; Botvin, Baker, Filazzola, & Botvin, 1990; Botvin, Baker, Renick, Filazzola, & Botvin, 1984; Caplan et al., 1992; Gersick, Grady, & Snow, 1988; Kim, 1988; Pentz, 1985; Snow, Tebes, Arthur, & Tapasak, 1992). The foci of these studies include self-efficacy, problem solving, decision making, coping, interpersonal and group interactive skills; and therefore reflect the components in our personal–social competence model. All but two of the studies measured respective competence variables in addition to drug-related knowledge, attitudes, and behavior, thus providing measures of protective or mediating variables as well as drug-related criteria. Measures of personal–social competence included responses to hypothetical social situations, self-reports, and teacher ratings. Pentz (1985) included measures of academic adjustment as well. All but one of the studies measured long-term outcomes, up to 2 years following the intervention. In general, these studies provided support for a competence enhancement approach to drug prevention, although long-term effects on substance use were mixed. That is, programs consistently documented short-term effects on personal–social competence, drug-related knowledge and attitudes, and self-reported drug use. Drug-use effects were not always maintained and in some cases treatment groups showed negative effects; that is, participants reported higher use rates compared to nonparticipants. The mixed findings regarding long-term effects may reflect variations in program design or implementation. That is, in programs in which long-term gains were evident (Botvin, Pentz), program developers were consistently involved in implementation (e.g., through cofacilitation, consultation, or monitoring) and used peer leaders as program facilitators. Furthermore, Botvin's studies suggest that the use of both peer leaders and boosters (review) sessions can facilitate long-term program effectiveness.

The issue of preventing substance use through enhancement of personal–social competence was addressed directly in one study (Pentz, 1985). Using data collected at 6-month intervals over 2 years from a subsample of the control group, Pentz validated a bidirectional relationship between drug (cigarettes, alcohol) use and social competence (self-efficacy and social skills). Prior drug use predicted lower self-efficacy and social skills and higher levels of subsequent drug use. Although prior drug use was the best predictor, social competence also predicted subsequent drug use. Drug availability, peer drug use, adult sanctions for use, and intention to use were weak predictors of subsequent drug use; however, in combination with social competence, these variables strengthened prediction. Pentz concluded that these findings supported a stress-response model of drug use; that is, drug use increases rather than alleviates stress. This model contradicts the commonly held belief in a stress-coping model of drug use (i.e., drug use is a coping method in response to stress). Regression analyses of prospective data from Pentz's intervention study suggest that drug use is influenced by multiple factors, including social competence, attitudes, and environmental influences. That is, demographic variables (male sex, higher age), poor social competence (skills and self-efficacy), negative social attitudes, and strong external influences (peer use, parent use, sanction, availability) all contributed to actual and intended use. These findings emphasize the complexity of drug use prediction and prevention.

One school-based prevention program specifically designed for COAs—Stress Management and Alcohol Awareness Program (SMAAP)—focused on the enhancement of coping skills and personal–social competence to prevent adjustment difficulties characteristic of this population (Roosa, Gensheimer, et al., 1990; see Appendix 2B). The SMAAP also included a knowledge acquisition component about alcoholism and its effects on the family. A unique aspect of this program was its systematic approach to program design. Unlike the majority of such interventions, the SMAAP used a problem analysis model to guide intervention design. This included systematic data collection procedures (e.g., self-report, interviews, checklists) with the target school population to address the following questions: Are COAs at risk if the alcoholic does not seek treatment? What factors distinguish COAs with and without adjustment difficulties? At what age is prevention realistic/necessary? How does one identify COAs? Roosa and colleagues concluded that (1) children of untreated alcoholics are at risk for adjustment difficulties; (2) the key mediators of adjustment are family conflict and self-esteem; (3) the optimal age for prevention is preadolescence (students under the age of 12 rarely exhibited adjustment problems); and (4) self-selection is a viable approach to identification in school settings. Thus, school-based interventions should include goals relevant to enhancing coping strategies (e.g., to cope with family stressors) and self-esteem. Second, voluntary participation is advisable. Realistic identification procedures involve the following steps: (1) provide information about family alcoholism to all students; (2) invite students to attend a discussion session about family alcoholism; (3) provide additional information about the COA intervention program and distribute parental consent forms; and (4) administer self-report measures to determine level of concern about parental drinking. These conclusions guided SMAAP program development and implementation. Consistent with program goals, SMAAP resulted in increased use of problem- and emotion-focused coping strategies, which were correlated with teacher reports of adaptive classroom behavior.

In conclusion, research supports the application of cognitive–behavioral approaches to substance abuse prevention, with primary focus on enhancement of specific resistance skills or more general personal–social competencies. Such approaches also hold promise for preventing adjustment difficulties among COAs. In the next section, we briefly review research on cognitive–behavioral interventions for developing social competence with both general and at-risk populations. In particular, we address the use of interpersonal cognitive problem-solving training, an integral part of the ESCAPE approach.

Efficacy of Personal–Social Competence Enhancement Programs

Consistent with the substance abuse prevention research, cognitive–behavioral interventions have been shown to be effective for promoting behavioral adjustment of children and adolescents in general and at-risk populations (Camp & Bash, 1985; Durlak, 1983; Gesten & Weissberg, 1986; Goldstein, 1988; Goldstein, Reagles, & Amann, 1990; Oden, 1986; Pellegrini & Urbain, 1985; Rotheram-Borus, 1988; Shure & Spivack, 1988; Spivack & Shure, 1974; Weissberg, Caplan, & Harwood, 1991; Weissberg & Gesten, 1982). Many of the cognitive–behavioral programs include structured interpersonal cognitive problem-solving training as a key component; for example, the programs developed by Camp and Bash, Gesten and Weissberg, Goldstein and colleagues, Shure and Spivack, and Urbain. Research documents the efficacy of such programs for enhancing cognitive and behavioral skill components (e.g., problem-solving strategies, perspective taking, conflict resolution, collaboration, and social interactions). For example, Goldstein's Skillstreaming program has successfully helped adolescents develop prosocial skills of empathy, negotiation, assertiveness, self-control, conflict resolution, perspective taking, and cooperation. This approach uses modeling, role-playing, performance feedback, and transfer training through structured homework focused on application of new skills to real-life settings.

The research of Weissberg and colleagues further illustrates the effectiveness of collateral cognitive problem solving and behavioral social skills training for improving problem-solving skills, prosocial attitudes toward conflict resolution, and self-reported behavioral adjustment of school-age (grades 2–6) populations (Gesten & Weissberg, 1986; Weissberg et al., 1991). An additional year of training enhanced long-term effects, supporting the utility of booster sessions suggested by the substance abuse prevention research of Botvin and colleagues (Botvin et al., 1990). The importance of booster sessions for maintaining program effects is documented also by Lochman (1992). A problem-solving program for fourth through sixth grade aggressive males resulted in long-term (3-year) effects for social problem solving, self-esteem, and substance use. Only participants who received booster sessions (18 vs. 12 weekly sessions) maintained classroom adjustment effects on off-task behavior.

The Interpersonal Cognitive Problem Solving (ICPS) model developed by Shure and Spivack (1988) has been used effectively to improve interpersonal problem solving and behavioral adjustment of young children (preschool–kindergarten). This program is designed to be implemented in classrooms by teachers and involves the use of such facilitation techniques as explication (verbalizing the child's strategy use) and scaffolding (prompting the child to apply problem solving to real-life situations). (We discuss the use of facilitation techniques in Chapter 3.) These features may account for the consistent generalization of skills to real-life situations, in contrast to many other cognitive–behavioral programs. For example, Skillstreaming programs result in skill acquisition by more than 90% of the participants, but the skills transfer to real-world settings for only 45–50% (Goldstein et al., 1990).

Similarly, risk prevention research with children and adolescents frequently has focused on enhancing individual competencies (e.g., communication, problem solving, conflict resolution, and resistance skills) within the context of group-based interventions such as small groups or classrooms (Caplan et al., 1992; Goldstein et al., 1990; Hawkins et al., 1992; Rhodes & Jason, 1988; Weissberg et al., 1991). Such programs have been successful in enhancing target skills and reducing or preventing substance use and abuse. Transfer to real-world settings, however, is typically much lower than direct effects on program-specific outcomes (e.g., Goldstein et al., 1990). Such limitations suggest the need to create environments that encourage and reinforce normative values and behaviors consistent with program goals (e.g., engagement in competence-promoting behaviors) and thereby foster generalization and maintenance. In addition, research suggests that peer engagement in high-risk behaviors such as substance abuse is among the strongest predictors of such behaviors among adolescents (Hawkins et al., 1992). Thus, development of peer norms that are antithetical to engagement in high-risk behaviors is a critical goal for intervention.

School-based programs that have modified classroom instructional strategies, roles of school personnel, and school organization (e.g., scheduling, home–school collaboration, shared decision making) have documented positive effects on substance use, personal–social and academic competence, compliance with school regulations, and attitudes toward school (Felner & Adan, 1988; Fry & Addington, 1984; Graves & Graves, 1985; Hawkins et al., 1992; Solomon, Watson, Delucchi, Schaps, & Battistich, 1988). Classroom- and school-based programs are commonly group focused, thus making the development of group norms possible. Solomon et al. (1988) developed a multiyear classroom-based program to enhance prosocial behavior. The effects of this program most likely reflect the creation of norms consistent with prosocial responding. Prosocial interactions (e.g., helping, sharing, comforting, cooperation) were promoted through the creation of a classroom environment that used cooperative learning, supportive teacher–student relationships, student participation in rule setting and decision making, modeling and discussion of prosocial behavior, and opportunities to engage in prosocial behaviors such as helping. Thus, the classroom environment was designed to encourage prosocial reasoning and behavior and to provide support of prosocial interactions by adults and peers. Elementary students who participated in this program over 5 years (grades K–4) exhibited more frequent prosocial interactions than students in comparison groups; findings were replicated in a 2-year program. Although we can explain these results from a social construction perspective (e.g., participants constructed norms supporting prosocial interaction), such programs typically do not include an explicit focus on co-construction of norms through a guided negotiation process (e.g., explictly encouraging peers to guide and reinforce the behavioral change of partners).

The context provided by collaborative interactions might be particularly effective for both promoting and reinforcing change in interpersonal skills (cf. D. W. Johnson, 1981). For example, research supports the collaborative application of interpersonal problem solving to promote conflict resolution and peer mediation (D. W. Johnson, Johnson, & Dudley, 1991; D. W. Johnson, Johnson, Dudley, & Acikgoz, 1991; D. W. Johnson, Johnson, Dudley & Burnett, 1991). D. W. Johnson and colleagues used a collaborative approach successfully to teach negotiation and mediation skills, having students practice in pairs. Students generalized skills to conflicts on the playground. School personnel reported a reduction in discipline problems that required their attention, as students became more autonomous in collaborative problem resolution. A unique aspect of this intervention is the focus on dyads, which increases the opportunities for practice with similarly skilled individuals, peer modeling, and prompting and social reinforcement by peers. Classrooms are optimal contexts for interventions focused on social dynamics. In the next section, we discuss the efficacy of cooperative learning environments for enhancing both personal–social and cognitive–academic competencies.

COOPERATIVE LEARNING

Research has documented the comprehensive efficacy of cooperative learning for enhancing cognitive, academic, social, and emotional competence (Nastasi & Clements, 1991, provide a research review). Participation in cooperative learning experiences has been shown to enhance higher-order cognitive skills, such as reasoning and problem solving, and learning of specific academic content (e.g., reading, mathematics, science, social studies). In addition, cooperative learning fosters active involvement in learning, increased motivation, and positive attitudes toward learning, teachers, and school. Cooperative learning experiences encourage reciprocal interactions (e.g., sharing ideas, mutual helping), prosocial orientation, and perspective taking. Such interactions promote improvements in interpersonal relationships and acceptance of individuals from diverse cultural backgrounds. Furthermore, these learning contexts enhance students' self-efficacy regarding academic and social competence. Such advantages seem to be universal. Effectiveness has been demonstrated with children, adolescents, and adults of varying ability levels and from diverse ethnic and cultural backgrounds. (For additional reviews of cooperative learning research, see D. W. Johnson & Johnson, 1983, 1989; D. W. Johnson, Johnson, & Maruyama, 1983; D. W. Johnson, Maruyama, Johnson, Nelson, & Skon, 1981; Slavin, 1986; Slavin et al., 1985.)

Collaborative Problem Solving

In cooperative learning situations, the goals of individuals are interdependent; that is, the attainment of one person's goals positively influences the attainment of another's goals. Typically, students work toward common goals. In collaborative problem solving, individuals work together as they engage in the process of solving assigned or self-selected problems. When solving problems collaboratively (in simulated or real-life contexts), students are responsible for every step of the problem-solving process, from problem identification and definition, to generating and identifying potentially effective solutions, to implementing and evaluating the solutions.

Collaborative problem solving is especially effective for enhancing higher-level cognitive skills, competence motivation, and interpersonal relations (Nastasi & Clements, 1991; Slavin, 1986). Nastasi and Clements distinguish between collaborative interactions characterized by *reciprocal sense making* (i.e., partners generate ideas and build meaning through discourse) from those characterized by *cognitive conflict and resolution* (i.e., partners pose and resolve discrepant viewpoints). In reciprocal sense making, partners exchange information, explain ideas, and attempt to build consensus. Such interactions facilitate higher-level problem solving and transfer, and are more beneficial for learning than individualistic or competitive learning experiences (D. W. Johnson, Johnson, Roy, & Zaidman, 1985; D. W. Johnson, Johnson, & Scott, 1978; D. W. Johnson et al., 1981; R. T. Johnson, Johnson, & Stanne, 1985; Nastasi & Clements, 1991; Slavin, 1980). Specifically, explicit requests for help and elaborate explanations are associated with enhanced learning (Peterson, Wilkinson, Spinelli, & Swing, 1984; Wilkinson & Spinelli, 1983).

Opportunities for posing and resolving alternative perspectives (cognitive conflicts) may be the optimal context for learning. That is, interactions involving cognitive conflict are more likely to foster cognitive growth and effectance motivation than those involving consensus building while avoiding disagreement (Doise & Mugny, 1984; D. W. Johnson & Johnson, 1985; D. W. Johnson, Johnson, Pierson, & Lyons, 1985; Nastasi & Clements, 1992, in press; Nastasi, Clements, & Battista, 1990). Furthermore, conflict resolution seems to be the critical variable for promoting cognitive change (Bearison, 1982; Doise & Mugny, 1979; D. W. Johnson, Johnson, Pierson & Lyons, 1985; Lindow, Wilkinson, & Peterson, 1985; Nastasi & Clements, 1992; Nastasi et al., 1990; Smith, Peterson, Johnson, & Johnson, 1986). Thus, it is not so much the conflict itself but the manner in which the disagreement is resolved that accounts for the cognitive benefits of collaborative problem solving. These benefits are most likely when the process of resolution involves equal participation of partners, discussion of the quality or validity of ideas, and negotiation towards a compromise or synthesis (Bearison, Magzamen, & Filardo, 1986; Lindow et al., 1985; Nastasi & Clements, 1992).

Conflicts of ideas provide individuals with opportunities to consider multiple perspectives and synthesize discrepant ideas, a critical process for cognitive growth and co-construction of norms. Such interactions are possible in learning contexts that engender (1) *self-directed collaborative problem solving*—students working with partners define and solve self-selected problems; (2) *conflicting perspectives*—students are encouraged to consider alternative perspectives and have access to information necessary to generate alternative problem solutions; and (3) *conflict resolution*—resolution of discrepant views is necessary to proceed successfully (Forman & Cazden, 1985; Nastasi & Clements, 1992; Nastasi et al., 1990).

Cognitive change occurs even after short-term (e.g., single-session) laboratory-based collaborative interventions (Damon, 1983) and has been associated with infrequent conflictive interactions (e.g., that occur less than 10% of the time; Nastasi & Clements, 1993). Both cooperative learning and prevention research, however, suggest that long-term interventions may be necessary to achieve stable conceptual and behavioral change. For example, although gains in basic academic (mathematics) skills occur after participation in cooperative learning for 8 weeks, gains in conceptual skills are found only after 24 weeks (Slavin, 1986; Slavin et al., 1985). In addition, the conflictive interactions associated with cognitive gains (reported by Nastasi and Clements) occurred after 40–60 collaborative sessions. Similarly, primary mental health prevention programs consisting of short-term (a few hours) interventions are effective for increasing knowledge; however, stable improvements across multiple indices—knowledge, attitudes, and behaviors—require longer-term interventions (40–50 hours; Weissberg et al., 1991). Furthermore, booster or review sessions facilitate long-term maintenance of these cognitive–behavioral preventive interventions (Botvin et al., 1990; Weissberg et al., 1991). *Thus, consolidation of conceptual and behavioral gains may require longer-term interventions or extended opportunities for practice.*

In sum, cooperative learning approaches that encourage collaborative problem solving are especially effective for enhancing higher-level thinking (e.g., reasoning, critical thinking, problem solving), competence motivation (related to self-efficacy), and interpersonal relationships among individuals from diverse backgrounds. The most beneficial collaborative contexts for promoting cognitive change are those that encourage consideration and resolution of divergent viewpoints. Such settings also provide contexts for the co-construction of social norms that promote personal–social well-being; for example, through opportunities for enhancing perceived competence, effectance motivation, and self-esteem.

Perceived Competence and Effectance Motivation

Social interactions during collaborative problem solving provide occasions for enhancing perceived competence and effectance motivation. Cooperative learning has been shown to influence perceived social and cognitive competence, goal orientation, intrinsic motivation, and positive attitudes toward learning (D. W. Johnson, Johnson, Pierson, & Lyons, 1985; D. W. Johnson et al., 1978; R. T. Johnson, Brooker, Stuztman, Hultman, & Johnson, 1985; R. T. Johnson, Johnson, & Stanne, 1985; Nastasi & Clements, 1991; Slavin, 1980). That is, students working with partners, compared to those working alone or in competition, perceive themselves as more academically competent and more accepted by peers, and display greater interest in learning. Increased self-efficacy and motivation regarding academic pursuits promote active engagement in learning activities and influence future academic performance, perhaps more so than actual ability (Pokay & Blumenfeld, 1990; Schunk, 1990b; Skinner, Wellborn, & Connell, 1990). Similarly, improved social self-efficacy fosters social interaction, particularly in similar collaborative endeavors. Success in these subsequent endeavors further enhances self-efficacy and effectance motivation in respective domains (Schunk, 1989a, 1990b); however, attempts to engender self-efficacy must be linked to specific competencies. Furthermore, perceptions of competence in domains that are socially valued (e.g., valued by peers) and the availability of social support both influence global self-worth, which in turn influences social–emotional adjustment (Harter, 1990a, 1990b; Harter & Marold, 1991). Thus, collaborative environments provide valuable contexts for enhancing self-efficacy, effectance motivation, and self-worth and for promoting social–emotional well-being.

Research provides guidelines for structuring contexts in which students can develop perceived competence, effectance motivation, and self-esteem (Harter, 1990a, 1990b; Harter & Marold, 1991). In facilitative environments, varied competencies are valued. Individuals are offered opportunities to identify and use their competencies, and they can make social comparison with others who have similar competencies. In addition, social support from adults and peers is available. Furthermore, individuals are provided opportunities for independence as well as connectedness. These same contextual variables have been identified as critical for promoting academic success and empowerment of minority students (Cummins, 1986). Cummins suggests that empowered students "develop the ability, confidence, and motivation to succeed academically" (p. 23). Thus, the classroom social climate may facilitate or inhibit the development of an individual's sense of competence, intrinsic motivation, and self-esteem.

Peers influence self-efficacy, both as sources for social comparison and as models (Schunk, 1990b). Perceptions of competence are more likely to be influenced by peer than adult models. Models who attempt and persist at difficult tasks (i.e., coping models) are more important for promoting self-efficacy than models of successful performance (i.e., mastery models). Although models are an important source of efficacy information, feedback about one's own performance is more effective for increasing self-efficacy than the same information obtained vicariously (i.e., observing a model). Next, we examine task-related variables that can be modified to facilitate successful performance and enhance perceived competence.

Students' experiences with goal setting and attainment can influence their sense of competence and subsequent performance (Schunk, 1989a, 1989b, 1990a, 1990b, 1991; Schunk & Rice, 1991). Self-efficacy is likely to be enhanced through the use of process-, rather than product-oriented, goals; by setting challenging but attainable goals; by making goals specific; and by self-selection of goals. A combination of proximal (short-term) and distal (long-term) goals may be optimal. Short-term goal setting can enhance self-efficacy, whereas long-term goal setting increases interest. The availability and use of effective strategies are also critical. That is, self-efficacy is enhanced by teaching students the necessary strategies for goal attainment and providing information about the value of specific strategies. During task performance, perceived competence can be fostered by encouraging students to verbalize strategies, providing explicit feedback about strategy mastery, and giving performance-based feedback about progress toward goal attainment. Such feedback is especially critical in the early stages of mastery. The combination of goal setting and feedback can foster both self-efficacy and academic performance. Furthermore, instruction can improve both skill and self-efficacy, which in turn improve skill and persistence.

The self-efficacy and motivational benefits of cooperative learning have been attributed to both social and task-related factors (Nastasi & Clements, 1991). The continuous availability of partners increases the opportunities for social support and peer acceptance, social comparison with peers, peer feedback about performance, and modeling of motivational orientation and perceived competence. Interactions with a partner over time provide opportunities for observing examples of coping, particularly if the process of goal attainment is emphasized. In addition, the need to communicate with partners facilitates explication of strategies and of progress toward goal attainment. Active participation and explication of strategies during collaborative problem solving are critical determinants of cognitive gains (Rogoff, 1990).

Cooperative learning situations that foster controversy (cognitive conflict), rather than consensus seeking, are more likely to engender task-involvement, motivation, and self-efficacy (D. W. Johnson, Johnson, Pierson, & Lyons, 1985; R. T. Johnson, Brooker, et al., 1985). For example, children who worked together in a context in which conflict resolution occurred more frequently also exhibited higher frequencies of self-directed task formulation and pleasure at intellectual discovery (Clements & Nastasi, 1988; Nastasi et al., 1990). In addition, they verbalized problem-solving strategies more often and performed better on a transfer task of higher-order thinking than did their counterparts in situations where conflict resolution occurred less frequently. Enhanced competence motivation resulting from collaborative problem solving within such environments has been shown to account for cognitive gains (Nastasi & Clements, 1993). Thus, cooperative problem-solving environments that encourage engaging in cognitive conflict and its resolution may provide optimal settings for enhancing motivation and a sense of competence as well as facilitating cognitive growth.

Collaborative problem-solving activities can easily be structured to incorporate facilitative task-related factors such as performance-contingent feedback, strategy teaching, and goal setting. Dyads working in a context in which evaluative feedback was provided by a computer exhibited positive self-statements more frequently than those in contexts in which such feedback was not provided (Clements & Nastasi, 1988; Nastasi et al., 1990). The students in the latter condition more frequently sought approval from the teacher, suggesting the need for some external feedback. The extent to which collaborative activities are self-directed, and thus rely on intrinsic motivation, may also be important. Dyads working collaboratively with self-selected projects more frequently engaged in self-directed task formulation and displays of pleasure at mastery, than those working with teacher- or computer-selected activities (Clements & Nastasi, 1988; Nastasi et al., 1990). Such self-directed activity within a single domain may engender a greater sense of control and mastery than such activity across multiple domains (Nastasi et al., 1990; Schunk, 1990b). "The path to self-direction and mastery might be paved with failed plans, seeking of external feedback, and enhanced self-evaluation of work once success is achieved" (Nastasi & Clements, in press). This scenario characterized the work of students who also were rated by teachers as exhibiting more indications of effectance motivation (e.g., initiates tasks, is interested in a variety of activities, enjoys problem solving, is proud of accomplishments, seeks information, considers alternative perspectives). Furthermore, the enhanced effectance motivation resulting from their collaborative problem-solving mediated cognitive gains. Thus, opportunities for self-directed mastery in collaborative problem-solving contexts may foster both effectance motivation and cognitive gains. Even within such contexts, however, performance-contingent feedback may be necessary.

In sum, collaborative problem-solving contexts provide opportunities to foster personal–social and cognitive–academic competencies. The facilitator plays a critical role in forming the sociocultural context in which learning takes place.

Facilitating Collaborative Interactions

Certain characteristics of cooperative learning environments contribute to attainment of both personal–social and cognitive–academic goals (Nastasi & Clements, 1991). These include the following:

1. *Positive group interdependence.* Partners share goals and resources, have specific roles that are flexible, communicate about the task, and encourage each other's learning.

2. *Individual accountability.* Each person is responsible for contributing to goal attainment and for his/her own learning. Thus, each person must fulfill responsibilities of agreed-upon roles, question partners to ensure understanding, and participate in such a manner that task completion and learning are assured.

3. *Reciprocal sense making.* Partners contribute equally to generating ideas and problem solving, and they strive for consensus and shared meaning. They attempt to understand and extend each other's ideas. Each person contributes ideas and listens to the ideas of others, seeks clarification, answers questions, and explains ideas fully.

4. *Cognitive conflict resolution.* Partners pose alternative perspectives, engage in perspective taking, and work toward resolving discrepant viewpoints through negotiation and synthesis. That is, each person strives to generate and consider alternative views, discuss the viability of alternate

ideas/solutions, and seek resolutions that reflect the combining of discrepant ideas. At a minimum, resolution involves consensus (i.e., all members agree) following discussion and consideration of each idea. Optimally, resolution is a synthesis or combining of divergent ideas into a new and better idea (cf. the dialectic integration of the thesis and antithesis into a higher-level idea).

5. *Group processing.* Individually and collectively, participants make explicit and evaluate dyadic and/or group dynamics. Participants examine their social interactions, attempt to identify what interactive behaviors facilitated or inhibited collaboration, and discuss ways to promote facilitative interactions and to alter inhibitory ones. This process of evaluation is an ongoing component of collaboration.

A collaborative environment with these features helps to ensure that (1) all members participate in and benefit from collaborative interaction; (2) all members are valued; (3) a sense of social responsibility is encouraged; (4) co-construction of ideas is facilitated; and (5) participants address both social and task-related aspects of collaboration. In environments that engender self-directed collaborative problem solving and co-construction of meaning, the facilitator assumes a mediational, rather than a directive, role. This mediational role may be especially important for enhancing problem solving and higher-level thinking skills. As participants gain mastery and assume control over their learning, peer collaboration and mediation increase, and teacher direction and mediation decrease (Clements & Nastasi, 1992; Emihovich & Miller, 1988; Riel, 1985).

Peer-mediated learning may be more beneficial than teacher-mediated learning. Prevention research focused on enhancing personal–social competence, for example, indicates that peer-led interventions are more effective than those led by adults (Botvin et al., 1990). The efficacy of cooperative learning provides further support for the cognitive and academic benefits of peer interactions. Even preschoolers may benefit more from peer-mediated learning. In one study, for example, peer-mediated problem solving was found to be positively correlated with post-treatment achievement, whereas teacher-mediated learning was negatively correlated with achievement (Perlmutter, Behrend, Kuo, & Muller, 1986). These young children, however, had difficulty balancing the cognitive and social demands of collaborative problem solving. Thus, peer-mediated learning does not preclude the need for adult facilitation of collaborative interactions.

Balancing the task-related and social demands of collaboration is challenging at any age level, particularly for those individuals with limited experience or skill. Effective management of both aspects is necessary for success in collaborative problem solving (Nastasi & Clements, 1991). Indeed, attention to social dynamics may enhance academic gains. In one

study, students who evaluated with partners the social aspects of collaboration and discussed strategies for improvement of social dynamics scored
higher on achievement tests than those who did not (Yager, Johnson,
Johnson, & Snider, 1986). The facilitator plays an important role in guiding such evaluative activities. For example, the facilitator might initially
assess the social interaction skills of participants, provide opportunities for
participants to improve their interpersonal skills, guide participants in
evaluating and discussing group dynamics, and facilitate the enhancement
of group dynamics. Such mediation can be decreased gradually as participants become more successful in peer-mediation of group process.
(Nastasi and Clements, 1991, provide additional suggestions for facilitating collaboration.)

Facilitators mediate collaborative peer interactions through explication and modeling of target processes, scaffolding or prompting to elicit
target processes, and reflective evaluation of performance. We detail these
facilitative (mediational) techniques in Chapter 3. Such methods have been
used successfully to facilitate collaborative problem solving and to assess
problem solving processes (Bruner & Haste, 1987; Campione & Brown,
1987; Clements, 1990; Clements & Nastasi, 1990; Rogoff, 1990). Use of
these methods can help the facilitator to assess participants' understanding
or mastery of target processes and provide the supports necessary to
promote success. Within collaborative problem-solving activities, mediation applies to social interactions (dyadic or group dynamics) and cognitive
requirements (e.g., goal setting, mathematical problem solving). Especially
when participants have had minimal experience with collaboration, it is
important to monitor their reactions to both the collaborative process and
task demands. For example, problem-solving gains from a cognitive–behavioral social skills program were greater when group leaders took a
facilitative role; however, participants reported less enjoyment of the program than participants in groups with a more directive leader (Rotheram-
Borus, 1988). Thus, the facilitator may need to assess participant reactions,
address their concerns, and explain task requirements and potential
benefits that may not be readily apparent. By doing so the facilitator can
help to ensure that participants view activities favorably, thus fostering
acceptance of intervention and perceptions of effectiveness. Research suggests that the extent to which recipients view interventions as acceptable is
related to perceived effectiveness (Elliott, Witt, & Kratochwill, 1991). Thus,
it behooves the facilitator to assess participant perceptions and make explicit the purpose, process, and expected benefits of program activities. We
have found that attention to these issues early in the implementation of
collaborative activities facilitates understanding and cooperation, and
provides a frame of reference for subsequent discussion and evaluation. In
addition, continual monitoring of group process (e.g., through self-evaluation by participants) helps to ensure that social dynamics do not inhibit

effective task completion and provides opportunities for developing interpersonal skills (i.e., for teaching and practicing skills). We return to the topics of facilitation and intervention acceptability in Chapter 3, as we provide guidelines for program implementation and evaluation.

In the ESCAPE curriculum, we use collaborative and story contexts to enhance interpersonal problem solving, social interaction skills, self-efficacy, and self-esteem. In the next section, we provide the rationale for *story* as a mechanism for facilitating communication and co-construction of meaning, and promoting the development of personal–social competence.

USE OF STORY

We began with the stories of Maggie and Robert, two children who like all of us live storied lives. Story is communication about specific life experiences and has the potential for fostering a "sense of connection with others in the world" (Vandergrift, 1980, p. 1). It "is a means of reaching out to others, of sharing ideas and life experiences; as such, it can influence the way one perceives and responds to people and situations in 'real life'" (p. 38). Sharing of stories from diverse experiences fosters understanding and perspective taking. Furthermore, use of stories relevant to students' own lives facilitates awareness and connections to their respective sociocultural histories, thus facilitating self-definitions that include cultural identity. Our culture stories facilitate coping in our worlds (Howard, 1991) and help us better to understand the worlds of others. The use of story is central to the ESCAPE curriculum presented in Chapter 4. In this section, we define story and discuss its role in promoting personal–social competence. We describe the use of various story forms—literature, film, and story writing—and examine the efficacy of such applications.

Story is ubiquitous and is central to making meaning. We all have stories to tell. Think for a moment about Monday morning conversations with our colleagues. "How was your week-end? Tell me about the party. What did you think of the 'big game'?" Consistent with the dialectical process, through stories we communicate our ideas, consider alternative views, and negotiate the integration of diverse perspectives. It is through this process that individuals co-construct values, knowledge, and behavioral norms within a given sociocultural context. Furthermore, we learn social mores and cultural heritage through stories. Much of our human memory is story-based, and according to Schank (1990), "Knowledge, then, is experiences and stories, and intelligence is the apt use of experience and the creation and telling of stories ... What we know is embodied in what we tell" (p. 12).

Consistent with the notion of co-construction, social and physical sciences are replete with storied constructions of culture, thinking processes, beliefs, and theories (cf. Howard, 1991). It is through story, then, that we communicate concepts and experiences. The storied approach allows us to investigate the taken-for-granted and tacit premises from which people operate and construct and reconstruct meaning. Researchers have used story forms such as prescribed or self-generated moral dilemmas, fables, self-constructed stories, and literature to examine how people construct meaning (Garrod et al., 1990; Gilligan, 1982; Johnston, 1988; Tetenbaum & Pearson, 1989). For example, children's self-generated stories were used to examine their experiences and conceptions of caring student-teacher relationships (DeZolt, 1992). In their real-life stories first, sixth, and twelfth graders described teachers in a helping or nurturing role either in terms of instruction of academic content or promotion of personal–social competence. Excerpts from two interviews describe caring teacher behaviors.

One sixth grade student describes the teacher's role in helping her to resolve a peer conflict. She emphasized the importance of maintaining the relationship with her peer as well as resolving the conflict. From this student's perspective, the caring teacher provided the emotional support and opportunities for connectedness that are considered to be critical factors in facilitating children's coping (Anthony & Cohler, 1987; Garbarino et al., 1992; Rutter, 1979).

CHILD: This one teacher, she was my fifth grade teacher and at first we were—some friends—we were, like, getting in an argument and she went over and tried to help us figure it out. And she, like, you know, asked each of us, you know, what was the matter and how we thought we might be able to work it out on our own. And so she was trying to get us to talk to each other to see, you know, if we could work something out. That would make us stop arguing about it.

EVALUATOR: What was caring about that?

C: That we didn't have to do it on our own—that she was there. She would try to help us work it out.

E: Why is that caring?

C: Because she, like, cares about us.

E: How did you know that?

C: She tried to help us instead of having us go to another person or just not even bother with it. (DeZolt, 1992, p. 68)

In the words of the second student, we hear the juxtaposition of the interpersonal and the academic. He articulates the teacher's ability to relate academic content to students' personal experiences.

STUDENT: Well, my third grade teacher . . . was the best friend I had ever had as, for a teacher, and she did a lot of good stuff with me and we went and we had dinner with each other and we went around on outings and she really paid attention to math and I thought that was caring because every job you do you have to know math or else you can't be very successful at it.

E: So, what was the specific situation then that you thought that what the teacher did was really caring?

S: . . . I gave the wrong answer

E: You didn't, there's not a wrong answer, I'm asking, I'm just asking you a question about it.

S: OK.

E: What was caring about what that person did?

S: Well, she taught that system worldly and I thought it was really helpful to every student in the whole class. (DeZolt, 1992, p. 69)

We use story to facilitate understanding and communication of individual perspectives, interpersonal problem solving, modeling of self-efficacy and coping, and the social construction of norms that support the development of personal–social competence. In the next section, we discuss the value of story for enhancing the specific aspects of personal–social competence—self-efficacy, interpersonal problem solving, and social interaction skills.

Using Story to Enhance Personal–Social Competence

Story provides vicarious human experiences through its characters, which can substitute for actual experiences (Tucker, 1981). For example, a reader can learn about the nature of the world and the limits of human potential without the penalty of following the mistaken notions and misconceived fantasies of fictional characters. Stories also provide models of personal–social competence through fictional or real-world accounts, and provide scenarios for discussion and role-play of hypothetical or real-life situations. Furthermore, stories contribute alternative frames of reference for interpreting interpersonal experiences.

Stories can become scripts or mental representations of social behavior relevant to specific situations. Repetition of story themes facilitates rehearsal and elaboration of scripts, which become instantiated through real-world application. This cumulative process has been used to explain the long-term effects of viewing violent media scenes on aggressive behavior (Huesmann, 1986; Huesmann & Malamuth, 1986). The results of one study suggest that televised programming may contribute to a commonly held script about alcohol use (i.e., that alcohol use is an adult activity). Children (ages 8 to 11) who viewed a syndicated television show in which adults were drinking alcohol were more likely to choose alcoholic beverages for adults in a hypothetical scenario, than those who viewed nondrinking shows or no television (Rychtarik, Fairbank, Allen, Foy, &

Drabman, 1983). These effects were not evident, however, in children's choices of drinks for other children in hypothetical scenarios.

Story is a context for facilitating or inhibiting development of personal–social competence. Using story effectively requires careful selection and mediation of story content. Mediation can facilitate co-construction of normative behavior and counteract the potential effects of negative models. Sociocultural and historical experiences, however, may differentially influence the impact of story because of the availability of extant scripts for interpreting current experiences. That is, children with an alcoholic parent may have different perceptions of parental approval and use of alcohol, which may influence their response to models of alcohol use and prevention efforts (Baer et al., 1988; Chipperfield & Vogel-Sprott, 1988). Thus, mediation of individuals' experiences with story requires attention to extant scripts. We return to the issue of mediation in a later section. First, we examine the use of story for each aspect of personal–social competence.

Self-Efficacy

Guided experiences with story enhance self-efficacy to the extent that they provide models of effective coping and of an enhanced sense of efficacy. Most importantly, through story we can present models of individuals who confront and overcome adversity, and who take credit for their successes. These models are often child or adolescent characters such as those seen in adventure stories or fairy tales (Bettelheim, 1977; Tucker, 1981). Bettelheim says of fairy tales:

> This is exactly the message that fairy tales get across to the child in manifold form: that a struggle against severe difficulties in life is unavoidable, is an intrinsic part of human existence—but that if one does not shy away, but steadfastly meets unexpected and often unjust hardships, one masters all obstacles and at the end emerges victorious. (p. 8)

Furthermore, story can extend personal experiences and enhance the sense of power over the environment through the characters' exploration of the world. "[A]s the child dwells in and wonders at the lives lived in story, she comes to know both herself and the world and begins to see that world as something over which she, as a character in life, might exercise some control" (Vandergrift, 1980; pp. 1–2). These vicarious experiences might be especially important for children who perceive aspects of their lives as being beyond their control. Stories of characters who meet similar challenges and cope effectively provide contexts for children to explore strategies for coping with seemingly insurmountable obstacles and to re-create their own stories.

Creating stories helps individuals exercise ownership of their decision making (Tappan & Brown, 1989). Keeping a journal, for example, helps to organize and label thoughts and feelings, and structure goal setting. Indeed, committing thoughts to paper can be characterized as attempting to make explicit what is implicit. The mathematics journals of fifth and sixth graders, for example, helped students to make explicit their level of understanding about specific mathematics concepts and their anxiety about performance, as well as to identify necessary resources for task completion (Gordon & Macinnis, 1993). This use of story can thus facilitate goal setting, task performance, and a sense of efficacy in academics.

Interpersonal Problem Solving

Story can facilitate emotional awareness and understanding of social situations, present hypothetical or real-life problems, teach problem solving strategies, and provide models of effective problem-solving and coping with crisis. For example, children as young as 3 years of age infer emotions of story characters, particularly when stories are presented visually (Tucker, 1981). Books with pictures, even without words, provide a medium for teaching young children awareness of feelings in self and others (e.g., through recognition of relevant facial expressions). Pictures alone are used in social skills training programs to facilitate identification of emotions and problem solving (e.g., Shure, 1992; Urbain, 1982). Stories provide scenarios for applying interpersonal or collaborative problem solving to hypothetical and real-life situations. Alternatively, children can use their own stories as contexts for problem solving.

Daily journal writing by kindergarten students in one classroom provided the context for problem solving and social interaction (Hipple, 1985). Students were encouraged to record (i. e., write, dictate, or draw) their ideas, feelings, and real-life experiences; to create their own stories; and to share journal entries with each other. In this context, the teacher observed heightened student interest in each other's work.

Especially for the preschool child, story provides a way to extend real-life experience. Even 6-year-olds have difficulty separating real-life experiences from those presented through fictional stories (Applebee, 1978). In Applebee's study, 73% of the 6-year-olds remained uncertain about whether story characters and events were real, and 50% tended to think they probably were real. By age 9, children exhibited a firm recognition of fiction, with only l0% reporting that fairy tales were probably real. This lack of differentiation between the real world and the story world makes story a powerful tool for extending the limited real-life experience of the young child. For the older child or adolescent, story can extend sociocultural experiences and enhance understanding of others' experiences. In this manner, story can foster consideration and negotiation of multiple perspectives.

Story can facilitate coping through distancing or depersonalizing a crisis situation (Applebee, 1978; Bettelheim, 1977; Gumaer, 1984; Tucker, 1981), in order to reappraise the situation or develop a strategy for changing it. Through depersonalization, the individual is able to analyze the situation, gather information, explore alternatives for coping, and develop a plan of action, in a more objective manner.

Social Interaction Skills

Vandergrift (1980) views story as "a primary means of connection between children and the world" (p. 297). Story is a medium for discussing problems and ideas, for verifying thoughts and feelings, and for practicing communication and relationship skills. Story can facilitate prosocial responding. Sharing behaviors among preschoolers increased following five 30-minute sessions of reading books about sharing, with subsequent role play and discussion of story themes (Shepherd & Koberstein, 1989). Children's prosocial behaviors increase after viewing televised programming that depicts such behaviors as helping, sharing, empathic responding, cooperation, and constructive conflict resolution. Clements and Nastasi (1993) and Van Evra (1990) provide reviews of the effects of televised programming on personal–social development.

Repeated collaborative experiences with story facilitate the establishment and maintenance of relationships. For example, in a social skills group a school psychologist had used children's books for several months to introduce, discuss, and role play personal–social competencies. During discussion of a story about friendship, one 8-year-old girl commented that she considered the other participants to be her friends, explaining, "We got to know each other when we read stories together and talked about things that happened to us."

Exploration of story from diverse cultures can foster understanding and perspective taking regarding the variety of sociocultural experiences within a given group, thereby facilitating the co-construction of meaning and norms. Such exploration also can extend one's experiences beyond those of the group and encourage critical examination of the self in relationship to others from a more global perspective. For example, the life of Gandhi (depicted in literature or film) provides the context for discussing peaceful conflict resolution and the notion of a global community in addition to examining the social and political history of India.

With regard to teaching specific social interaction skills, story provides both characters who model target skills and scenarios for rehearsal through role play. The distancing or removal of the story's characters and setting from the immediate sphere of experience furnishes a way to explore the violation of behavioral norms and the consequences of transgressions, without the real-life experience of sanction or reprisal. Thus, story gives adults a way to teach potential consequences of undesirable behaviors. Caution must be exercised, however, regarding the presentation of inappropriate models; for example, through depictions of positive outcomes of undesirable behaviors. Research provides unequivocal support for the relationship between excessive violence in media and increases in the violent behavior of some viewers (Clements & Nastasi, 1993; Huesmann, 1986; Huesmann & Malamuth, 1986; Van Evra, 1990). This relationship, however, can be mediated by cognitive–behavioral interventions directed at changing perceptions about and teaching alternatives to aggression (Eron, 1986; Marton & Acker, 1981). Thus, story provides a context for facilitating social behavior change; however, effective use depends on mediating individuals' encounters with story.

In addition to viewing storied models of social behavior, individuals can create their own stories to depict target social interaction skills. For example, individuals can create and role play their own stories to be videotaped and used as personalized models of effective social interactions. Such use—viewing oneself on edited videotapes exhibiting exemplary behaviors—is supported by research on self-modeling (Kehle & Gonzales, 1991). The use of self-modeling from a social construction perspective requires the involvement of the participants in creating and editing personalized models.

Stories, in a variety of forms, provide contexts for promoting personal–social competence. We use story in the ESCAPE curriculum to enhance self-efficacy, interpersonal problem solving, and social interaction skills. Mediation of individuals' encounters with story is essential.

Planning Encounters with Story

Story is the context for exploring emotions, discussing problems, and engaging in interpersonal cognitive problem solving. Stories also provide scenarios for role playing hypothetical or real-life experiences and trying alternative solutions in a protective environment. Through such discussion and role play, story can be used to enhance personal–social competencies within the context of existing school curricula. This use of story facilitates integration of social skills or drug education curricula with academic curricula such as reading, language arts, and social studies. The method of implementation is likely to vary depending on the developmental level of students. For example, the teacher is likely to present stories orally to preschool and early elementary students, whereas older students are likely to read stories independently. Discussions of stories can be conducted as a group process and may occur at the end of the story or at critical points throughout the narrative.

The recommended scheme for using story, presented in Chapter 3, can be easily integrated into instructional sessions focused on assessing and facilitating story (language, reading) comprehension. The sequence for discussing story involves (1) focus on the story in a depersonalized manner, (2) focus on personalized application of the story, and (3) use of the story as a stimulus for engaging in interpersonal problem solving. The facilitator questions participants about affective, cognitive, and behavioral components of both the story characters' and the students' personal experiences. The goal of such questioning is to facilitate learning and application of interpersonal problem-solving strategies within objective (e.g., literature) and subjective (related personal experiences) contexts of story. The facilitator uses questioning, prompting, modeling, explaining, and clarifying (see Chapter 3). Initial discussion of the story content provides a means for integrating academic and personal–social competence goals, through the focus on story comprehension framed in a problem-solving perspective. This allows students to think about problem situations in an objective manner and to discuss the emotions, cognitions, and behaviors as belonging to the story characters. Some students, however, might immediately relate the story to personal experiences.

As one structures children's encounters with stories, it is important to heed the warning of Vandergrift (1980). She defines the therapeutic use of children's literature as "at its best, a means of helping one make connections between books and his own life" (p. 281), and warns that merely trying to match problem books to problem children, or to children's specific problems, is the basic cause of disconnection of child and story. Concerning the therapeutic value of story, Vandergrift states:

> In the sense that literature takes a reader outside of himself and enables him to think about what it feels like to be in another time, place, and situation, or even what a character feels like in a situation similar to his own, all story is therapeutic. (1980, pp. 281–282)

Similarly, to the extent that story provides opportunities to (1) enhance one's sense of mastery over the environment, (2) explore alternative problem solutions and consequences, (3) establish connections with other individuals and cultures, and (4) enhance self-definition, all story has the potential for enhancing personal–social competence. In Chapters 3 and 4, we provide specific guidelines and activities for such use of story.

Thus far, we have provided the theoretical and empirical basis for developing school-based programs for children of alcoholics. In subsequent chapters, we present the practical considerations for program development, implementation, and evaluation; a K–12 curriculum designed to enhance generalizable coping skills of COAs; and resource materials for school-based programming.

APPENDIX 2A

Review of Selected Studies on Characteristics of COAs or COSAs

Reference	Subjects	Method/Criteria	Results[a]
Ballard & Cummings (1990)	35 children, ages 6–10; 13 COAs (12 with alcoholic father); Caucasian[b]; mixed socioeconomic status (SES). All volunteers; COAs recruited through alcohol treatment centers, AA, ACOA,[c] or Al-Anon; non-COAs recruited by newspaper or flyers. Alcoholic parents diagnosed or self-identified.	Compared COAs' and non-COAs' responses to analogue (videotape) presentation of hypothetical angry and friendly adult interactions, including their perceptions of adult anger, emotional reactions to adult anger, and proposed solutions to adult interactions; parental ratings of child adjustment, CBCL[d] (Achenbach, 1991b); parental self-report of marital adjustment/distress and conflict management.	Analogue—COAs, compared with non-COAs, more often proposed solutions to adult interactions, particularly indirect solutions (e.g., minimize the distress of adult). Male COAs responded with less anger than female COAs; male non-COAs with more anger than female non-COAs. Parental reports—for COAs, more child behavior problems; greater marital distress, verbal and physical conflict. Marital distress and conflict accounted for the relationship between COA status and behavior problems. Across groups, children (1) perceived anger as more negative than friendly interactions; (2) perceived physical anger as most negative, and indirect anger as least; (3) responded with more anger to angry than friendly interactions, with the greatest anger toward destructive adult anger; (4) responded with more distress to anger than to friendly interactions; and (5) perceived angry adults as having more negative feelings toward children, especially for displays of aggressive anger.

Reference	Subjects	Method/Criteria	Results[a]
Barnard & Spoentgen (1986)	368 college students, ages 18–21, at small Midwestern state university.	Compared COAs seeking treatment (educational support group), COAs not seeking treatment, and non-COAs on self-report measures of inner-directedness, self-regard, self-acceptance, feeling reactivity, and capacity for intimate contact.	COAs seeking treatment scored lower on all self-report measures compared to those not seeking treatment and to non-COAs. COAs not seeking treatment scored higher on capacity for intimate contact, compared with non-COAs.
Berkowitz & Perkins (1988)	860 liberal arts college students, ages 16–23 from Northeastern region, upper-middle class.	Compared self-identified with non-identified COAs on self-report measures of emotional adjustment (impulsiveness, lack of tension, self-depreciation), interpersonal orientation (independence/autonomy, need for social support, directiveness, sociability), and other-directedness.	COAs reported higher self-depreciation, independence/autonomy. Male COAs higher than male non-COAs on independence/autonomy. Female COAs higher than female non-COAs on self-depreciation.
Calder & Kostyniuk (1989)	62 parents (33 fathers, 29 mothers) in treatment for alcohol problems; children ages 6–16 (data provided for the eldest child, under the age of 17); Canadian.	Compared alcoholic parents' ratings of children's personality with published norms of the PIC[d] (Wirt et al., 1984); 12 clinical scales—achievement, intellectual, development, somatic concerns, depression, family relations, delinquency, withdrawal, anxiety, psychosis, hyperactivity, social skills.	COAs exhibited elevated scores (significantly different from the norms; indicative of maladjustment) on 11 of 12 scales (excluding Intellectual); mean COA scores greater than 1 standard deviation (sd) above the mean of norm sample on family relations, delinquency, depression, withdrawal; overrepresented in the clinical range by 4:1. Majority of COAs had scores in the normal range; 50% of COAs had no elevated scores.

Reference	Subjects	Method/Criteria	Results[a]
Clair & Genest (1987)	70 adults, ages 18–23, primarily female (F); 30 (28F) with alcoholic fathers, 40 (34F) from non-alcoholic families; self-selected Canadian sample. COAs solicited through newspapers, posters, and community AA and Al-Anon contacts; non-COAs, university undergraduates.	Compared COAs with non-COAs on retrospective (adolescent experiences, ages 13–18) self-reports of family environment, coping strategies, and social support; and current self-ratings of depressive tendencies and self-concept. Examined relationship of prior (adolescent) family environment, social support, and coping to current (adulthood) depressive tendencies and self-concept.	COAs, compared with non-COAs, reported lower family cohesion and intellectual orientation; higher family conflict (family environment); less informational support (social support). COAs (vs. non-COAs) were more likely to view family problem situations as unchangeable; to use coping strategies of wishful thinking and help-seeking/ avoidance; and to report depressive tendencies. COAs were more likely to use emotion-focused than problem-focused coping; for non-COAs, comparison was non-significant. Greater depressive tendencies predicted by less independence from family (family environment), less informational support, greater self-blame (coping). Lower self-esteem predicted by lower family cohesion and greater use of emotion-focused coping.
Drake & Vaillant (1988)	At initiation, 456 non-delinquent, adolescent, inner-city males (mean age = 14).	Longitudinal (33-year) study of COA and non-COA males, from adolescence to adulthood. Predictor variables (at adolescence) based on interviews with subjects, parents, and teachers, and on social service records from multiple agencies—familial use of and attitude toward alcohol; social, economic, and family environment; adolescent adjustment.	At adolescence, COAs had more alcoholic relatives, more environmental stressors (e.g., known to 9+ social agencies, physical abuse, separation from parents for 6+ months), poor parent–child relationships, and poorer adjustment (emotional problems, poor physical health, general competence in age-appropriate skills); poor adjustment was associated with poor maternal relationship.

Reference	Subjects	Method/Criteria	Results[a]
Drake & Vaillant (*cont.*)	At 33-year follow-up, $n = 399$.	Outcome variables (at adulthood), based on semistructured interview with subjects and recent psychiatric, medical, and arrest records—DSM-III[d] alcoholism and personality disorder criteria.	At adulthood, 28% of COAs were diagnosed with alcohol dependence—predicted by number of alcoholic relatives, low SES[c], school behavior problems; 25% diagnosed with personality disorder—predicted by environmental weaknesses, poor maternal relationships, feelings of inadequacy.
Fisher et al. (1992)	174 adults, median age range 31–40; White. Three groups: 97 ACOAs; 36 with other dysfunctional family history (e.g., divorce, death, sexual or physical abuse); 41 controls. Solicited through announcements in public locations for study of individuals with/without family history of dysfunction.	Compared ACOAs, those with other dysfunctional family histories, and control group on self-reports of problem events in family of origin, participation in social support organizations (e.g., AA, Al-Anon), frequency of adult problems (including common ACOA personality characteristics based on clinical reports).	Greater frequency for ACOAs, compared with controls, of common ACOA characteristics—guesses at normal, lies, has difficulty having fun, overreacts to changes over which one has no control. ACOAs, compared with dysfunctional family group, reported higher frequency of difficulties with intimate relationships.
Gross & McCaul (1990–91)	88 adolescents; ages 12–17; high-risk, urban, low SES, 60% Black.	Compared COSAs[c] (70%, alcohol) with non-COSAs, on self-report measures of self-concept, behavior problems, depression, substance use; parental marital status.	COSAs reported higher somatic complaints and delinquent behaviors. Fewer COSAs living in intact, nuclear family.
Jarmas & Kazak (1992)	207 college students, large, urban, Northeastern university; 84 with alcoholic fathers (parental adaptation of SMAST[d]),	Compared ACOAs and non-ACOAs on self-reports of (1) indivi- dual functioning—defense mechanisms (turning against others/self), depressive experiences (dependen-	ACOA (vs. non-ACOA) males reported more alcohol-related problems (26% met criteria for alcoholism on SMAST; non-ACOA males, 9%) and used alcohol and drugs more frequently. ACOAs

Reference	Subjects	Method/Criteria	Results[a]
Jarmas & Kazak (*cont.*)	cy, self-criticism, 123 with nonalcoholic parents.	self-criticism, efficacy), alcohol-related problems (SMAST); and (2) family environment— socio-environmental family characteristics (cohesion, expressiveness, conflict, organization, achievement orientation), problematic family functioning (communication), parental inconsistency of love (separate ratings for mother and father).	reported greater degree of introjective depression (self-critical, prone to guilt), excessive self-criticism, turning against others as defense; perceived families as having greater inconsistency, less cohesion, less expressiveness, more conflict, less organization, poorer communication. Father's inconsistency was single best discriminator between ACOAs versus non-ACOAs.
J. L. Johnson, Boney, & Brown, (1990–91)	72 children, ages 8–14; Eastern metropolitan area; 57% Caucasian, 43% Black.	Compared COSAs to non-COSAs on self-report measures of depression, state and trait anxiety, and standardized tests of academic ability.	COSAs scored higher on measures of depression and trait anxiety, and lower on arithmetic.
Knoblauch & Bowers (1989)	655 college students (mean age = 18.3), randomly selected from freshmen at Midwestern university.	Compared self-identified COAs and non-COAs; self-reports of problem drinking and need to control.	COAs reported higher levels of problem drinking and need to control.
Manning et al. (1986) *Three studies*	*Study 1*: 62 families (21 alcoholic, 41 nonalcoholic), mothers and children (ages 5–17); Caucasian, blue collar, New England urban community; 50% of COAs, single parent (35%, non-COA); with mother 50% of the time. Sampling—alcoholic, in treatment program for spouses of alco-	Examined the prevalence of Type A behavior pattern in COAs versus non-COAs. Type A—relatively chronic struggle to achieve poorly defined goals in shortest period of time; marked by competitive achievement, striving, time urgency, impatience, aggression, hostility. Type B—do not exhibit these traits. Parents' ratings and child self-report. *Study 1*:	*Study 1*: COAs scored higher on impatience/aggression; no birth order effects.

Reference	Subjects	Method/Criteria	Results[a]
Manning et al. (*cont.*)	holics; non-alcoholic, parent's night at public school.	Compared mothers' reports of children's Type A characteristics (competition and impatience/aggression).	
	Study 2: 58 recovering alcoholic fathers and 81 male controls; U. S. military personnel. All children ages 5–17 (95 COAs, 143 non-COAs); matched age, race, sex.	*Study 2*: Compared fathers' reports of children's Type A characteristics (competition, impatience/aggression).	*Study 2*: First-born COAs higher than siblings on competition.
	Study 3: 70 children, 35 children of recovering alcoholic, 35 nonalcoholic parents; Grades 4–12; Southern metropolitan area; Caucasian, middle to upper-middle class; matched age/grade, race, sex. Recruitment—social group for recovering alcoholics; non-COAs from private school, same community and SES.	*Study 3*: Compared children's self-reports of Type A characteristics (energy, impatience/aggression, leadership, alienation).	*Study 3*: No significant differences.
Pease & Hurlbert (1988)	60 adults, male veterans; 27% Black, 73% White.	Compared non-alcoholic (employees of VA medical center) and alcoholic (DSM-III diagnosis of alcohol dependence; patients at alcohol treatment center of VA medical center); self-report measures of child-rearing attitudes.	Alcoholics less supportive of child-rearing practices that encouraged verbalization and emotional expression, and avoided harsh punishment; more tolerant of aggression in children, irresponsibility by father, and inconsiderateness toward spouse.

Reference	Subjects	Method/Criteria	Results[a]
Perkins & Berkowitz (1991)	860 college freshmen and sophomores; upper-middle class, ages 16–23; Northeastern region. 15% reported having at least one parent or grandparent diagnosed or treated for alcoholism. Groups: Diagnosed/ treated alcoholic parent, $n = 41$; grandparent, 77; both, 10; neither, 727.	Compared children of alcohol parents and grandparents with non-COAs; self-reports of problem drinking and family alcoholism (parents, grandparents).	Higher rates of problem drinking for those with alcoholic parent or grandparent, compared with non-COAs. Highest rates if both alcoholic parent and grandparent. Self-concern about drinking and reports of negative consequences of their drinking more prevalent for those with more stressful family situations related to alcohol use. Majority (63%) who reported experiencing the greatest stress and discord related to parental alcohol abuse had parents not diagnosed/treated for alcoholism.
Reich et al. (1988)	54 children ages 6–17, and their parents; Midwestern, middle or working class families.	Compared COAs with non-COA hospitalized medical controls; part of ongoing family genetic study of alcoholism. Structured interviews with children and parents regarding child adjustment and family environment.	Based on child interview data, 72% of COAs and 27% of non-COAs received at least one DSM-III diagnosis (mostly behavioral). COA family environments were characterized by more marital conflict, parent–child conflict, maladaptive parental functioning, and physical and emotional abuse than non-COA environments. Presence of psychiatric diagnosis was associated with greater exposure to effects of parental drinking, more parent–child conflict, less parent–child interaction.

Reference	Subjects	Method/Criteria	Results[a]
Roosa, Sandler, Beals, & Short (1988) *Two studies*	*Study 1:* 208 high school students, Grades 9–12 (38 COAs; self-identified, CAST[d]); one public school, Southwestern metropolitan community, multiracial/ ethnic sample. Sampling: solicited through informed consent letters to parents (for study of stress and mental health, without mention of substance abuse focus). *Study 2:* 75 students, Grades 9–12 at five public high schools in a Southwestern city; multiracial/ ethnic sample; 32 (45%) self-identified as COAs (CAST). Sampling: volunteers from school-based support groups for students concerned with chemical abuse by parents, siblings, friends.	In both studies, compared COAs and non-COAs on self-reports of depression, anxiety, self-esteem, alcohol use.	*Study 1:* COAs higher on depression, lower on self-esteem, and (trend) higher on alcohol use. *Study 2:* COAs higher on drinking (trend). Non-COA participants in support groups higher on depression and lower on self-esteem compared to non-COAs from general school population.
Roosa, Beals, Sandler, & Pillow, (1990); Roosa, Gensheimer, Ayers, & Short (1990)	145 adolescents (mean age = 15 years, 9th and 10th grade, Anglo), recruited from general high school population and self-help groups; South-western metropolitan area; 43 self-identified COAs (70% female).	Compared self-identified COAs with general sample to test a stress process model for predicting mental health symptoms. Two administrations (3-month interval) of self-reports of stressors (positive and negative life events; COALES[d]), and psychological adjustment (depression and anxiety).	COA status was related to depression, anxiety, higher number of negative events, and lower number of positive events. Positive and negative events had immediate but not long-term (3-month) relationship to symptoms. Best predictor of later adjustment was earlier adjustment.

Reference	Subjects	Method/Criteria	Results[a]
Slavkin et al. (1992)	152 college students (61 COPDs,[c] identified with F/M-SMAST[d]; 91 non-COPDs); Eastern state university.	Compared COPDs and non-COPDs on analogue measures of problem-solving performance (number of solutions generated for hypothetical interpersonal and non-interpersonal problems; observer ratings of solution adequacy) and self-appraisal of problem-solving ability. Other independent variables were birth order and self-reported personal alcohol abuse (MAST[d]).	Solution effectiveness was higher for COPDs than non-COPDs, for first solution only, with later-born COPDs having the highest ratings. Alcohol-abusing COPDs reported less positive self-appraisal compared with alcohol-abusing non-COPDs; alcohol-abusing non-COPDs had the highest self-appraisal.
Stern et al. (1991)	90 children, Grades 1–5, and their parents; Western community; predominantly Caucasian, 25% Hispanic.	Compared proportion of COAs in three groups: regular education, emotional disturbance, learning disability. Identified COAs through children's perceptions of parental drinking, and parental perceptions of substance use within the family and codependency concerns.	Failed to find differences in proportion of COAs with regard to educational placement.
Weintraub (1990–91)	474 children, ages 7–16; White, lower-middle class, intact families; part of longitudinal study of schizophrenia.	Longitudinal study of children in three groups— at risk for alcohol abuse and psychiatric disorder (Comorbid; $n = 138$), at risk for psychiatric disorder alone (PD, 227), parents are diagnosis-free (Dx-Free, 109). Assessments at childhood (ages 7–16), following parental hospitalization for psychiatric problems; and 10 years later in adulthood (over age 18).	In childhood, both at-risk groups more maladjusted (social–emotional, academic) than controls. Comorbid group had highest rate of alcohol/drug use; externalizing, conduct problems; academic problems, school dropout. At adulthood, higher proportion of at-risk groups (Comorbid, 40%; PD, 30%; Dx-Free, 9%) exhibited DSM-III diagnosis compared with controls. Diagnoses of

Reference	Subjects	Method/Criteria	Results[a]
Weintraub (*cont.*)		Teacher and peer ratings in childhood (social–emotional and academic competence); self-reports in adulthood (social–emotional and occupational competence, alcohol/drug use, family environment). Home visit interviews with patient and spouse (family environment) and reports from offspring.	substance abuse disorder, depression, and antisocial personality more prevalent; and social and occupational competence more deviant in Comorbid group, compared to both PD and Dx-Free. Greater family disorganization (conflict, cohesiveness, marital adjustment, problems with family warmth and family stability) in at-risk groups.

[a]Only statistically significant differences are reported, unless otherwise indicated.
[b]Terms denoting race reflect the terminology of the original authors (e.g., African American, Anglo, Black, White, Caucasian).
[c]*Note*: COAs = children of alcoholics; COSAs = children of substance abusers, including alcohol; COPDs = children of problem drinkers; ACOAs = adult children of alcoholics; AA = Alcoholics Anonymous; SES = socioeconomic status.
[d]*Measures*: CAST = Children of Alcoholics Screening Test (Jones, 1981); CBCL = Child Behavior Checklist (Achenbach, 1991b); COALES = Children of Alcoholics Life Events Schedule (Roosa, Sandler, Gehring, Beals, & Cappo, 1988); DSM-III = Diagnostic and Statistical Manual of Mental Disorders (3rd ed.) (American Psychiatric Association, 1982); F/M-SMAST, parental (father/mother) versions of SMAST (Sher & Descutner, 1986); MAST = Michigan Alcoholism Screening Test (Selzer, 1971); PIC = Personality Inventory for Children (Wirt, Lachar, Klainedinst, & Seat, 1984); SMAST = Short Michigan Alcoholism Screening Test (Selzer, Vinokur, & Van Rooijen, 1975).

APPENDIX 2B

Review of Selected Efficacy Studies of Substance Abuse Prevention Programs: Resistance Skills and Personal–Social Competence

Reference	Goals[a]	Subjects[b]	Methods[c]	Outcome criteria[d]	Results[e]
			Resistance Skills		
Baer et al. (1988) *Two samples*	Substance use prevention. *Foci:* Resistance skill training; attitude change and decision making.	*Sample 1:* 1,307 7th graders in four junior high schools; Caucasian/ middle-class, suburb of Southwestern metropolitan community. *Sample 2:* 1,461 high school students (primarily 10th graders) from the same school district as Sample 1.	*Design:* Pre–post, control group design, with 1-year (Sample 2) and 2-year (Sample 1) follow-up. Quasi-experimental. Nonrandom assignment of classes (94% of students participated): (1) resistance training; (2) attitude change and decision making; (3) no-treatment control, program schools; (4) no-treatment, nonprogram schools. *Programs:* 22 sessions, 9 in common (self-expression, drug education, daily life alternatives to substance abuse). *Resistance training:* Recognition and resistance to peers, family, adults, media; self-esteem; assertiveness.	*Self-reported attitudes/beliefs:* Perceived adverse social consequences of substance use, estimate of peer influence, judgments about functions of substance use, tolerance of deviance, perceived peer/adult modeling of substance use (perceived approval, use of substances), negative self-judgments. *Self-reported behavior:* Frequency and quantity of substance use, academic grade point average (GPA), participation in extracurricular activities, deviant behavior during the previous year.	*7th graders* (at 2-yr follow-up): Positive effects of both interventions for participation in extracurricular activities and estimate of peer influence on substance use. For quantity of alcohol use, resistance training more effective with high levels of perceived peer/ parent modeling; attitude change and decision making more effective with low levels of perceived modeling. *10th graders* (at 1-yr follow-up): Positive effects of both interventions for quantity and perceived value of substance use.

Study	Focus	Sample	Design/Program	Measures	Results
Dielman et al. (1986)	Prevention of alcohol misuse. *Foci*: Knowledge (alcohol and its consequences) and resistance (peer and media influence) skills.	5,635 5th and 6th grade students from 213 classrooms in 6 school districts (each school with 1 to 7 classes per grade level) in Southeastern Michigan.	*Design*: Pre–post, control group. Randomized block; schools (matched on SES, racial mix, achievement scores) randomly assigned to treatment, treatment plus booster, or control. Half in each condition assigned to pretest or no pretest condition. *Program*: Classroom-based intervention in 5th grade, with booster in 6th, by project staff working in pairs. Four 45-min sessions; discussion, audiovisual presentation, practice, role play, videotaping and viewing of own successful refusals.	Self-reported knowledge (curriculum content), alcohol use and misuse (validated self-report with bogus pipeline procedure).	Positive results for knowledge of curriculum content 8 weeks after the intervention. Failed to document immediate effects on self-reported use.

Attitude change and decision making: Relationships among attitudes, beliefs, and behaviors regarding substance use, decision making, problem solving, life goals. Non-authoritarian group process, implemented by masters/predoctoral-level psychologists.

Reference	Goals[a]	Subjects[b]	Methods[c]	Outcome criteria[d]	Results[e]
Duryea (1983, 1985; Duryea et al. (1984); Duryea & Okwumabua (1988)	Alcohol education and prevention. Knowledge and skills focus.	Entire 9th grade of Midwestern parochial school (n = 155). At 6 months follow-up, n = 83; at 3 years, n = 130.	*Design:* Pre-, post- (2-week), and follow-up at 6 months and 3 years. Random assignment to educational program or control group; both with/without pretest (Solomon four-group). *Program:* Film presentation, question and answer, role play with feedback and discussion; six daily sessions, 1-hour each. Booster, school activities, and posters for an additional month. One-day teacher training.	*Knowledge* (alcohol effects on performance); *attitudes* (toward drinking and driving); *behavior-skills* (self-reported ability to refute arguments, intended non-compliance to risky alcohol situations, and drinking or riding with drinking drivers).	*2-week:* Positive effects on knowledge; ability to refute arguments, intended non-compliance with risky alcohol situations, attitude toward riding with drinking driver, frequency of drinking and riding with drinking drivers. *6-month:* Effects sustained for knowledge, refutation, non-compliance, and riding with drinking drivers. *3-year:* Groups not significantly different; all drinking less than initially.
Ellickson & Bell (1990)	Drug prevention program. *Foci:* Knowledge, attitudes, and behaviors (resistance skills) related to use of gateway drugs (tobacco, alcohol, marijuana).	7th and 8th graders from 30 schools, 8 districts in California and Oregon; urban, suburban, rural; wide range of SES and racial/ethnic groups (9 schools—50% or more minority; 18 schools—low income).	*Design:* Pre-, multiple posttest (3, 6, 12, 15 months), control group. Schools blocked by district and characteristics (test scores, primary language, ethnicity, income, drug use by 8th graders) and randomly assigned to 3 conditions: (1) 7th grade prevention curriculum	Self-reported *beliefs* about and *use* of tobacco, alcohol, marijuana; *saliva samples* (tobacco use). Based on pretest self-reported drug use, 3 groups were identified—nonusers, experimenters, users.	Positive short- and long-term program effects for substance use indices; for both adult-only and adult-plus-peer-leader programs. Variation in program effects by drug use level.

			with booster in 8th, conducted by adult health educator; (2) same program, conducted by adult health educator and high school peer leader; (3) control (school's existing drug education program). *Program*: Discussion, role playing, skills practice, small-group exercises. Eight weekly sessions in 7th grade; 3 booster sessions in 8th.	
Gilchrist et al. (1987)	Alcohol and other drug prevention. *Foci*: Person-environment fit; coping and resistance skills (interpersonal, problem-solving, stress management skills); knowledge and attitudes about drug use. Culturally sensitive; designed for Native American youth.	102 Native American youth (mean age = 11; 49% female) from 7 urban and rural sites in the Pacific Northwest.	*Design*: Pre-, multiple posttest (immediate and 6 month), control group. Random assignment by site to educational intervention or no-treatment control. *Program*: Ten 60-min sessions. Curriculum reflects specific cultural values and experiences. Implemented in school classrooms or tribal center, by two-person team (Native American project staff and indigenous professional). 10-hour staff training.	Self-reported *knowledge, attitudes*, and *behavior* related to substance use; *self-esteem* ; and *interpersonal skill* (response to hypothetical situation). Self-report *of consumer satisfaction* for program group.	*Immediate*: Positive effects for knowledge; interpersonal skills; frequency of tobacco use; and number of self-identified users of tobacco, alcohol, marijuana, inhalants. *Follow-up*: Positive effects for knowledge; interpersonal skills; frequency of substance use (alcohol, marijuana, inhalants); number of self-identified users of alcohol, marijuana, inhalants. (*cont.*)

Reference	Goals[a]	Subjects[b]	Methods[c]	Outcome criteria[d]	Results[e]
Gilchrist et al. (*cont.*)					*Consumer satisfaction:* High level of satisfaction with cultural sensitivity, immediate applicability to lives, overall drug use prevention effectiveness.
Hansen, Graham, et al. (1988)	Alcohol prevention program. *Foci:* Information (consequences of alcohol use); attitudes/beliefs (school/classroom norms about alcohol use); self-efficacy; resistance skills ("just say no").	718 5th graders and 710 7th graders from 10 elementary and 4 junior high schools; metropolitan West Coast community; predominantly Caucasian.	*Design:* Quasi-experimental. Schools assigned to one of three program components: information, resistance training, or normative education; 1 to 4 classrooms per school recruited. Compared differential effectiveness of three classroom.	Self-reported *knowledge* (consequences of alcohol use), *attitudes* (about alcohol use), *skill/behavior* (self-efficacy and ability to resist peer pressure).	Differential effects consistent with focus of the curricular component, for self-reported knowledge, attitude/beliefs, resistance skills. Failed to document effects for self-efficacy regarding resistance skills.
Hansen, Johnson, et al. (1988)	Prevention of onset of substance use. *Foci:* Affective education and social pressure resistance training.	2,863 7th graders from eight junior high schools in one West Coast metropolitan community; multiracial/ethnic sample with 38% Hispanic, 31% Black, 22% White, 6% Asian, 3% Other.	*Design:* Pre–post, control group design, with 12-month posttest and 24-month follow-up; each experimental condition compared separately with control, but not with each other. Random assignment of schools and classrooms to affective ($n = 24$ classrooms), social influence (25), no-treatment control groups (35).	*Behavior:* Self-reported substance use; that is, onset, incidence, prevalence.	Positive effects for onset of substance use for the social influence group only (compared with control). Negative long-term (at 24 months) effects for self-reported substance use, for the affective education group (compared with control).

Study	Program Focus	Sample/Design	Program Components	Measures	Results
Hansen, Malotte, & Fielding (1988)	Drug (tobacco and alcohol) education and prevention. *Foci:* Knowledge (parental influences, consequences of use); attitudes (norms, public commitment not to smoke or drink); resistance skills (peer and media influences).	Two samples, West Coast metropolitan community. *Sample 1* (over 4 years): 556 7th graders, ethnically diverse, lower middle to upper middle SES (District A); 665 7th graders, White, middle to upper-middle (District B). *Sample 2* (3-year): 1,379 7th graders (District A); 328 6th graders, high-income (District C). *Design:* Pre-, multiple posttest, quasi-experimental. Schools assigned to program or control. *Program:* Health or social studies teachers, minimally trained (1- to 2-day); 15 50-minute sessions. Peer leaders also. *Control:* Existing tobacco/alcohol education program.	*Programs:* 1-day staff training; 12 weekly sessions (3 months); didactic, active participation, peer opinion leaders. *Affective:* Personal development—self-esteem, assertiveness, stress reduction, goal setting, decision making. *Social influence:* Knowledge about sources of influence (peers, media); strategies for resistance ("say no," peer support).	*Behavior* (drug use): Saliva collection (tobacco use) and self-reported tobacco and alcohol use.	Experimental program reduced the onset and prevalence of tobacco use; failed to document effects for alcohol use.

Reference	Goals[a]	Subjects[b]	Methods[c]	Outcome criteria[d]	Results[e]
Newman et al. (1992)	Alcohol prevention (long-term). *Focus*: Knowledge and skill building related to resisting pressures associated with drinking (drinking, drinking and driving, riding with a drinking driver).	Two samples, approx. 3,500 each; entire 9th grade population of Midwestern urban school system, over 2 academic years; *Year 1*: 87 social studies classes (51 experimental, 36 control); *Year 2*: 84 English classes (48, 36), from same 9 junior high schools.	*Design*: Pre–post, control group design, with 1-year follow-up. *Program*: 10-session, didactic and videotape presentation, discussion, small group role play. 6-hour, 1-day teacher training.	Self-reported *knowledge* and *behavior* (perceived ability to resist, drinking behavior, incidences of riding with drinking driver).	Positive immediate effects on knowledge and perceived ability to resist; positive long-term effects on self-reported incidents of riding with drinking driver.
Schinke et al. (1988)	Substance abuse prevention. *Foci*: Bicultural competence (assertiveness in Native/non-Native American contexts); drug/alcohol resistance skills (communication, coping, decision making). Culture-specific content.	137 Native American youth (mean age 11.8; 54% girls), from two Western Washington reservation sites. Study conducted on reservation sites.	*Design*: Pre-, multiple posttest (immediate, 6-month), control group. Random assignment by reservation site to program or no-treatment control. *Program*: 10 sessions, with homework, by 2-person team (Native American counselors).	Self-reported *knowledge*, *attitudes*, and *interactive skills* (response to hypothetical, culturally relevant situations involving resistance to peer influence) related to substance use; also actual *substance use*.	Positive effects on self-reported knowledge, attitudes, interactive skills, and substance use (tobacco, alcohol, other drugs); at immediate and 6-month posttests.

Personal–Social Competence

Study	Focus	Sample	Design/Program/Control	Measures	Results
Botvin, Baker, Botvin, Filazzola, & Millman (1984)	Prevention of alcohol abuse. *Foci*: Information (consequences of alcohol misuse) and personal–social skills (decision making, coping, social, assertiveness, self-improvement).	239 7th graders; two schools in Eastern, metropolitan, ethnically diverse community.	*Design*: Pre-post, control group; 6-month follow-up. Random assignment (schools) to program or control. *Program*: 20 15-minute sessions; science teachers; 1-day training; alcohol information and personal–social skills. *Control*: Existing school drug prevention program.	*Behavior*: Self-reported drinking behavior.	No differences at immediate posttest; positive follow-up effects at 6-month follow-up for frequency of drinking, amount of drinking per occasion, frequency of drunkenness.
Botvin et al. (1990); Botvin, Baker, Renick, Filazzola, & Botvin (1984)	Multicomponent life skills training and substance abuse prevention. *Foci*: (Cognitive-behavioral) decision making, coping, social skills, assertiveness, resistance to peer/media influences, self-image, alcohol-related knowledge.	1,311 8th graders; 10 suburban junior high schools in Eastern region; primarily White, middle class, well-educated, two-parent families.	*Design*: Pre, multiple posttest (immediate, 1-year) control group. Schools randomly assigned to peer-led, with/without booster; teacher-led, with/without booster; no-treatment control. *Program*: 20 sessions, 7th grade; with/without 10 boosters, 8th grade. *Program techniques*: Discussion, modeling, practice, role play, goal setting, homework. Teacher training, 1-day. Peer leaders (*cont.*)	Self-reported *knowledge, attitudes*, and *behavior* regarding substance use (tobacco, marijuana, alcohol). *Personality*: Locus of control, self-esteem, self-confidence, assertiveness, social anxiety, and general and smoking influenceability.	*Posttest*: Peer-led most effective for substance knowledge, attitudes, and use; and personality variables. Teacher-led had positive effects on knowledge and social anxiety. *Follow-up*: Peer-led with booster most effective for knowledge, attitudes, use, personality. Teacher-led, implemented with fidelity, effective for substance use (for female students only).

Reference	Goals[a]	Subjects[b]	Methods[c]	Outcome criteria[d]	Results[e]
Botvin et al.; Botvin, Baker, Renick, Filazzola, & Botvin (cont.)			(10th–11th graders), 4-hour training; meeting before each session; detailed manual. Monitoring for most peer-led; periodic teacher-led.		
Caplan et al. (1992)	Prevention, classroom-based program. *Foci:* General personal–social competence and domain-specific coping strategies.	282 inner-city (72 experimental and 134 control, 90% Black) and suburban (37 experimental and 39 control, 99% White) 6th and 7th graders; two Southern New England schools.	*Design:* Pre-post, control group. Subjects stratified by ability, randomly assigned to intervention/control. *Program:* Biweekly, 15 weeks; six units: self-esteem, stress management, problem solving, assertiveness, social networks, drug and health information. *Program techniques:* Didactic, discussion, diaries, group role play, worksheets, homework; co-led by teachers and community health educators. Six (2-hour) teacher training workshops, weekly on-site consultation. *Control:* (science class) instruction on physical effects of substance use.	Self-reported coping *skills* (quantity, effectiveness of solutions to hypothetical vignettes about peer pressure and real-life stressors); social and emotional *adjustment* (general emotional state; self-perceptions of behavioral conduct, problem-solving skill, self-worth). *Attitudes* (smoking and drinking); *substance use* (frequency in past 2 months). Self-reports of program acceptability. Teacher ratings of *behavior* (conflict resolution with peers, impulse control, popularity, assertiveness with adults).	Positive program effects on self-reported coping skills, self-efficacy of problem solving, intention to use, and alcohol use; teacher-reported conflict resolution, impulse control, popularity. Effectiveness varied across classrooms. Over 90% liked the program, learned and used target skills, would recommend to peers.

Reference	Program description	Sample/Design	Measures	Results
Gersick et al. (1988); Snow et al. (1992)	Multiyear, classroom-based prevention of substance abuse. *Focus*: (Coping skills) decision making, conflict resolution, group process, social network utilization skills.	1,372 6th graders (2 samples); 698 in program group, 674 control (1,075 at 2-year follow-up). Each sample included all students in 32 6th grade classes in 20 public schools; two working/lower-middle class, racially/ethnically diverse New England communities.	*Design*: Immediate post-test, control group; 2-year follow-up. Schools grouped by SES and ethnicity; classrooms randomly assigned to program/control. *Program*: (12 weekly, 40-minute) Didactic, discussion, role play of target/focus skills.	*Skills/behavior*: Decision-making process (applied to hypothetical situations), knowledge of group dynamics (applied to audiotaped group discussion), self-reported substance use. At follow-up, only substance use measured.	*Immediate*: Positive effects on knowledge of decision making, group dynamics; self-reported tobacco use. *2-year*: Effect on tobacco use maintained. Negative effect on alcohol use (higher use for program).
Kim (1988)	Alcohol education and prevention, K–12 school curriculum (Here's Looking at You, HLAY); evaluation of short- and long-term effects. *Focus*: Alcohol use and personal–social skills (self-esteem, coping, interpersonal).	*Short-term*: (Immediate posttest) 900 students in HLAY, 135 in control; Grades 4–6, North Carolina metropolitan school system. *Long-term*: (1982–1987) 6,545 students, Grades 5–10, same school district.	*Short-term*: Pre–post control group design. *Long-term*: Compared alcohol use by self-identified program participants ($n = 310$) and nonparticipants (6,235). (Records of program participation not consistent).	*Short-term: Knowledge, alcohol use; attitudes*, alcohol use, intention to use; and *behavior*, self-reported alcohol use. *Long-term: Behavior*, self-reported alcohol use.	*Short-term*: Positive program effects on attitudes about alcohol use. *Long-term*: Negative effects on behavior (monthly alcohol use higher for self-identified 8th grade participants).

Reference	Goals[a]	Subjects[b]	Methods[c]	Outcome criteria[d]	Results[e]
Pentz (1985)	Social competence (self-efficacy and social skills) enhancement with primary focus on assertiveness; and decreasing drug use. Compare prevention training vs. prevention instruction vs. no-intervention.	$n = 1,193$ (originally, 1,472), Grades 6–9; eight public schools (four rural, four suburban) in one Southern county; 96% Caucasian; 51% female. Sample characterized by initially low rate of drug use at Grade 6 (5%) with sharp increases by Grade 9 (38%); consistent with national data.	Design: Pre-, multiple posttest (immediate, 6-month intervals over 2 years), control group. 25% of school population randomly selected by classroom within grade. Teams of four to five classrooms randomly assigned to prevention training, prevention instruction, or no-intervention. Prevention training: Skill-streaming; trained teacher and program asst.; nine 55-minute sessions; live/audiotaped models, rehearsal, feedback, reinforcement. Peer-led small group practice on every-day social situations. Instruction: Didactic, content and use of social competence (two sessions).	Drug-related attitudes, beliefs, behavior; personal–social skills: Self-reported drug use, intention to use, peer and parent use, availability, adult sanctions; self-efficacy regarding assertiveness and resistance skills in familiar/unfamiliar interpersonal situations. Social skills (audio-taped role play, hypothetical social situations). Self-reported social attitudes (e.g., school values, rebelliousness, student–teacher relationships, family cohesiveness). Achievement, truancy, absence.	Positive effects of training (vs. instruction and control) on self-efficacy, social skills, GPA. Positive effects on drug use for both training and instruction (vs. control). Training effects on drug use declined over time. Training and instruction groups significantly better than control after 2 years. Training effects greatest at Grade 9 for social competence; at grades 6 and 9, for drug use and intention.

Roosa, Gensheimer, Ayers, & Short (1990)	Alcohol education, and enhancement of coping skills and personal–social competence of COAs. *Foci:* Knowledge of alcoholism and its effects on family; social support; self-esteem (through cognitive mediation); coping/ personal-social skills (communication, problem solving, help seeking, emotion-focused coping).	81 4th–6th graders (26 experimental, 55 control) from 3 elementary schools; primarily low income, Hispanic population.	*Design:* Pre–post control group, random assignment of volunteers to treatment or control. One school, also personal trainers (generalization). *Program:* 8 weekly, 1-hour; small group (6–8), research and school staff cofacilitate. Discussion, didactic instruction, video demo, modeling, behavioral rehearsal, role play, homework. Personal trainer, 8 weekly (3–4 hrs) sessions, adult role model for specific skill.	Self-reported coping (problem- and emotion-focused), self-esteem, help seeking. Teacher report of classroom behavior. *Program acceptability:* Staff and student perceptions of and satisfaction with program; feedback from group leaders on session activities. *Program integrity (adherence):* Audiotaped all sessions. Community advisory board (professionals) reviewed program procedures/content.	Positive effects for problem- and emotion-focused coping; negative correlation of coping with teacher reports of problem classroom behavior. Personnel and students highly supportive of program. Effects of personal trainer component not evaluated, but acceptability by trainers and students high.

[a]*Goals* are the program foci, specifically resistance skills or personal–social competence. Other program goals included changing drug-related knowledge, attitudes, and behavior. Drugs refer to alcohol and other drugs such as tobacco and marijuana; the specific drugs are indicated when such information was available.

[b]*Subjects* are the program participants.

[c]*Methods* includes the research design and program procedures related to implementation, training of program staff, and program evaluation.

[d]*Outcome criteria* include the target criteria (i.e., drug-related knowledge, attitudes, and behavior; specific resistance skills or personal–social competencies) and the procedures (e.g., self-report) for measuring these variables.

[e]*Results* include statistically significant findings, except where indicated.

[f]Terms denoting race reflect the terminology of the original author (e.g., African American, Anglo, Black, White, Caucasian).

3

Designing, Implementing, and Evaluating School-based Prevention Programs

In this chapter, we provide information necessary for the development, implementation, and evaluation of school-based programs to enhance the personal–social competence of COAs. First, we review the general rationale for the ESCAPE program presented in the next chapter. Second, we describe intervention, assessment, and evaluation methods for implementing the ESCAPE program. Third, we discuss practical and ethical issues related to program design and implementation. We conclude with the characteristics of a school culture that promotes personal–social competence.

RATIONALE

The general strategies used in the ESCAPE program are based on a synthesis of the psychological and educational theory and research described in Chapters 1 and 2. These strategies are designed to foster development of personal–social functioning in general. The program is designed for implementation at a primary prevention level. In addition to the potential benefit for the general population, we encourage a preventive focus for several reasons:

1. Children in families affected by alcohol do not always identify themselves as COAs because of family denial systems.

2. An educative, curriculum-based focus is most consistent with goals of public education and is likely to facilitate integration into existing drug education and social skills programs.
3. Information presented in a nonthreatening educational setting facilitates acceptance by parents and school personnel and provides a context in which COAs may self-identify.

Although we focus on prevention, we provide guidelines to assist school personnel in securing services for COAs at secondary (i.e., for those identified as at-risk) and tertiary (i.e., for those experiencing adjustment difficulties) levels.

The ESCAPE program integrates strategies for enhancing personal–social competence with those that promote academic and cognitive competence. The recommended strategies reflect the synergism of self-efficacy, interpersonal problem solving, and social interaction skills; that is, many of the strategies address all three components simultaneously. For example, social feedback about progress toward a collaborative goal serves to enhance self-efficacy, to model communication of constructive feedback (i.e., social interaction skill), and to encourage the reflection and explication of collaborative problem solving. Although the program is designed as a classroom-based intervention, activities can be modified for individual or small group application.

Implementation in real-life group contexts strengthens ecological validity and facilitates generalization. In particular, the inclusion of familiar peers and adults (e.g., classmates and teachers) increases the potential for environmental support of target skills and minimizes the need to provide explicitly for transfer to real-life contexts. Our program's focus on co-construction of norms through a guided negotiation process further facilitates social support and reinforcement of target skills. The likelihood of skill acquisition resulting from group-based personal–social competence programs is high, with up to 90% of the participants acquiring target skills in some programs. Transfer to real-world settings, however, is typically much lower; for example, only 50% of the participants use skills outside of the intervention context (Goldstein et al., 1990). Such limitations suggest that we need to create environments that encourage and reinforce normative values and behaviors consistent with program goals, especially for adolescents, who are most likely to be influenced by peer behavior (Hawkins et al., 1992; Weissberg et al., 1991).

INTERVENTION METHODS

The curriculum-based intervention program we propose includes a variety of procedures for introducing concepts, facilitating knowledge and skill acquisition, influencing beliefs and attitudes, practicing target skills, and facilitating generalization. The role of the facilitator (e.g., teacher, school psychologist, counselor, social worker, peer facilitator) is to provide a context in which target skills can be learned, practiced, and generalized. As described in Chapter 1, our program is based on the premise that learning occurs as individuals within a specific sociocultural context co-construct knowledge and norms of behavior. From this perspective, social interaction and the coordination of divergent viewpoints are essential to the development of individual cognitions and behaviors and to the formation of group norms of behavior. Through repeated social exchanges within a given sociocultural context, newly acquired cognitions and behaviors are internalized. Adults and peers are important mediating agents (facilitators) in this socialization process.

The intent of our program is to facilitate social construction of cognitions, behaviors, and norms that foster development of individual personal–social competence. Rather than attempting to impose adult ideas and norms of behavior through a didactic approach, facilitators guide learning, using a set of facilitation techniques. In addition, facilitators provide practice using methods such as story, journal writing, role play, and cooperative learning. Furthermore, they foster generalization through integrating and extending activities within the academic curriculum, encouraging self-evaluation and self-monitoring, and using real-life experiences as foci for discussion and role play. Program implementation requires a classroom environment that fosters development of personal–social competence. Ideally, the classroom environment is supported by a school culture that promotes such development. In this section, we describe the methods for creating the classroom context; that is, facilitation, journal writing, role play, cooperative learning, use of story, social norms construction, goal setting, and generalization methods. In a later section, we describe the characteristics of a school culture that supports the development of personal–social competence.

Facilitation

The curriculum is implemented using facilitative, or guided instruction, methods. That is, rather than using direct instruction, the facilitator guides students to use target processes or skills through prompts and feedback. The four primary instructional techniques—modeling, scaffolding, explication, and reflection—are used to promote knowledge and skill acquisition, metacognitive awareness, and generalization. Content-relevant information is presented using these techniques in conjunction with didactic instruction and written and audiovisual materials.

Table 3.1 provides definitions and examples of both direct and guided instruction using modeling, scaffolding, explication, and reflection (cf.

TABLE 3.1. Facilitator Behavior Observation Scheme

Category	Definition
	Methods
Direct instruction	Instructs student(s) regarding target process or skill. For example, in response to a request for help, tells student(s) the problem-solving steps.
Guided instruction	Guides student(s) to use target process or skill, without giving direct instructions. For example, reminds student(s) to think about possible alternatives to solving a problem without providing explicit information. Categorized as follows:
General prompt	Poses question or statement to elicit use of *general* target process or skill. For example, "What do *you* think you need to do?"; "Think of the problem-solving steps."
Specific prompt	Poses question or statement to elicit use of *specific* target process or skill. For example, "What are ways to express anger?"; "Think of what is likely to happen if you hit someone."
Feedback	Gives performance-contingent feedback; that is, provides evaluative information about use of target process or skill. For example, says "Now you're getting the idea about how to solve problems."
	Techniques
Modeling	Provides a model (adult, peer, story character) of target process or skill; or provides performance-contingent feedback about (or reinforcement of) model's use of target process or skill.
	Example of Guided Instruction: Referring to the main character in the film, *Boyz 'n the Hood*, the facilitator says, "His decision *not* to seek revenge against the guys who killed his friend is a good example of what can happen when you think about the consequences of your actions. How do you think he came to this decision?" [The facilitator guides the students to engage in consequential thinking through additional general and specific prompts, as needed.]
	Example of Direct Instruction: Referring to the main character in the film, *Boyz 'n the Hood*, the facilitator says, "He made a good decision *not* to seek revenge against the guys who killed his friend. He probably said to himself, 'If I do this, I might get killed or end up in jail. This won't solve the problem.'"

(cont.)

TABLE 3.1. (*continued*)

Category	Definition
Scaffolding	Identifies current level of knowledge or skill and provides support (through cues, questions, prompts, feedback) to elicit use of target process or skill beyond the current level.
	Example of Guided Instruction (reflects a Vygotskian [1978] interpretation): The facilitator, recognizing that a student is having difficulty developing a work plan for a long-term project, uses the following prompts to guide the student's goal setting: "Tell me what needs to be done. What are the necessary steps? How long do you have to complete the work? What could you do next? How can you find out how long it will take to do each part? What information is provided in your textbook that might help? Who else in the class has figured out a plan? You might ask them how they figured out what to do next. I thought the way you planned your last science project was effective. Think about what you did then."
	Example of Direct Instruction (an analogue of successive approximation or shaping procedure): The facilitator, recognizing that a student is having difficulty developing a work plan for a long-term project, provides the following instructions: "You have figured out that there are four major parts to this project and that it must be completed in three weeks. It looks like you're not sure what to do next. These are the steps that you need to follow to figure it out. . . ." The facilitator directs the student through a step-by-step process of goal setting.
Explication	Poses questions or statements to elicit articulation of target process or skill.
	Example of Guided Instruction: As two students resolve a conflict about sharing materials, the facilitator uses prompts to help them state the strategies they used: "What did you decide? How did you decide?" [The facilitator guides the students to verbalize the steps they took to resolve the conflict, using additional general and specific prompts as needed.]
	Example of Direct Instruction: As two students resolve a conflict about sharing materials, the facilitator says: "I noticed you decided to take turns. You each said why you needed the materials and for how long. Then Joey said you could go first, and Billy said that maybe you could split up the materials."

TABLE 3.1. *(continued)*

Category	Definition
Reflection	Poses questions or statements to elicit identification and evaluation of target process or skill.
	Example of Guided Instruction: Following a cooperative learning activity, the facilitator asks students to record individually their use of conflict resolution strategies (e.g., using a checklist of strategies, or in journals). The facilitator then guides discussion of the effectiveness of those strategies, using questions such as: "What strategies did you use? How did they work? Was the goal accomplished? What else could you have done? What might you do in a similar situation in your neighborhood?"
	Example of Direct Instruction: Following a cooperative learning activity, the facilitator asks students to record individually their use of conflict resolution strategies (e.g., using a checklist of strategies, or in journals). The facilitator then identifies and evaluates the students' strategy use, saying, for example, "I noticed that one group used negotiation to answer the first question. Each person stated their ideas and then tried each one to see what worked best. That seemed to work well, because everyone got a chance to participate and they got the right answer. But it took a long time and they did not finish the second problem. That was OK, because working together requires that you figure out how to resolve conflicts. The group could have come to the same answer in less time by working in pairs to try different solutions. Negotiation might be a good way for students to resolve conflicts at recess when they all want to play something different."

Clements, 1990; Clements & Nastasi, 1990. In the following sections, we describe the four instructional techniques in the context of guided instruction.

Modeling

The facilitator provides live (adult, peer) or vicarious (e.g., story characters) models of target processes or skills. Effective modeling depends in part on making explicit the behaviors to be imitated, providing reinforcement of the model's behavior, and ensuring similarity between the model and observer (Bandura, 1977). Examples of how the facilitator implements modeling within our program are as follows: (1) verbalizes the steps while demonstrating solutions to actual problems that occur within the group context; (2) provides performance-contingent feedback and reinforcement to students (or peers) engaging in problem solving; (3) selects a diverse representation of story models that reflect group composition and a broad array of competencies (e.g., academic, social, athletic); and (4) provides not only models of mastery or goal attainment, but also models of the process of coping or progress toward goal attainment. In addition, the facilitator provides models that reflect seemingly discrepant characteristics such as self-assertion and perspective taking (cf. Harter, 1990c). For example, the facilitator expresses his/her personal viewpoint about a current social issue and encourages students to express alternate views.

Scaffolding

The facilitator provides the necessary support (cues, prompts, questions) to help students reach beyond current knowledge or skill levels. This requires that the facilitator is able to determine a student's current level of understanding or mastery, and provide just enough support so that the student progresses toward a higher level. Both adults and peers with more advanced skills can provide scaffolding. From a Vygotskian (Vygotsky, 1978) perspective, scaffolding makes it possible for students to perform tasks that are not currently in their repertoire. In addition, scaffolding provides the context for skill acquisition (i.e., students then perform independently tasks that initially required support). Guided scaffolding includes (1) questioning students to explain their thinking or strategies, (2) prompting them to think about general strategies or attend to specific information relevant to problem solution, (3) suggesting resources for additional information, and (4) providing feedback contingent upon performance. For example, the facilitator who recognizes that a group of students are focused on a single problem solution suggests that they generate a list of alternatives through brainstorming, reading stories about how others have solved the problem, or asking peers how they solved similar problems.

Explication

The facilitator attempts to bring target processes and skills to an explicit level of awareness. For example, as the group solves a problem, the facilitator questions the students to help them identify the strategies they are using. In addition, students are encouraged to verbalize their thinking to each other and/or to make a written record of the strategies they are using. To facilitate explication, the facilitator encourages students to develop visual and/or verbal cues depicting target processes, and to use these cues as explicit reminders to engage in the target process. For example, students individually or as a group might draw pictures and/or identify key words to depict each step of interpersonal problem solving. Many of the published programs use such cues. Urbain (1982), for example, uses a stop sign and the slogan, "Stop and Think: What might happen next?" (p. 52), to signal consideration of consequences. Camp and Bash (1985) use pictures of Ralph the Bear to signal the problem-solving steps; a thought bubble with a light bulb depicts Ralph's thought, "What are some plans?" (p. 49), as a way of signaling alternative-solution thinking. McGinnis and Goldstein (1990) depict alternative solution thinking with line drawings of alternative activities (book, crayons, ball and bat; p. 153) for the young child to consider when he/she is told "no" regarding a preferred activity. To ensure individualized meaning, we suggest that students be encouraged to develop their own visual and verbal cues.

Reflection

The facilitator encourages students to explicate and evaluate their use of target processes and strategies. Reflection involves a process of self-monitoring and self-evaluation that can be used to facilitate generalization. The facilitator promotes reflection through (1) guiding group discussion and evaluation of problem solving and collaborative processes, (2) asking individual students to identify and evaluate their use of problem solving and collaborative strategies, (3) promoting regular use of journals for continued explication and evaluation of target processes and skills, and (4) modeling explication and reflection of his/her own teaching approach (i.e., the teacher makes explicit the goals of the activity and the process of goal attainment). Explicit reflection by the facilitator also may help to inform participants about the purpose, process, and potential benefits of activities, and provide a model for participant evaluation of activities. For example, participants can be asked to make explicit and evaluate the purpose, process, and perceived effectiveness (e.g., personal and group benefits) of activities by responding, in journals and/or discussion, to questions such as the following: What was the purpose of the activity? What did we do to achieve that purpose? What have you learned? This reflective process can facilitate assessment and promotion of intervention acceptability.

Cooperative Learning

Cooperative learning is an essential instructional component of our intervention approach. Certain characteristics of cooperative learning environments contribute to attainment of both personal–social and cognitive–academic goals (Nastasi & Clements, 1991). These characteristics include positive group interdependence, individual accountability, reciprocal sense-making, cognitive conflict resolution (particularly through negotiation and synthesis), and group processing (explication and evaluation of group dynamics). In this section, we provide guidelines for facilitating these types of collaborative interactions and for assessing and promoting personal–social competence.

Positive Group Interdependence

Positive group interdependence is facilitated by forming groups with clearly defined and interdependent individual roles, such that every member's contribution is essential to task completion. This is best accomplished in a context in which diverse competencies are both necessary and valued, and individuals provide mutual social–emotional support. Guide students to (1) identify resources and activities necessary for task completion, (2) determine roles and responsibilities for each activity, (3) designate roles and responsibilities to group members based on competencies and interests, and (4) ensure that each member has a necessary part. In addition, encourage students to discuss their work, share information and resources, provide constructive feedback and encouragement, and challenge ideas (not people). To further facilitate interdependence among students, institute the "ask three before me" policy; that is, to ask three other students before asking the facilitator.

Individual Accountability

Individual accountability ensures knowledge and skill acquisition by all group members. Each student is responsible for understanding concepts and mastering target skills. Individual participation and group norms influence accountability. Help students to self-monitor, identify and use available resources, discuss understanding with peers, and self-evaluate. Provide individual feedback and reinforcement of progress toward acquiring knowledge and skill, especially during the initial stages of mastery. Encourage group responsibility for monitoring individual contributions and outcomes. Establish individual accountability criteria based on current skill level.

Reciprocal Sense-Making

Reciprocal sense-making involves the co-construction of ideas such that all members contribute ideas, attempt to understand others' perspectives, and build upon others' ideas as they work toward a mutual goal. Promote negotiation of perspectives and consensus building, using the steps of collaborative problem solving (Table 3.2). Encourage students to (1) be receptive to diverse perspectives, (2) explain their ideas to each other, (3)

TABLE 3.2. Problem-Solving Steps Applied to Interpersonal and Collaborative Situations

Steps of interpersonal problem solving	Steps of collaborative problem solving
1. Recognize feelings in self and others 2. Identify and define the problem 3. Generate alternative solutions 4. Consider the consequences of each solution, to self and others 5. Choose the "best" solution 6. Implement the solution 7. Evaluate solution effectiveness	1. State feelings (each person) 2. Define and clarify the problem in terms of needs and views of each person 3. Brainstorm possible solutions 4. Consider how the solutions meet the needs or integrate the views of participants 5. Choose the "best" solution, seeking consensus or synthesis 6. Implement the solution 7. Evaluate the solution process

try to make sense of other's explanations, (4) ask specific questions when seeking clarification, and (5) give more elaborate explanations when others seek clarification.

Cognitive Conflict Resolution

The facilitator plays a critical role in promoting engagement in and resolution of cognitive (idea) conflicts through negotiation and attempts to synthesize discrepant ideas. Students may be uncomfortable with conflict. Emphasize that better ideas can result from contributions of multiple perspectives. Encourage students to propose alternative ideas, consider the varied perspectives, and work toward consensus. Using the collaborative problem-solving model (Table 3.2; also described in Chapters 2 and 3), encourage students to reflect upon the discrepancies and similarities between their own and others' ideas and to consider possible resolutions; for example, through acceptance of one person's idea, a compromise among several ideas, or integration of multiple ideas. (For additional information and specific procedures for facilitating conflict resolution among children and adults, see Bolton, 1979; Drew, 1987; Friend & Cook, 1992; D. W. Johnson & Johnson, 1987; D. W. Johnson, Johnson, Dudley, & Burnett, 1991; Kreidler, 1984; Shrumpf et al., 1991).

Group Processing

Following cooperative activities, the facilitator guides group discussion of the collaborative process using questions from Table 3.3 (cf. Nastasi &

TABLE 3.3. Questions to Facilitate Self-Evaluation of Group Process

Positive group interdependence

What was the purpose (goal) of the activity?
What were the necessary roles? How did you divide up roles?
What resources were necessary? How did you obtain and share resources?
What did you need to do to accomplish the task?
What steps did you take?
How did you help each other?
How did you let someone know you liked/didn't like what they said or did?
How did you react when someone liked/didn't what you said or did?

Individual accountability

When you did not understand, what did you do?
When someone in the group did not understand or made a mistake, what did you do?
How did you make sure each person participated?
What did you do if someone didn't participate?

Reciprocal sense-making

How did you include everyone's ideas?
When you had a question what did you do? Whom did you ask? What if that person did not know?
What kind of questions did you ask when you did not understand? What if you still did not understand even after someone answered your question?
How did you answer another person's questions?
How did you explain your ideas to each other? How did you add on to each others' ideas?
If someone did not understand your explanation, what did you do?
How did you know if others understood your explanation?

Cognitive conflict resolution

How did you encourage each other to think of different ways to solve the problem?
How did you make sure that everyone's ideas were presented? How did you make sure all group members had a chance to explain their ideas?
How did you tell others you disagreed with their ideas?
What did you do when group members disagreed on how to solve the problem?
How did you come to an agreement?
Which of these best describes how you resolved the disagreement? Give me an example.
    One person was the boss and made the decision.
    Everyone was nice to each other and quickly gave in.
    We gave each person a turn to make the decision.

TABLE 3.3. (*continued*)

We talked about all the ideas and agreed with one person's idea.
Each of us gave in a little to come up with a solution.
We tried to include part of everyone's ideas, to come up with a different
solution.
Other ways?
Was everyone satisfied with the resolution? Why or why not? What else could
you have done so that everyone's ideas were included?

General group process

What was the purpose of working together (vs. individually)?
What did you like most/least about working together?
What have you learned from working together?
What would you do differently next time? In general, how well did you work
together?
What difficulties (conflicts) did you have in working together?
How did you overcome (resolve) those? If difficulties were unresolved, how do
you plan to overcome (resolve) them?
Rate yourselves as cooperative problem solvers on 1–10 scale (10 = We are
excellent problem solvers). Explain the rating.

Generalization

To other interpersonal interactions:
What does cooperative problem solving mean?
What are the qualities of a good cooperative problem-solving partner (group)?
What have you learned from your cooperative work (in the classroom) that has
helped you to cooperate in other situations?
Tell me about how you used good cooperative problem solving in another situation.
Do you work better individually or with a partner? Why?

To academic domain-specific problem solving:
What does [academic area; e.g., mathematical] problem solving mean? What
are the qualities of a good [academic area; e.g., mathematical] problem-
solving partner?
What have you learned from [academic area; e.g., mathematical] problem solving
in the classroom that has helped you to solve problems in other situations?
Tell me about another time when you used good [academic area; e.g., mathe-
matical] problem-solving strategies.
Rate yourselves as [academic area; e.g., mathematical] problem solvers on 1–10
scale (10 = We are excellent problem solvers). Explain your rating.
How is [academic area; e.g., mathematical] problem solving similar to cooperative problem solving?
How is [academic area; e.g., mathematical] problem solving different from cooperative problem solving?

Clements, 1991). The purpose of discussion is to help students make explicit and evaluate their individual participation in the group process and the overall functioning of the group. When using the suggested questions, encourage students to give examples of situations that occurred during the activity. To facilitate generalization, encourage students to think of similar experiences in other situations. Encourage them to make explicit the link between academic domain-specific problem solving strategies and interpersonal problem solving. Appendix 3A consists of interviews with two pairs of fifth graders regarding their collaboration on a mathematics problem-solving task (Nastasi, 1993).

The rating scale in Table 3.4 can be used to facilitate group self-evaluation. The scale can be completed individually or collectively. For example, students complete ratings individually and reflect in their journals on their individual contributions to the group's functioning. The questions in Table 3.3 could be used to facilitate individual reflections in journals. Using the individual ratings and reflections, participants discuss their evaluations within their respective groups, thus facilitating intragroup evaluation and reflection. Alternatively, group members could collaborate on initial ratings. In addition, whole class discussion can facilitate intergroup evaluation and reflection, and promote the creation of classroom norms for collaboration. Effective intergroup discussion requires that the facilitator encourage cooperation and discourage competition among groups. Focus such discussions on the students' evaluation of their own cooperative strategies; for example, encouraging students to identify what strategies they used and the consequences of specific strategies for group functioning. In addition, encourage discussion of how to improve group functioning and promote the sharing of ideas across groups about successful collaborative interactions. Emphasize the uniqueness of each group and the concomitant need to develop specific strategies for the dynamics of each group.

Personal–Social Competence Assessment and Intervention

Cooperative learning activities provide a context for identifying target skills, evaluating progress toward the objectives of the personal–social competence program, and facilitating development and generalization of target skills. Successful participation in cooperative learning depends on a wide range of personal–social skills such as self-efficacy (e.g., perceived social and academic competence), coping strategies (e.g., for handling frustration, failure, or constructive feedback), social communication (e.g., active listening, asking questions, giving information, sharing ideas, nonverbal messages, giving constructive feedback), adherence to group norms (e.g., awareness and adherence to implicit or explicit group rules), problem solving (e.g., defining and solving problems individually or in colla-

TABLE 3.4. Group Process Self-Evaluation Rating Scale

[Instructions to group facilitator: Ask group members to rate the extent to which each statement describes the interactions or functioning of the group.] How well does each of the following statements describe your group? Circle the appropriate number:

We shared materials.			
1 = not at all	2 = sometimes	3 = most of the time	4 = all of the time

Each person had a role.			
1 = not at all	2 = sometimes	3 = most of the time	4 = all of the time

Roles were flexible.			
1 = not at all	2 = sometimes	3 = most of the time	4 = all of the time

We helped each other.			
1 = not at all	2 = sometimes	3 = most of the time	4 = all of the time

We encouraged everyone to participate.			
1 = not at all	2 = sometimes	3 = most of the time	4 = all of the time

Everyone did her/his part.			
1 = not at all	2 = sometimes	3 = most of the time	4 = all of the time

We criticized ideas, not people.			
1 = not at all	2 = sometimes	3 = most of the time	4 = all of the time

Each person had a chance to give her/his ideas.			
1 = not at all	2 = sometimes	3 = most of the time	4 = all of the time

We complimented members for their good ideas.			
1 = not at all	2 = sometimes	3 = most of the time	4 = all of the time

We tried to combine ideas.			
1 = not at all	2 = sometimes	3 = most of the time	4 = all of the time

(cont.)

TABLE 3.4. (*continued*)

We asked questions when we did not understand someone's ideas.			
1 = not at all	2 = sometimes	3 = most of the time	4 = all of the time

We tried to see each other's point of view.			
1 = not at all	2 = sometimes	3 = most of the time	4 = all of the time

We explained our ideas to each other.			
1 = not at all	2 = sometimes	3 = most of the time	4 = all of the time

We encouraged members to think of different ideas.			
1 = not at all	2 = sometimes	3 = most of the time	4 = all of the time

We tried to include part of everyone's ideas in our solutions.			
1 = not at all	2 = sometimes	3 = most of the time	4 = all of the time

boration), and conflict resolution (e.g., negotiation, perspective taking). The facilitator can gather information about the skill level of individual students through observations conducted during cooperative learning activities and through participants' self-evaluations of individual and group functioning. Furthermore, the facilitator can foster development and generalization of target skills using situations that occur during cooperative learning activities; for example, by guiding discussion and role play of alternative ways to resolve conflicts between partners. Observations and self-evaluations also provide information for helping students set personal goals and devise action plans. In Chapter 6, we provide an annotated bibliography of structured programs for teaching specific social skills.

A cooperative learning activity implemented with first graders provides an example of integrating assessment–intervention data. In the early stages of a social skills program, students participated in a collage activity that was integrated into the social studies (Alaskan culture) and science (winter weather) curricula. The teacher assigned students to three groups of eight, and guided them through the following: (1) selecting a theme for the collage related to Alaskan life and/or winter weather; (2) deciding on the steps and necessary materials; and (3) deciding who does what (e.g., who gets materials together, who draws what). Once these decisions were made, the teacher provided the materials and directed students to construct the collages. Each group's unique approach was reflected in the products. One group divided the collage into eight sections and each student did his/her own depiction of Alaskan life or winter scenes. The second group divided the collage into two sections; four students constructed a winter scene and four an Alaskan scene. The third group constructed an Eskimo wearing native garb and surrounded him with depictions of winter in an Alaskan village, thus integrating both themes. The first group had great difficulty negotiating different perspectives and resorted to individualized but parallel contributions. The second generated two themes and after unsuccessful attempts to choose one, decided to form two teams. Each team then worked cooperatively to construct half of the collage. The third group successfully negotiated diverse ideas into a synthesized theme. Observations of these interactions provided the teacher with data for planning subsequent activities. Specifically, she gave additional support to students who had difficulty with critical aspects of collaboration (i.e., perspective taking, communicating ideas, and conflict resolution) and regrouped students to provide peer models of successful negotiation.

Use of Story

A primary component of our intervention program is the use of story for exploring emotions, discussing problems, and engaging in interpersonal cognitive problem solving. In this section, we provide a format for effectively utilizing story. Table 3.5 presents a series of questions for guiding the use of story. The sequence proceeds from discussing the story in a depersonalized manner to a more personalized application of the story (cf. Gumaer, 1984). This progression allows students initially to discuss the emotions, cognitions, and behaviors of the story characters, and then to relate the story to their own personal experiences. Discussions of stories can be conducted as a group process and might occur at the end of the story or at critical points throughout the narrative. Although discussion would typically begin with an objective description of the characters' experiences, some students might immediately relate the story to personal experiences.

The facilitator then poses questions to guide an analysis of hypothetical and real-life contexts from a problem-solving perspective. This analytical approach, consistent with instructional strategies for promoting and evaluating language comprehension, integrates academic and personal–social competence goals. Thus, for example, interpersonal problem solving can be taught within extant reading, language arts, and social studies curricula. Likewise, the use of story in social skills and health curricula can facilitate language development.

In the ESCAPE program, we use visual, oral, and written forms of

TABLE 3.5 Using Story to Enhance Personal–Social Competence

Focus on the story in a *depersonalized* manner.
　Reconstruct the story (characters, events).
　　Who were the characters?
　　What happened in the story?
　Identify feelings and behavior of characters.
　　How do you think she/he was feeling? How could you tell?
　　What did she/he do?
　Identify alternative behaviors.
　　What would happen if . . . ?
　　How else could she/he have handled the situation?

Focus on real-life experiences in a *personalized* manner.
　How does this relate to your own experiences?
　Have you ever encountered anything like this?
　How did you feel?
　What did you do?

Focus on *effectiveness of coping strategies* (depersonalized and personalized).
　What was the problem the character encountered, or the goal the character
　　was trying to reach?
　How effective were the character's strategies for solving the problem, or
　　reaching the goal?
　How effective were your strategies in a similar situation?
　What other strategies may have worked for the character? for you?
　What might you do in the future in a similar situation? How effective are
　　those strategies likely to be?

story. Facilitators present story through literature, film, pictures, and storytelling. Students relate their own stories in oral, written, pictorial, and dramatic (e.g., role play) forms. In addition, students elicit stories from others (e.g., family and community members) through interviewing. We selected specific stories for the ESCAPE curriculum using the guidelines presented in Table 3.6. (See Chapter 5 for recommended literature and films, with developmental level and topic annotations. Stories used as examples in this chapter are listed there also.) Facilitators are encouraged to use these guidelines for critiquing and selecting additional stories. The application of selection guidelines to Cynthia Rylant's (1985) book, *The Relatives Came*, is shown in Table 3.7.

　　Story also is useful for identifying target skills, evaluating progress toward program objectives, and facilitating development and generalization of target skills. For example, during discussion of *The Relatives Came* in a social studies unit on family, the teacher assessed student understanding of the steps of interpersonal problem solving. For homework, he asked students to write in their journals about an interpersonal conflict that occurred during their own experiences with relatives. In the next session,

TABLE 3.6. Guidelines for Story Selection

- Developmental level (reading, conceptual, vocabulary)
- Type (fiction, nonfiction, biography, self-help)
- Form (book, movie, play, photo essay, newspaper, etc.)
- Relevance of theme or topic to program objectives
- Depiction of competencies related to the curriculum
- Perspectives of the author or characters
- Sociohistorical culture, including gender, race, ethnicity, language
- Mediation needed from the facilitator?

he guided students through role plays of solutions to these conflicts, using the assessment data collected during the preceding session.

Social Construction

The purpose of social construction activities is to facilitate the development of cognitions, behaviors, and group norms that promote individual personal–social competence. The facilitator guides the dialectic process in which students explore relevant hypothetical or real-life dilemmas, are encouraged to consider alternative perspectives regarding solutions, and

TABLE 3.7. Example of the Application of Guidelines for Story Selection

Rylant, C. (1985). *The Relatives Came.* New York: Bradbury Press.
- Developmental level (reading, conceptual, vocabulary)
    Elementary—Grades 3 to 5
- Type (fiction, nonfiction, biography, self-help)
    Fiction
- Form (e.g., book, movie, play, photo essay, newspaper)
    Book
- Relevance of theme or topic to program objectives
    Family relationships, problem solving
- Depiction of competencies related to the curriculum
    Extended family members display caring and use collaborative problem solving to maintain relationships during summer visit
- Perspectives of the author or characters
    Told from the perspective of a child who views self and family as caring for each other by helping, sharing, problem solving, and hugging
- Sociohistorical culture, including gender, race, ethnicity, language
    Rural mountain community, Caucasian, English-speaking; relatives from Virginia
- Mediation needed from the facilitator
    Facilitator guides discussion of family composition and relationships, helping students to relate to their own family experiences

as a group arrive at mutually agreeable solutions that are viable and consistent with norms of promoting competence. Information necessary to engage in informed decision making is presented in the context of discussing dilemmas. The processes of reciprocal sense-making and cognitive conflict resolution are integral to the norm construction process. Thus, students are encouraged to engage in consensus building through integration of compatible ideas (reciprocal sense-making) and synthesis of discrepant ideas (conflict resolution). Considering the highly contextual nature of much of the decision making related to personal–social competence, we recommend that students be encouraged to consider dilemmas within specific contexts that are relevant to their own life experiences. In an attempt to develop more generalized norms for social functioning, it may be necessary to consider multiple contexts.

The following is an example of perspective taking related to norms construction that occurred during a junior high health class focused on promoting mental health. We used the book, *The True Story of the 3 Little Pigs* by Jon Scieszka (1989), to introduce the dilemma posed by conflicting perspectives of individuals from different cultures (using the sequence in Table 3.5). Initially students discussed the story from the perspective of the characters (wolf and pigs), emphasizing the discrepancy between this version (the wolf's) and the traditional story (the pigs'). When we asked students to apply the theme to personal experiences, they first gave examples of situations in which adults (e.g., teachers and school administrators) misperceived their actions. They then talked about experiences with racial discrimination in the community and school. Finally, they focused on perceptions across gender lines, citing examples of immature behaviors exhibited by opposite-sex peers within their own group. Through discussion of their own shared experiences, male and female students discovered inconsistencies in their explanations of each others' behaviors. Specifically, female students perceived male roughhousing as immature and competitive, whereas male students described this behavior as a means of physical release similar to the girls' participation in games such as double-dutch. Boys perceived the girls' discussions about others as gossip, whereas the girls described this behavior as an expression of concern for self in relation to others and as a method for obtaining or providing social support. Through discussion of their discrepant views, students were able to clarify their expectations of each other in specific contexts. For example, they discussed differing views about standards of conduct on field trips. The girls expressed concern about boys' roughhousing, saying that they felt responsible for the boys' behavior and that the behavior of each member reflected on the group as a whole. The girls were also able to connect this sense of responsibility to their roles as babysitters of younger siblings. The boys expressed dismay over the girls' sense of responsibility, indicating that they did not experience the same concerns. Indeed, they thought that each person was to be held account-able for his/her own behavior and the actions of any individual in no way reflected on the group as a whole. For homework, students were directed to define maturity and give examples of mature behavior of same-age peers. The health educator used this information in the next session to continue discussion of establishing mutually agreeable norms for mature behavior and to further facilitate communication among the students.

We were impressed by the students' openness and willingness to discuss their views and to confront each other about apparent mispercep-tions. We provided scaffolding to facilitate perspective taking and con-sensus building, and mediated discussion to ensure that all views were represented (e.g., that each student had an opportunity to participate). Furthermore, we observed that as we moved from the hypothetical to the more personal dilemma, the students' enthusiasm and investment in re-solving the dilemma increased. This was in part exemplified by increased student participation in and direction of discussion. Students also began to talk directly to each other instead of to the facilitators. As the discussion progressed, we assumed the role of mediators rather than directors of discussion; eventually two students (one male and one female) began to take leadership roles as mediators of the discussion.

Journal Writing

Journal writing provides an opportunity for students to record descrip-tions of situations, their reactions and thoughts, and alternative solutions to dilemmas posed in those situations. It also allows students to reflect on the situation as it relates to their real-world experiences. Effective use of journals is facilitated by encouraging students to (1) maintain their jour-nals in ringed or spiral bound notebooks, (2) date all entries, (3) record their responses as soon after the event or situation as possible, and (4) share their work with others. Facilitators need to provide students with time to write in their journals, a variety of writing opportunities, an atmo-sphere of acceptance of their ideas, and encouragement to assume control of their writing experience. Use both structured and open-ended writing activities. Table 3.8 provides a structured format for application of inter-personal problem solving through journal writing. The use of journals for reflecting on group process (e.g., using questions in Table 3.3) exemplifies a more open-ended approach. Consider also the use of dialogue journals in which the facilitator and student converse on paper with each other, or in which students converse with each other (e.g., in reference to collabo-rative activities or resolution of disagreements). Journals may also contain drawings, photographs, and other student selected materials.

Facilitator and student readers are reminded to be genuine in their feedback, though not corrective, evaluative, or judgmental. For example,

TABLE 3.8. Journal Format for Applying Interpersonal Problem Solving

Actual	Future/alternative
(In this column, the focus is on documenting what has occurred. This information is used to plan the "future/alternative" scenario.)	*(In this column, the focus is on determining a different end and then generating alternative ways to handle the situation in order to accomplish that end.)*
[Feelings identification] How did you feel? How do you think others were feeling? How did you know what they felt?	[Feelings identification] How might you identify feelings? Your own? Those of others?
[Problem identification] What happened? What was the problem or situation?	[Problem identification] What is another way to define the problem? Have you experienced similar problems in other situations?
[Alternative solution thinking] What solutions did you think of?	[Alternative solution thinking] Generate as many solutions as you can.
[Means–end thinking] What was your goal? What steps did you think about taking to solve the problem (to reach the goal)?	[Means–end thinking] What is the goal? Short term? long term? Devise a plan for reaching the goal (solving the problem). What are the steps?
[Perspective taking] Who else did you have to consider? What were the other perspectives you needed to consider? How did you know what others thought?	[Perspective taking] What can you do to ensure that others' perspectives are considered?
[Causal thinking] Describe the chain of events. How did one thing lead to another? How did your behavior contribute to the situation? What else do you think contributed to the situation?	[Causal thinking] What is another possible sequence of events? What if you had done something different? What might have happened? Describe the chain of events you would like to see happen. What might you do to make that happen?
[Consequential thinking] What were the actual effects of your actions? What were other possible effects of your actions?	[Consequential thinking] What are the possible consequences of the solutions you generated? Short term? Long term?
[Implementation] What did you actually do to solve the problem (reach the goal)?	[Implementation] What will you do to solve the problem (reach the goal)?
[Evaluation of solutions] Did it work? How do you know?	[Evaluation of solutions] How will you know if it worked?

Note. The problem solving strategies correspond to those described in Chapter 1. Consider the developmental levels of the participants in selecting journal questions.

the facilitator might pose questions or ideas for consideration as alternatives, without commenting on the accuracy of student ideas. This approach is consistent with an emphasis on guiding students to develop competence-promoting norms, rather than imposing external standards. In addition, focus should be on idea generation, not technical quality (i.e., journals should not be substituted for academic writing activities). Although this is important at all grade levels, it is especially necessary in the early elementary grades where students' drawing and writing skills are less well developed. The importance of respecting the personal, even confidential, nature of journal contents needs to be stressed and must also be given consideration when deciding who will read the journals, how they will be discussed or processed, and where they will be stored.

The following is an example of using journal writing in a self-contained program with six elementary students with behavior disorders. This activity was incorporated into an existing social skills program. As part of a collaborative project, one of the authors (B. N., a school psychologist) discussed with the classroom teacher the use of story to accomplish the objectives of the program. The teacher and psychologist then modified the social skills curriculum to incorporate the use of story. The program was implemented in group format on a daily basis for the entire school year. Group sessions were cofacilitated by the classroom teacher and either a school psychologist or classroom aide. Cofacilitators shared the responsibilities for presenting information, facilitating discussion and journal writing, and behavior management. As the students' personal–social skills improved, the roles of facilitators and students changed. Initially, the facilitators focused on directing student participation and managing their behavior. As the year progressed, the students became more self-directed. The change from teacher- to peer-mediation became evident as students started reading stories, assisting each other with writing, directing feedback, and providing support to each other. They also facilitated generalization by helping each other to analyze and solve problems that occurred outside of the classroom. At the conclusion of the school year, the students commented on the friendships they had developed within the program. The following activity occurred in the early part of the program.

The teacher read Judy Viorst's (1972) book, *Alexander and the Terrible, Horrible, No Good, Very Bad Day*, to the group, and facilitated discussion using the sequence in Table 3.5. The teacher guided discussion of "bad days" experienced by the story character and by the students, with a focus on the steps of problem solving—identifying feelings, defining the problem, generating alternative solutions, and considering consequences. Using their journals, each student drew a picture and/or wrote a short story describing a relevant personal experience. The facilitators assisted students in writing as needed; for example, the student related the story and the facilitator recorded it verbatim, or the facilitator responded to requests for help with technical aspects (spelling, grammar, punctuation). The journal entries became the focus of subsequent application of problem solving, through group discussion and role play. To facilitate generalization, the students recorded in their journals coping strategies used on difficult days. The teacher structured this journal activity with the following questions (a variation of Table 3.8): What happened? What did you do? How did it end? What else could you do? How might it end? These entries were used in subsequent discussion and role play. As we will discuss in a later sections, the use of journals for recording daily experiences provides the context for self-monitoring and generalization. In addition, a consistent format for journal entries facilitates assessment of current functioning and evaluation of program effectiveness.

Role Play

Role play provides the context for rehearsal and practice of target processes and skills. For example, students can (1) rehearse verbal mediators, such as positive self-statements to enhance self-efficacy; (2) enact social interactions related to friendship making; and (3) practice problem-solving steps leading to assertive expression of anger. In addition, role play affords the opportunity to give direct instruction or prompting, assess skill level, and provide feedback and reinforcement. Furthermore, role play activities give students the opportunity to observe peer models and to encounter alternative perspectives. Videotaped role plays allow students to engage in self-modeling. Story serves multiple purposes in conducting role play: (1) story characters model target skills, (2) story plots supply role play content, and (3) students' stories provide role play scripts.

In structuring role play activities, the facilitator provides (e.g., through stories) or guides students to develop scripts. Students also can improvise as the role play progresses; for example, switching roles or enacting alternatives to predetermined scripts. All students should have opportunities to participate. It is critical that the facilitator monitors the role play activity in order to guide students through the process (e.g., prompting the student to think of the next step) and to support reluctant students. Props may be helpful for motivating participation. Puppets are particularly useful for engaging the early elementary student. We encourage collaboration with art, drama, and instructional resource personnel in developing content and materials for role play activities.

The following is an example of how role play facilitated perspective taking, decision making, and engaging in appropriate classroom behavior. In addition, the situation afforded an opportunity to reinforce desired behavior. The activity was part of a classroom-based social skills lesson in a program for elementary students with behavior disorders. To address a target student's oppositional behavior in response to teacher directives, we engaged the teacher (Ms. T) and the student (Jeff) in a reverse role play. We planned with Jeff and Ms. T an enactment of what typically transpired. The teacher (played by Jeff) asked the student (played by Ms. T) to complete a mathematics assignment. Ms. T refused, threw a temper tantrum, and was placed in time-out. Ms. T then returned to her desk and ultimately completed the assignment. Following enactment of this scene, Jeff was asked to demonstrate immediate compliance to Ms. T's request (i.e., to show Ms. T how it should be done). The reenactment transpired as follows: Ms. T asked Jeff to complete his math assignment. Jeff said, "OK, I'll do it"; simulated completion of the assignment; and said, "I'm finished, Ms. T." Ms. T then praised Jeff for his immediate compliance and simulated review and feedback about his work. The other students in the group, who had been observing the role play, cheered at Jeff's successful behavior. Group discussion and feedback then (1) reinforced Jeff for generating and implementing a successful alternative to noncompliance; (2) emphasized the connections between Jeff's decisions, his behavior, and the consequences; and (3) focused on Jeff's understanding of Ms. T's frustration in response to his noncompliance. Indeed, Jeff verbalized his frustration at Ms. T's noncompliance during the first scenario.

Goal Setting

Goal setting can be integrated into academic and social competence objectives. Goals should be (1) specific, (2) proximal (short-term) and distal (long-term), (3) process- and product-oriented, (4) difficult enough to challenge the individual, and (5) realistic enough to be attainable. To facilitate goal attainment, make sure that students have prerequisite skills and help them divide tasks into manageable components or steps. Make explicit students' capabilities for goal attainment and provide feedback or rewards for progress toward and following goal attainment. Encourage students to select their own goals, monitor their own progress, and evaluate their own performance. Table 3.9 provides a checklist for self-regulation of planning and goal setting. Teach and model coping strategies for handling barriers to goal attainment. For example, emphasize optimistic thinking ("I know this is going to be hard, but if I take it one step at a time I can do it.") and persistence ("If at first you don't succeed, try, try again."). Demonstrate strategies for overcoming difficulty; for example, by redefining proximal goals or revising the plan for attainment.

Promote collaborative goal setting and attainment by grouping students with similar goals, and encouraging partners to provide suggestions, feedback, and support. Students with more advanced skills could provide scaffolding for their peers; for example, through modeling effective strategies for attaining goals and for coping with difficulty.

TABLE 3.9. Checklist for Goal Setting

What is the long-term goal?

What are the short-term goals?
#1
#2
#3

What materials do I need? How will I get them?

What help or information will I need? How will I get that?

Answer the following questions for each short-term goal:

Short-term goal #____

What are the steps for reaching short-term goal #____? (check off each step as you do it)
____ 1.
____ 2.
____ 3.
____ 4.
____ 5.

How confident are you that you can reach short-term goal #____? Rate on a scale of 1 to 5 (1 = I don't think I can; 5 = I know for sure I can). _____

If you don't rate this a 4 or 5, what help (information, materials) do you think you need?

How will you get it?

Foster exploration of a broad array of goals related to self-identity, including social relationships, education, career, and other domains of competence. Solicit involvement of teachers of specific content areas, pupil support personnel, family members, and community representatives to serve as information resources, role models, and mentors.

Generalization

Implementing interventions within the naturalistic context of the classroom helps to ensure generalization because of the likelihood of support and reinforcement by teachers and peers. In addition, a classroom-based program that is integrated into the curriculum provides opportunities for repetition, practice, and intermittent reinforcement of target processes and skills across multiple contexts. Such a program facilitates generalization across time, setting, and domain. The emphasis on social support and group implementation enhances the likelihood of modeling and social reinforcement of target processes and skills. The opportunities for skill application within the classroom and community strengthens the ecological validity of target processes and skills, and thus furthers generalization.

Specific cognitive strategies for fostering generalization include cognitive mediators, self-monitoring and -reinforcement, and efficacy expectations. (For an extensive discussion of the development and functions self-regulatory mechanisms, see Bandura, 1986.) For example, the explication of interpersonal problem solving provides individuals with strategies for applying problem solving across multiple problems and contexts. Visual and verbal cues can also be used to signal the application of problem-solving strategies in other settings (e.g., playground, cafeteria, at home). Including self-monitoring, -reinforcement, and -evaluation of target skills facilitates application and reinforcement across setting and time. Realistic goal setting, task structuring, and performance-based feedback foster successful performance and development of self-efficacy. In addition, reflection and explication regarding strategy use, goal attainment, and competencies are likely to further enhance expectations of success; for example, by facilitating awareness and cognitive mediation.

Thus far we have described the methods for implementing our primary prevention approach to enhancing social competence and personal efficacy. Effective program design and implementation also requires assessment of target competencies, identification of program participants, and program evaluation.

ASSESSMENT AND PROGRAM EVALUATION

A primary issue in assessment and evaluation is the concurrent consideration of interpretive and consequential validity (Moss, 1992). That is, evaluators need to establish the construct validity and relevance of selected assessment techniques with respect to intended use. In addition, they must consider the potential consequences of decisions based on assessment data (e.g., Will the data result in ecologically valid interventions?). These considerations are consistent with a multidimensional approach to assessment, which includes the use of multiple methods and sources of data to collect information across multiple settings and for multiple purposes. In this section, we describe the assessment process that leads to identifying and providing service to COAs within school contexts. In addition, we describe procedures for evaluating programs.

Assessment of COAs

We return to the stories of Maggie and Robert to illustrate the assessment process in the context of classroom-based prevention programs and in the evaluation of children referred for school adjustment difficulties.

Rewriting Maggie's Story

We first encountered Maggie as an adult struggling to deal with the consequences of growing up in an alcoholic family. Let's return to Maggie's adolescent years, during which she first sought help for sadness, anxiety, and fear. Recall that from outside appearances, Maggie seemed to be well adjusted socially and academically. Thus, her emotional concerns seemed unwarranted and were dismissed by professionals. Now, let's rewrite her story. . . .

Maggie's school had integrated the ESCAPE program into the drug education and academic curricula. The drug education specialist and school psychologist collaborated on a presentation of family alcoholism. They used the educational film, *Soft Is the Heart of a Child* (1978), to discuss the characteristics of the family affected by alcohol and to generate a list of strategies and resources for coping with family alcoholism. During this discussion, Maggie asked specific questions about how to determine if a person is an alcoholic and seemed particularly interested in the reactions of children to parental alcoholism. In a follow-up journal activity, Maggie wrote about her identification with the feelings of the family hero depicted in the film and her relief that there was help for families affected by alcohol. In a subsequent class session, after reading the students' journals, the school psychologist distributed the CAST (Jones, 1981) so that students could record their perceptions of alcohol use within their own families. The psychologist then indicated that she was starting a support and educational group for students with concerns about family alcoholism, and suggested that those who checked 6 or more of the 30 items should consider joining the group.

Maggie talked to the school psychologist, expressing interest in the group, but apprehension about discussing the group with her mother. The school psychologist agreed to meet with Maggie and her mother to discuss Maggie's concerns about her father's drinking and her participation in the group. Maggie's mother denied any specific problems with alcohol in their family, but consented to Maggie's participation in the group with assurance of confidentiality. The school psychologist provided Maggie's mother with information about services in the community, including support groups (e.g., Al-Anon, Alateen) and counseling for families affected by alcohol. Several months later Maggie was still participating in the group at school and learning how to cope with her father's drinking. In a follow-up meeting with Maggie's mother, the school psychologist learned that although Maggie's father was still drinking, her mother was attending Al-Anon meetings. Her mother indicated that Maggie's experiences in the group and the information the school psychologist had provided served as the impetus for her to attend Al-Anon. Maggie now views herself as a personally and professionally successful adult.

Elaborating Robert's Story

We pick up Robert's story at the time when he was referred to the school psychologist for academic problems. In an initial interview with Robert's father, the school psychologist gathered information about developmental and family history. In this context, Robert's father revealed a history of family alcoholism. Specifically, Robert's maternal and paternal grandfathers, two uncles, and an aunt were all recovering alcoholics. Although Robert's father openly discussed the details of the divorce and custody arrangements, he made no mention of his former wife's alcohol use. The school psychologist asked the father to complete the Child Behavior Checklist (CBCL; Achenbach, 1991b) to assess social–behavioral adjustment. Robert's mother was not available for an interview but agreed to complete the CBCL. The school psychologist observed Robert in a collaborative classroom activity and on the playground to assess peer interactions. She also interviewed Robert's teacher and asked the teacher to complete the Teacher Report Form (TRF; Achenbach, 1991c) to assess Robert's social–behavioral adjustment at school. The school psychologist interviewed Robert about his concerns and perceptions, using the Structured Pediatric Psychosocial Interview (SPPI; Webb & Van Devere, 1985, 1990) and several Harter scales (Harter, 1980, 1985a, 1985b). In addition, the psychologist administered norm-referenced measures of intelligence and achievement, and conducted a curriculum-based assessment in reading and mathematics.

Results revealed high average intellectual functioning, achievement scores commensurate with ability, and teacher and parent reports of behavioral functioning within a normal range. Robert's self-reports indicated concerns about family discord (e.g., conflict between parents), maternal drinking, peer acceptance and support, and self-worth. In addition, he indicated a reliance on external motivators for academic performance. In a follow-up interview, Robert's father confirmed the concerns about family discord and maternal alcoholism, and indicated an interest in securing family intervention. The school psychologist's recommendations included referrals to a community agency that worked with families affected by alcohol and to child protective services to determine alternatives to the current visitation arrangements. The psychologist and the teacher designed classroom-based interventions to address academic performance and motivation. In addition, Robert agreed to join a school-based COA support group.

Denial, a common defense used by members of alcoholic families, often precludes identification of COAs. Instead, information that suggests parental alcoholism may be revealed in a number of indirect ways; for example, in children's responses during formal testing, during interviews with the child or parent, or during drug education or other classroom activities. The following indicators facilitate identification of COAs (DeZolt & Nastasi, 1991): (1) concern, fear, or embarrassment about parental drinking; (2) desire to control parental drinking; (3) reference to family problems or conflict involving parental drinking; (4) reticence about discussing family-related issues; (5) negativism about alcohol use or alcoholics; (6) view of intoxication as inevitable outcome of alcohol consumption; (7) greater familiarity, compared with same-age peers, with alcohol and alcohol-related behaviors and situations; (8) inordinate reference to alcohol in situations in which it plays a minor role; and (9) behavioral changes or evidence of anxiety during alcohol education activities.

When such indicators are present, the school psychologist should conduct further assessment of the child's concerns and family environment. The CAST (Jones, 1981) is a 30-item self-report measure of concerns and emotional distress associated with parental alcohol use. Clinical interviews, such as the SPPI (Webb & Van Devere, 1985, 1990), provide an opportunity to explore the nature and extent of psychosocial stress related to family and peer relationships. As standard practice, school psychologists should include in all parent interviews questions about family history of alcohol use. When family alcoholism is suspected, the child's reactions or perceptions of parental drinking should be the focus of concern, as other family members may deny alcohol-related problems (DiCicco, Davis, & Orenstein, 1984). However, it is still essential that the psychologist conduct a follow-up conference with the child's parent(s) to discuss the concerns about parental drinking; provide information about alcoholism and intervention (e.g., through reading materials); and facilitate referral for appropriate services such as treatment for the alcoholic, family counseling, and community and school-based support groups. A more comprehensive assessment of the family environment may provide a better understanding of contextual variables related to alcoholism (e.g., family conflict, parent–child relationships, child-rearing practices). Such comprehensive assessment of the family is critical to design of family interventions, but not necessary for identification of COAs and referral for family services. (For additional information on family assessment techniques, see Copeland & White, 1991; Grotevant & Carlson, 1989.)

Measures of children's social–emotional adjustment should include self-reports as well as informant reports (e.g., by parents and teachers) of personal–social competence and behavioral adjustment. Multiple-informant approaches provide information about variations of the individual's functioning across settings and/or variations in perspectives of the informants. Examples of multiple-informant behavior rating scales include those developed by Achenbach, CBCL, TRF, and Youth Self-Report (Achenbach, 1991a, 1991b, 1991c); Gresham and Elliott, Social Skills Rating System (Gresham & Elliott, 1990); and Reynolds and Kamphaus, the Behavior Assessment System for Children (Reynolds & Kamphaus, 1992).

Self-report measures can also provide information about children's self-perceptions of their competencies. For example, scales developed by Harter and colleagues (Harter, 1985a, 1988; Harter & Pike, 1984b; Neemann & Harter, 1986) measure perceived competence in multiple domains and global self-worth. (See Chapter 6 for reviews of selected measures.)

The manifested social–emotional and academic difficulties of COAs do not necessarily distinguish them from referred non-COA children (e.g., Robert's story). Furthermore, COAs may exhibit behaviors that are adaptive in school and peer settings, but still express concerns about parental drinking (e.g., Maggie's story). Therefore, attention to indicators of family alcoholism facilitates proper identification and intervention.

Program Evaluation

Evaluation is an integral and guiding component of program development and implementation. Valid program evaluation can facilitate acceptability (consumer satisfaction), integrity (adherence to the prescribed program), and effectiveness (outcome). Acceptability and integrity measures are essential for evaluating program efficacy (Elliott et al., 1991). Measures should be obtained at several points in time, including pre- and post-intervention, long-term follow-up (e.g., 6 months, 1 year); and on a formative basis (e.g., intermittent probes and through the process of consultation). Additional information relevant to program evaluation includes demographic data about participants, program costs, staff time, resources, management of program activities, logistics of data collection, and documentation of professional development activities.

Consistent with a multidimensional approach, we use both qualitative (e.g., interviews, journals, observations) and quantitative (e.g., rating scales, systematic observations) measures gathered from all participants (e.g., students, parents, school staff). The combined use of qualitative and quantitative methods capitalizes on the benefits of both approaches. Quantification objectifies and standardizes the measurement of program goals and objectives, thus facilitating replicability and generalizability. The sole use of quantitative methods, however, does not capture the complex dynamics inherent in program acceptability, implementation, and efficacy. Qualitative techniques provide the means for examining (1) the meaning of program-specific constructs; (2) the individual and contextual variability in manifestations (i.e., operational definitions) of constructs; (3) the construction and co-construction of knowledge, behavior, and norms; and (4) individual and contextual factors that facilitate or inhibit the change process. Furthermore, integrating quantitative and qualitative methods not only enhances our understanding of these complex variables, but facilitates applying theory and research to practice (Nastasi, Bingham, & Clements, 1993).

In the next section, we describe evaluation methods specific to each focus. Although we examine acceptability, integrity, and effectiveness separately, the three foci are inextricably linked such that some measures serve multiple purposes. Chapter 6 provides a bibliography of readings about program evaluation, qualitative and observational methods, and annotations of standardized assessment measures.

Program Acceptability

Measures of program acceptability or consumer satisfaction provide information about the extent to which program participants (i.e., facilitators, students) find program activities useful, feasible, and effective. Standardized rating scales, such as those designed to assess teachers' and students' perceptions of the acceptability of behavioral interventions, provide quantitative measures (Elliott et al., 1991). It may be necessary to adapt such measures to reflect program goals and objectives. We recommend the use of focus groups with representative students and facilitators to identify initial acceptability and to devise questions for interviewing and surveying all participants. (Stewart and Shamdasani, 1990, provide guidelines for conducting focus groups.) Periodic interviews with all facilitators and randomly selected students can provide in-depth qualitative data about program acceptability. (For information on ethnographic interviewing techniques, see Spradley, 1979.) Facilitators' records of program implementation (described in the next section) also provide information about reactions to specific activities. Furthermore, we encourage facilitators to maintain journals, using the format in Table 3.8, to promote reflective practice. That is, facilitators record experiences and reactions regarding their involvement in all phases of the program, and use these records to facilitate discussion during regular collaborative sessions with other program staff. The facilitators' journals provide the model for students' journals about program acceptability. Content analysis and coding of participant interviews and journal entries provide both qualitative and quantitative measures of program acceptability. In addition, use of these techniques in the early phases of multiyear projects can facilitate development of program-specific standardized measures of acceptability.

Program Integrity

Assessment of program implementation can serve several purposes. First, it documents program integrity; that is, the extent to which program components are implemented as planned. Second, measures of program implementation provide information to guide ongoing professional development and collaborative consultation. Third, such measures facilitate process evaluation; that is, identifying factors that contribute to program efficacy. Fourth, data about program implementation can guide development of program-specific standardized measures of integrity. Systematic observations, self-report rating scales, interviews, journals, and program artifacts (e.g., materials, permanent products) comprise a multimeasure, multisource approach to assessing program implementation. Observations provide detailed descriptions of program activities and are the primary mechanism for systematically evaluating person–environment and person–person interactions. This form of data collection is particularly important in programs such as ESCAPE that rely on specific student–student and facilitator–student interactions to promote change. Table 3.1 provides coding schemes (i.e., operational definitions and examples) for systematic observation of facilitator behavior. (For information on conducting and analyzing field observations, see Bakeman and Gottman, 1986; Lofland & Lofland, 1984; Sanjek, 1990; and Spradley, 1980.) Information from self-report measures (i.e., rating scales, interviews, journals) reflects the perspective of program participants and supplements observational records of program activities. To provide ecologically valid data, observational and self-report measures must incorporate the key components of the program (Elliott et al., 1991; Gresham, 1989). We provide examples of both types of measures for documenting the implementation of the key components of the ESCAPE program: (1) a record form for conducting a frequency count of observed (*in vivo* or videotaped) instructional methods and facilitation techniques (Table 3.10); and (2) a facilitator self-report checklist (Table 3.11). In addition, we use the group-process questions in Table 3.3 to guide narrative observations and analysis of field notes. This approach to observational data collection permits the investigation of contextual variations and individual differences in manifestation of group process (Nastasi et al., 1993). Alternatively, program evaluators could use these same questions to develop program-specific observation schemes for conducting

TABLE 3.10. Facilitator Behavior Observation Record Form[a]

Directions: Tally the occurrence of each type of facilitator behavior.

	Guided instruction (GP, SP, FB)[b]	Direct instruction
Modeling		
Scaffolding		
Explication		
Reflection		

[a]Table 3.1 provides operational definitions of facilitator behavior.
[b]Indicate type of guidance: GP, general prompt; SP, specific prompt; FB, feedback.

TABLE 3.11. Facilitator Self-Report Checklist

Directions: Provide the following information for each lesson.
Goal and objective (#):

Activity description (include duration):

Materials:

Using the chart, indicate what program components were used? (Check all that apply.) In the comments section, include your reactions to the ease of implementation, appropriateness for the intended purpose and students, and effectiveness.

Component	Implemented? (yes/no)	Comments/reactions (use reverse side as needed):
Story		(Circle) book film other
Journal writing		
Role play		
Cooperative learning		
Norms construction		
Group processing		(Circle) oral written
Individual student self-evaluation		
Integration with existing curriculum		Area(s)?

frequency counts or time sampling of participant behaviors (e.g., see Nastasi & Clements, 1992). The observational measures and self-report checklist, in conjunction with journals, interviews, and program artifacts, provide records of the manner in which specific program activities are implemented and the facilitators' and participants' reactions to these activities.

Program Effectiveness

Selection of program efficacy measures is guided by specific program goals and objectives. Evaluation of programs such as ESCAPE requires the use of multiple measures designed to assess knowledge, attitudinal, and skill-based outcomes related to program objectives. Curriculum-based assessment (CBA) provides content-valid measures of target knowledge and skills, demonstrates assessment–intervention links, and facilitates functional and time-series analyses (Shapiro, 1989; Shinn, 1989). CBA, which provides a common metric across varied content areas, is especially relevant to evaluating programs that use existing curricula. Self-report measures provide information about attitudes and beliefs and may be most appropriate for assessing the cognitive and affective aspects of personal–social competence. Within a multisource model, such measures complement observations and ratings by significant others. We recommend a combination of self-report techniques such as standardized rating scales, interviews, journals, and analogue measures (e.g., self-reported efficacy beliefs or generation of problem solutions, in response to hypothetical dilemmas). To assess skill-based outcomes, we recommend direct observation, analogue measures, self-report instruments (e.g., journals, interviews, rating scales) and a combination of norm- and criterion-referenced teacher and parent rating scales. This multisource, multimethod approach is consistent with best practice models of social–emotional assessment (Knoff, 1986; Reynolds & Kamphaus, 1990; Shapiro & Kratochwill, 1988).

In Chapter 6, we provide an annotated bibliography of measures relevant to the goals and objectives of ESCAPE. These include self-report and parent and teacher rating measures of perceived competence, social interaction, behavioral adjustment, psychosocial and affective distress, and perceptions and attitudes. We also use hypothetical dilemmas and the application of problem-solving strategies to real-life dilemmas to assess interpersonal problem solving as well as observations during collaborative program activities to assess collaborative problem solving and social interaction skills. In addition to pre- and multiple post- (immediate and follow-up) measurement, intermittent probes (e.g., observations) are used for monitoring program effects. Furthermore, measurement of target processes and skill application outside of the intervention context (e.g., real-life application of problem solving, parental reports of behavioral adjustment) provides information about generalization.

PRACTICAL AND ETHICAL ISSUES

In this section, we consider professional standards regarding practical and ethical issues related to developing, implementing, and evaluating school-based programs. School support personnel are advised to consult the ethical standards specific to their respective professions. School psychologists should consult current guidelines set forth by the American Psychological Association (APA, 1992, 1993) and the National Association of

School Psychologists (NASP, 1992). In addition, school personnel should refer to relevant state laws and school policies.

The questions we pose to guide the decision making of program developers are not presented in order of importance or occurrence. Rather, they should be considered concurrently. Consistent monitoring of these practical and ethical issues during all phases of programming facilitates adherence to ethical guidelines, ensures program integrity, and preempts barriers to success.

What Are the Ecological Considerations? How Do We Address Resistance from an Ecological Perspective?

An ecological focus implies a comprehensive appraisal of the multiple contexts relevant to the target system. For example, school-based interventions require consideration of the immediate context of the classroom and the higher-order contexts of the school, the district, and the community. Of equal importance are other ecological systems such as peer group and family that indirectly affect the target system. Thus, program developers are well advised to include in all program phases students, teachers, support personnel, administrators, parents, and community representatives. We recommend a collaborative approach to program development as outlined in Table 3.12 (see accompanying worksheet, Appendix 3 B). This model is consistent with the collaborative problem-solving component of the ESCAPE program and with collaborative consultation models (Friend & Cook, 1992; Parsons & Meyers, 1984).

Identifying the ecological factors that support or inhibit program foci and activities is necessary for ensuring program acceptability and effectiveness. Factors that warrant consideration include values, needs, resources, and sources of support and resistance. The success of any program is contingent upon active participation of the target group and support from other constituent groups. Including representatives from constituent groups in the planning is likely to foster commitment to program goals, and ensure that goals and activities are relevant to the needs and interests of participants. Failure to involve relevant constituents in program development may preclude implementation or interfere with success of even the most well-documented programs. For example, pupil support personnel in one school district identified and documented the need for a substance abuse prevention program, based on the prevalence of drug abuse among adolescents in the district. With money from a parent organization, they purchased a program that had been implemented successfully in other schools. Teachers and counselors received training in program implementation. Prior to program initiation, the district superintendent at a school board meeting denied the existence of drug problems in the district and advised against implementing the program. As a result, the program was

TABLE 3.12.Steps for Collaborative Program Development

1. Define the problem.
   a. Describe as specifically as possible, in objective terms.
   b. Consider the following: What are the needs, views, concerns of target students? other students? teachers? administrators? parents? others?
   c. Identify the goal of problem solving: What needs to be accomplished, considering the needs, views, concerns of all parties?

2. Brainstorm solutions.
   a. Generate as many ideas as possible.
   b. Do not rule out any possibilities at this point.
   c. Do not stop to evaluate or critique. (That is your next step!)
   d. In brainstorming, think about the needs, views, concerns of all parties.

3. Consider and evaluate *each* solution.
   a. What are the likely consequences (for all parties involved)? Consider both short- and long-term consequences.
   b. What are potential outcomes? Does the solution meet the needs and/or address concerns of each party?
   c. How feasible is the solution? What resources (people, skills, materials, time) would you need? What are the facilitating factors (e.g., what resources are available)? What are the inhibiting factors (e.g., what roadblocks do you anticipate)? To what extent do the facilitating factors outweigh the inhibitors? How can you maximize the facilitating factors and minimize the inhibiting factors? What is the likelihood of success for solving the problem or reaching the goal?

4. Choose the "best" solution.
   a. Considering all the factors, which solution is likely to accomplish the goal or solve the problem?
   b. Remember that "best" is relative. There are likely to be many possible solutions, with "best" defined by the specific situation.

5. Design a plan for implementing and evaluating the solution.
   a. Devise a step-by-step plan. Consider the following: How will you implement the plan? Who does what? When? Where?
   b. How will you evaluate success? What measures will you use?

6. Implement the plan and collect evaluation data.

7. Evaluate the solution (formatively and summatively).
   a. How is it being implemented? (To what extent is the plan being followed?)
   b. Is it successful? (Does it meet the goals? How do you know?)
   c. Is it acceptable to all parties? (Do they think it will work? Are they comfortable participating?)

8. Review the evaluation data on a periodic basis (preferably as a team); revise plan as needed.
   a. Continue what is effective.
   b. Consider what revisions are needed, using the same problem-solving sequence.

Note. See the accompanying worksheet in Appendix 3B.

not adopted. The superintendent subsequently was asked to resign because of his own alcohol-related problems. The following year the district successfully instituted the program with administrative and community support.

An ecological approach to program design requires consideration of the relevant immediate, indirect, and higher-order contexts to ensure participation of the target system or group. To promote full participation of individuals from these contexts, it is important to assess their values and beliefs relevant to the program's theoretical basis, goals, and activities. We recommend that program developers conduct focus groups with representatives of constituent groups; for example, through meetings with administrators, school faculty, students, parents, community members (see Stewart & Shamdasani, 1990). Surveys can be used to assess the values and beliefs of the target population; for example, through the use of treatment acceptability measures (Elliott et al., 1991). A combination of these two methods is optimal in that focus groups provide the opportunity for indepth discussions, and surveys provide a broader sampling of the population.

To enhance commitment to program implementation, make explicit the goals and potential benefits of the program and involve participants in ongoing evaluation, with particular attention to program acceptability. During implementation, structure activities to ensure successful participation by all group members, providing scaffolding as needed. In addition, consider the ecological validity of instructional materials and activities. For example, in the ESCAPE program, we use popular literature and films that are relevant to student interests and link the hypothetical dilemmas in these story forms to students' real-life experiences.

As part of program planning, identify the needs and resources of staff members and involve them in securing the necessary resources. For example, identify (1) the necessary skills for effective implementation, (2) professional development needs, and (3) options for fostering professional development. In addition, identify staff consultation needs and explore alternatives for ongoing consultation. Involve administrators to ensure that necessary supports and resources are provided. For example, negotiate staff time for planning, evaluation, and collaborative consultation activities.

Most importantly, through a collaborative approach, promote a mutual sense of confidence in the competence of program staff. Establish a system of clear and open communication in the earliest phases of the program and continue communicating as a regular part of program implementation. For example, meet with the staff as a first step and set up a mechanism for regular meetings to discuss program implementation. In this way, problems can be prevented or addressed before they become unmanageable.

Consistent with an ecological focus, identify ways to modify the physical and social environment to achieve a good match between program goals and existing educational practice. As an essential first step, assess the following features of the system: (1) receptivity and readiness for change; (2) history of the system regarding change; (3) the sources of power, support, and resistance within the system; and (4) commitment to the proposed program. Inattention to potential sources of resistance can impede program implementation and success. For example, in one school system, staff members were reluctant to participate in a new program because of biases regarding target population (i.e., students with disabilities), anxiety about working with these students, concerns about having the necessary skills, and anger about perceived messages from the administration (e.g., "We are bringing in the experts because you cannot do your job.") (Kehle & Nastasi, 1993). These biases became apparent during the early phases of program development and hindered program implementation.

Using a collaborative approach to program design and attending to specific concerns in the early phases of program development can help to offset resistance to change. Especially where resistance is high, program developers should plan to conduct the project as a multiyear effort, with as much as one full year devoted to needs assessment, planning, and staff preparation. Start the implementation phase as a pilot project with a few highly motivated people. Through formative evaluation, examine the factors that facilitate and inhibit success and use those to inform subsequent phases. Staff members involved in the initial phase may be included in subsequent phases of the project; for example, in professional development of new program facilitators. Thus, to some extent, effective systems change requires attention to developmental considerations of the organization and the staff, in addition to the developmental needs of the target population. We discuss the needs of the target group in the next section.

What Are the Developmental Considerations of the Target Group?

Program goals, objectives, content, activities, and assessment techniques should be developmentally appropriate. That is, the cognitive, affective, and behavioral competencies of the target group should direct decision making about these aspects of program design and evaluation. In Chapter 1, we provide the developmental framework that guided design of the ESCAPE program. Developmental competence is linked to, but not defined by, chronological age. The grade-level focus of classroom-based programs such as ESCAPE implies a normative developmental progression. In addition, preassessment data facilitate individualizing the curricula based on the competence levels of participants.

How Do We Identify Target Populations?

Identification of program participants is often guided by factors such as predetermined program goals and the presumed needs and risk status of the population. We recommend that the previously discussed ecological and developmental considerations guide not only program development but also identification of the target population. Failure to consider ecological and developmental factors may result in resistance from program participants, misidentification of at-risk youth, and misplaced efforts.

What Levels of Intervention Does the Program Include?

The ESCAPE program is designed for implementation at the primary (prevention) level within the classroom. Many of the activities can be modified for use in small groups or individually at secondary (intervention) and tertiary (treatment) levels. For example, school psychologists can use the suggested activities in conducting support groups for self-identified COAs, in providing individual counseling for COAs with adjustment difficulties, or in facilitating the transition of adolescents returning from substance abuse treatment. Decisions about level of intervention are influenced by other issues such as needs, resources, and staff qualifications. Ideally, a comprehensive school-based program for COAs provides services at all three levels in collaboration with relevant community agencies.

What Are the Program Goals and Objectives? What Target Skills Does the Program Address?

Ideally a comprehensive school-based program would include goals and objectives relevant to enhancing personal–social competence and preventing substance abuse within the general student population, with a specific focus on COAs. The goals and objectives of the ESCAPE program are presented in Table 3.13. The ESCAPE program is designed to enhance generalizable coping skills of students in Grades K through 12 through fostering development of self-efficacy, interpersonal problem solving, and social interaction skills. In addition, the needs of COAs are addressed more directly through objectives related to developing skills for coping with family crises. Target skills include affective, cognitive, and behavioral competencies related to personal–social functioning and coping.

The goals and objectives of programs should be (1) specific to the needs of the target group, (2) integrated into existing curriculum, and (3) feasible with regard to available resources (e.g., staff, time, money). An important consideration is the complement to existing social skills, drug education, and health education programs. Thus, program goals should extend rather than supplant the goals of existing programs. For example,

TABLE 3.13. Goals and Objectives of the ESCAPE Program

Self-Efficacy

Goal 1: Enhancing self-perception
Objectives
1. Provide opportunities to develop healthy self-concept.
2. Provide social feedback to enhance sense of competence.
3. Provide opportunities for decision/choice making.
4. Facilitate realistic goal setting.
5. Structure tasks (e.g., proximal goal setting, performance-contingent reward).
6. Provide models of self-efficacy.

Goal 2: Defining self in relation to others (fostering interdependence)

Objectives
1. Provide opportunities to develop healthy self-concept.
2. Provide opportunities to identify common and unique characteristics within the group.
3. Provide opportunities to foster and discuss interdependence.
4. Provide opportunities for decision/choice making.
5. Facilitate realistic goal setting.

Goal 3: Recognizing and exercising the limits of personal control

Objectives
1. Provide opportunities for decision/choice making.
2. Facilitate realistic goal setting.
3. Encourage development of coping strategies for handling difficulties.
4. Ensure skill development to foster success.
5. Structure tasks through proximal goal setting.
6. Provide models of effective goal setting and decision making.

Social Interaction

Goal 1: Caring for self and others

Objectives
1. Promote an understanding of the importance of prosocial behavior (reciprocal helping, caring, empathy).
2. Promote an understanding of the importance of caring for self.
3. Promote an understanding of the connection between caring for self and caring for others.
4. Provide opportunities to apply prosocial interaction skills.
5. Foster a prosocial climate.
6. Provide models of prosocial behaviors.

(cont.)

TABLE 3.13. (*continued*)

Social Interaction (*continued*)

Goal 2: Relating in the private sphere (friends, family, and other intimate relationships)

Objectives

1. Promote an understanding of friendship, family, and other intimate relationships.
2. Promote an understanding of the role of prosocial behavior in developing and maintaining friendships, as well as family and other intimate relationships.
3. Promote an understanding of the behaviors that facilitate and interfere with establishing and maintaining relationships.
4. Provide opportunities to apply and evaluate skills related to initiating and maintaining relationships.
5. Provide models of prosocial behaviors in the private sphere.

Goal 3: Relating in the public sphere

Objectives

1. Foster development of social interaction skills (e.g., initiation, cooperation, communication, reciprocity).
2. Provide opportunities to apply social interaction skills within public contexts.
3. Promote an understanding of the importance of rules and the relevance of social norms to community functioning.
4. Provide opportunities to participate in the formulation of rules and the social construction of norms within public contexts.
5. Foster a sense of community (e.g., within the classroom and school).
6. Promote a recognition of diversity.
7. Provide models of prosocial behaviors in the public sphere.

Interpersonal Problem Solving

Goal 1: Recognizing feelings in self and others

Objectives:

1. Facilitate recognition and expression of feelings.
2. Provide models of affective expression.

Goal 2: Enhancing intra- and interpersonal problem solving (alone and in collaboration)

Objectives:

1. Facilitate understanding of problem-solving strategies.
2. Provide opportunities for application and evaluation of problem-solving strategies.
3. Provide models of effective problem solving.

TABLE 3.13. (*continued*)

Goal 3: Enhancing intra- and interpersonal conflict resolution

Objectives
1. Facilitate understanding of effective conflict resolution.
2. Foster an understanding of peaceful functioning of a diverse community.
3. Provide opportunities for application and evaluation of conflict resolution strategies.
4. Provide models of effective conflict resolution.

Goal 4: Coping with crises related to family alcoholism

Objectives:
1. Encourage appropriate expression of feeling.
2. Encourage social support by peer group.
3. Foster climate of acceptance and caring.
4. Explore strategies for coping with crisis.
5. Provide models of effective coping.

---

the goals of the current drug education curriculum might include providing knowledge about the effects of alcoholism on the individual (the alcoholic) without considering of the effects on family members. In this case, program developers would focus on ways to integrate information about family alcoholism into the existing drug education curriculum rather than creating a new drug education program or presenting the family alcoholism component as a separate curriculum. One school system with an established, comprehensive K–12 drug education and prevention program requested consultation regarding strategies for incorporating social and coping skills into the prevention program. Teachers indicated confidence in implementing the information components but expressed a need for additional training and consultation regarding the social skills component. This scenario reflects the importance of collaboration between teaching and support staff in program design and implementation.

What Content is Consistent with Program Goals and Objectives?

Story comprises much of the content of ESCAPE and includes specific problem-solving and conflict resolution strategies, social skills, and interpersonal dynamics related to peers, family, and community. We use stories depicted in literature, film, and hypothetical and real-life experiences as both the content and context for personal–social skill development. Story also provides the context for presenting family-oriented crises and developing coping skills. Curricular content regarding family alcoholism should include information about the biopsychosocial aspects of alcoholism; that is, etiology, characteristics, and impact on the individual, family, and community. This information is presented in Chapters 1 and 2. Additional sources of information are offered in Chapter 6.

Academic curricula provide real-life situations for practice and generalization of target skills. We extend the academic goals of cooperative learning activities to include personal–social goals by facilitating and examining group dynamics. That is, the facilitator guides both the academic and social aspects of the cooperative learning activity. The group-process self-evaluation questions presented in Table 3.3 are used to elaborate on the personal–social aspect of collaborative activities. Furthermore, academic curricula provide the context for developing self-efficacy; for example, through goal setting, feedback, and peer modeling.

Program developers are advised to examine not only the existing classroom curricula, but also to review available social skills and drug education programs such as those presented in Chapter 6. Few if any programs can be implemented without modification. Adoption and modification of available programs should be guided by considering target skills, developmental level, cultural representation, necessary facilitator skill, and existing curricula.

How Do We Use Copyrighted Material?

Program developers and implementers should follow legal guidelines regulating the use of copyrighted materials (e.g., curriculum, videotapes). We advise examining the stated restrictions on specific curricula with regard to permission to photocopy materials. For example, some publishers grant blanket permission to copy worksheets, whereas others require that users request specific permission to photocopy or that users purchase such materials. We also recommend that educators either purchase or rent videotapes or films for classroom use and follow copyright guidelines with regard to permissible use in educational institutions. Helm (1986) provides guidelines for educators regarding fair use of written and audiovisual copyrighted materials. We also suggest that program developers and implementors consult school media specialists for current legal guidelines and specific school policies regarding use of protected materials.

How Do We Integrate Program Goals, Objectives, and Content into Existing Curriculum?

In the ESCAPE program, the targeted curricular domains include language and creative arts, health and drug education, and the social sciences. For example, conflicts depicted in social studies are used as stimuli for teaching and practicing conflict resolution. Other curricular areas such as mathematics and the physical sciences are used to extend the application and practice of target skills (e.g., through cooperative learning activities in mathematics or science lab).

To facilitate integration of program goals, objectives, and content into existing curricula, program developers must systematically examine the match between the proposed program and the existing academic programs. Involving teachers as program developers is critical. Successful integration of personal–social and academic goals requires consideration of the extent to which the academic curriculum provides the context for instruction and practice of target personal–social skills. A system-wide K–12 personal–social competence program mandates a developmental progression of goals and objectives, repetition and extension of target skills, and ongoing assessment of the students' skills. Such coordination across grade levels is consistent with the scope and sequence of academic curricula. The goals, objectives, and content of the ESCAPE curriculum reflect this progression.

How Do We Link Assessment and Intervention?

Linking assessment to intervention requires clear articulation of goals and objectives, and ensures use of ecologically valid measures. Preassessment can guide program development, and facilitates individualization of program implementation. In addition, formative and summative assessments afford opportunities to monitor and evaluate program efficacy, integrity, and acceptability, and to modify program components accordingly. Consistent with a co-constructivist approach, in the ESCAPE program we emphasize learning through active participation and explication. Program participants are provided with opportunities for ongoing self-evaluation and reflection through structured journal writing, completion of self-evaluation forms, and collaborative evaluation of group process. Furthermore, staff development (described below) incorporates similar self-evaluation procedures. Thus, throughout all program components, both students and facilitators engage in reflective practice.

How Do We Best Serve Diverse Populations?

The American Psychological Association (APA, 1993) has set forth guidelines to ensure provision of quality psychological services to ethnically, linguistically, and culturally diverse populations. The APA Office of Ethnic Minorities recommends that service providers possess a sociocultural framework, as well as knowledge and skills relevant to assessment and intervention with diverse populations, including abilities to

- recognize cultural diversity;
- understand the role that culture and ethnicity/race play in the sociopsychological and economic development of ethnic and culturally diverse populations;
- understand that socioeconomic and political factors significantly impact

the psychosocial, political, and economic development of ethnic and culturally diverse groups;
- help clients to understand/maintain/resolve their own sociocultural
  identification;
- and understand the interaction of culture, gender, and sexual orientation
  on behavior and needs. (p. 45)

The ESCAPE program's objectives include recognizing diversity, fostering
an understanding of peaceful functioning in a diverse community, and
providing opportunities for the social construction of norms within multiple contexts. Our approach is consistent with the perspectives of educational and psychological theorists who advocate for the critical examination of existing paradigms and practices regarding the inclusion of
diversity in construction of social norms (Cummins, 1986; Giroux, 1988;
Graman, 1988; Rappaport, 1987). Thus, program developers are responsible for ensuring that all aspects of the program embrace the diversity of
the target population. That is, the program reflects the common and
unique characteristics of participants with regard to their individual and
sociocultural experiences. For example, in an ESCAPE program activity
focused on definition of family, high school students (1) examine how
media depicts and influences social norms about family; (2) consider discrepancies about norms within the media and amongst themselves; and (3)
discuss the influences of gender, race, ethnicity, family, religion, and other
cultural factors on social construction of norms. Such an activity makes
explicit the considerations of diversity and, when integrated into existing
curricula (e.g., language arts, social studies), promotes infusion of a multicultural perspective. Program developers and staff need to examine their
own knowledge, attitudes, and skills in the context of the APA guidelines
regarding diversity. In addition, staff training should address these issues
directly. Meaningful exploration of the sociopolitical influences on service
provision in a diverse culture requires a willingness to invite dialog and
controversy, rather than perpetuating the "walking on eggs" syndrome
(Frisby, 1992).

What Types of Services Can Program Staff Provide?

Program staff provide direct and indirect services depending on the nature of the program, needs of the system, and expertise of individual staff
members. Direct services include assessing and implementing activities
with individuals, small groups, and entire classrooms. Indirect services
include program development, coordination, and evaluation; training and
consultation with program staff; and complementary parent education.
For example, in one school the psychologist might provide direct services
by co-facilitating a classroom-based intervention or conducting a group for

self-identified COAs. In another school, the psychologist might provide indirect services by conducting staff in-service workshops and consulting with teachers during program implementation.

How Do We Distinguish Preventive Education from Therapeutic Intervention?

Prevention programs, such as ESCAPE, that address social–emotional, family, and substance abuse issues integrate educational and therapeutic interventions. Ideally, such programs require the collaboration of curricular (e.g., teachers, administrators) and mental health specialists (e.g., school psychologists, counselors, social workers). We caution against arbitrary and capricious program implementation. Program developers are responsible for ensuring that staff members have requisite knowledge of program content, skills for implementing program components (e.g., problem-solving process, group process), and awareness of their limitations. Inadequate preparation of staff could not only preclude effective program implementation but also potentially harm children. Limited knowledge of the content area can lead to misinformation and can create an environment that inhibits program effectiveness. Failure of program developers to address collaboration and integration across the curriculum can result in missed opportunities to pool resources and to reinforce concepts presented in multiple contexts (e.g., discussion of family alcoholism in drug education and science classes). Inattention to content areas in which therapeutic issues might arise (e.g., self-identification of COAs during health class) limits identification and referral of at-risk students. The following scenario exemplifies the misapplication of alcohol-related education.

In a high school health class, the teacher was presenting information from the text regarding the biological and psychological effects of alcohol. Students indicated they had learned this information in their drug education class and preferred to discuss experiences with peers and family related to alcohol abuse. The teacher, possibly unprepared to address students' experiences, chose to adhere to the prescribed curriculum. The students, however, continued to discuss their experiences with each other as the teacher presented facts about alcoholism and its effects on the family. Finally, in response to some of the students' comments, the teacher asked if any of them lived in an alcoholic family and stated that he understood such homes "are horrible places to live." At this point, discussion amongst students ceased.

Perhaps had the teacher collaborated with a colleague who had expertise in family alcoholism, he could have taken advantage of a teachable moment and helped students to apply health curriculum to their own lives. More importantly, the teacher's final comment may have prevented identification and referral of COAs. In this case, the school psychologist knew that some of the students in the class were COAs. Had the teacher and school psychologist (who had professional preparation for dealing with family alcoholism) consulted about the alcohol unit, the two of them could have conducted the class session collaboratively. Alternatively, the school psychologist, without violating the privacy of specific students, could have provided the teacher with the necessary information for addressing family alcoholism and been available for referral of students who self-identified as COAs. This example emphasizes the importance of collaboration amongst all school personnel in the design, integration, and implementation of COA curricula.

When Do We Obtain Consent?

The answer to this question depends on the level and nature of the intervention. Preventive education programs that are part of the state-mandated or board-approved curricula do not necessarily require parental consent for student participation. Thus classroom-based programs, such as ESCAPE, if approved by the school board would not necessarily require consent. Program developers are advised to consult with building and district policies regarding implementation of classroom or school-wide programs. Regardless of whether parental consent to participate is required, we always advise that parents be notified about the program.

Provision of services for at-risk students outside of the approved curriculum may require parental consent, depending on the nature of services and state and local policies. For example, few states explicitly authorize preventive treatment for COAs without parental consent, although some states permit counseling services to minors without consent (Woodside, Henderson, & Samuels, 1991). Thus, school personnel should refer to state statutes and school policies when planning individual or group intervention for COAs. When consent is not required, school personnel should weigh the merits of parental consent, in particular taking into account the denial typically associated with alcoholism and the potential impact on the student and the family. Consistent with the notion of home–school collaboration, it is advisable to involve parents whenever possible.

System-wide assessment and program evaluation procedures that are state mandated or board approved do not necessarily require parental consent. It is advisable for program developers to follow building and/or district level policy for conducting assessments that are not part of existing school practice. Ultimately, professional ethical standards should direct decision making about when parental consent is necessary. For example, use of psychological instruments measuring social–emotional functioning would warrant parental consent (e.g., National Association of School Psychologists, 1992).

How Do We Address Confidentiality?

In the context of preventive education programs, students are likely to reveal information about personal and family experiences. Thus, program developers should provide clear criteria for protecting the privacy of students and families. The nature and limits of confidentiality vary with the level of program implementation. Although classroom-based programs do not typically require assurance of confidentiality, it is advisable to encourage students to respect the privacy of classmates. In individual or small-group interventions, professionals are advised to follow ethical guidelines regarding privacy and confidentiality (e.g., APA, 1992). Furthermore, professionals are advised to follow their respective professional ethical standards and legal statutes regarding disclosure of confidential information.

What Are the Necessary Qualifications of Program Staff? What Comprises Staff Development?

The collaborative model implies participation of program staff who have complementary requisite skills, training, and experience. The necessary staff qualifications include knowledge, skills, attitudes, and beliefs relevant to program goals. That is, staff members should possess the following: (1) knowledge of the biopsychosocial aspects of alcoholism, including the etiology, characteristics, and impact with regard to the individual, family, and community; (2) knowledge of ecological–developmental influences on personal–social competence; (3) skills relevant to program design, implementation, and evaluation; (4) theoretical perspectives and attitudes consistent with program goals; and (5) self-efficacy regarding these qualifications.

Program design includes assessing the qualifications of program implementors and providing staff development. Assessing staff qualifications might best be accomplished through interviews and observations focusing on requisite knowledge, skills, attitudes, and beliefs (as discussed in the Program Evaluation section of this chapter). Staff development should be an analogue to program implementation. That is, the facilitator of staff development employs the strategies and relevant curriculum materials that program implementors will use. Within this context, program implementors are provided with the opportunity to incorporate program strategies into personal instructional styles and to examine congruence between program goals and personal beliefs and attitudes. Furthermore, cooperative activities provide the context for enhancing collaborative consultation skills. Most importantly, effective program implementation requires ongoing consultation through all phases of the program. The facilitator of staff development provides the necessary scaffolding for collaborative consultation until staff members assume full responsibility for the collaborative process.

How Can We Best Use Community Resources? What Community Resources Are Available?

When designing and implementing intervention programs, we encourage collaboration with existing community agencies to maximize use of available services and avoid duplication. For example, community-based substance abuse programs are invaluable resources, potentially supplementing existing curricula; providing consultation about program development, implementation, and evaluation; and assisting in staff training. In addition, having established relationships with personnel in such agencies eases the way for referral of program participants and/or their families in need of additional services. Types of community services include intervention programs, ranging from self-help groups to in-patient treatment facilities; educational resource centers; child protective service agencies; law enforcement substance abuse prevention programs; juvenile courts; and crisis hotlines. Chapter 6 includes resource lists of support groups, clearinghouses, and organizations.

How Do We Extend the Program Beyond the School System? How Do We Involve Families and Communities?

In addition to collaborating with community agencies and using community resources, we encourage establishing school–family–community partnerships to provide services to COAs. The ecological approach promotes the participation of family and community members in program planning. Parent education programs that parallel the school-based program can facilitate collaboration between schools and families, and promote generalization of target skills. Furthermore, extending classroom activities to the home and community can foster school–family–community partnerships and facilitate generalization. In the ESCAPE program, students apply program content and skills in home and community contexts. For example, they interview family and community members about relevant experiences, invite community representatives to participate in program activities, and conduct community service projects.

FINAL WORDS

We encourage the creation of a school culture that promotes the development of personal–social competence and thus directly addresses the needs of all students, including COAs. Specific attention to COAs as an at-risk population is best accomplished within a culture that fosters personal–social development, provides a safe environment for self-identification, and advocates for the protection of children and youth. In such a culture,

COAs are empowered to *escape* the potential negative consequences of family alcoholism through the development of specific personal–social competencies within a supportive context. The essential characteristics of this culture, described in Table 3.14, are embodied in the ESCAPE curriculum. The basis for these characteristics is provided in the literature review in Chapter 2.

Throughout this chapter we have presented a model for developing, implementing, and evaluating school-based prevention/intervention pro-

TABLE 3.14. Creating a School Culture to Enhance Social Competence and Personal Efficacy

A school culture that promotes the development of personal–social competencies—self-efficacy, interpersonal problem solving, social interaction—has the following characteristics:

- Multiple perspectives and competencies are mutually valued and encouraged. Individuals are encouraged to express opinions, consider multiple perspectives, appreciate common characteristics, and respect unique qualities. Individuals are provided with opportunities and support in developing unique competencies. Collaborative activities reflect the contributions of multiple competencies within and beyond the academic domain.
- Social support from peers and adults is the norm. Individuals are encouraged to provide mutual emotional support and practical assistance. Specifically, prosocial behaviors such as empathy, caring, helping, and sharing are cultivated. Opportunities for social support beyond the school community are available.
- Peaceful conflict resolution is customary. Individuals are encouraged to confront and reconcile discrepancies without fear of reproach or retaliation. Negotiation, compromise, mediation, and cooperative problem solving are common.
- Communication is characterized by perspective taking, active listening, and reciprocal sense-making, as well as by seeking clarification, providing explanations, and giving informational feedback and social reinforcement.
- Success is fostered through realistic goal setting and self-appraisal, performance-contingent feedback, and emphasis on progress rather than mastery. Coping through persistence and optimistic thinking is advocated.
- Diverse role models who embody personal–social competencies are manifest. Models include school pesonnel, older students, peers, family and community members, and story characters.
- Social responsibility for the mutual enhancement of personal–social competencies exists within and extends beyond the school. Members of the school and community at-large collaborate to create a culture that fosters the social competence and personal efficacy of all constituents.

grams for COAs. The ESCAPE curriculum detailed in Chapter 4 exemplifies the application of this model. The specific curricular activities can be modified to integrate them into existing curricula and to address the needs of specific populations. The information presented in this chapter should guide the adaptation of ESCAPE to the needs and resources of the population and the ecology.

APPENDIX 3A

Interview with Two Pairs of Fifth Graders about Their Collaboration

Pair 1 [E is the interviewer. B & C are the two children.]

E: Is it easier to work with a partner or to work by yourself?

C: Probably work with a partner.

E: Why is it easier to work with a partner?

C: Well, I think for working with a partner is like, um, if you don't get something on, like, a question or something, and you're working with a partner . . . then instead of asking for help, you could ask your partner to see if they understand, and . . . then they could, like, explain it.

E: OK.

B: Well, I think the same thing, but being by yourself is—is a little bit easier in different ways than . . . besides not understanding the problem, 'cuz you could ask the teacher also. You know, if you . . . didn't understand it. But, let's say if, um, you had, um, if you wanted to do a certain thing, an-an-an-and you thought, well that person probably didn't want to do that . . . you know, and you really had your heart set on doing that, you know. Then, when, if you were by yourself, you'd be able to do that, but I—I still like. . . being. . . working with partners.

E: So, what do you like about working with a partner?

B: Well, I like when, well, that—that, if, like she said about the, um, questions, you know. If you didn't understand the question, you could ask your partner instead of having to ask the teacher and bother her if she was doing something.

E: OK.

B: And, the other thing was you could learn to cooperate better.

Pair 2 [E is the interviewer. K & M are the two children.]

E: What does cooperative problem solving mean to you?

K: Well, um, like when you're working in, within a group. . . . Um, well, you have to be able to cooperate and understand each other. . . . And not fight a lot and, like, try to see the other person's point. . . . Like, if you only stay with your idea basically, then the other person might be right, and you have to try to figure out the problem between yourselves.

M: Um, I'd also say it's just learning to cooperate with others.

E: And, what does that mean to you, learning to cooperate?

M: Well, to, like, not fight all the time and to agree with others and, like, well, and to not always, um, think that if you're wrong, then the, um, like, some, then, like, it's the worst thing in the world or anything.

E: Why do you think that not thinking about being wrong is important when you're doing cooperative work together?

K: Well, I . . .

M: Well, it's good if you can just have fun. It would probably be.

E: And, what were you going to say?

K: Um, what was the question?

E: M said that she thought it was important not to think about if you're wrong, that would be the worst thing that could happen. Is that, am I saying that right?

M: Mm-hmm.

E: Yes. And I asked why is that important when you're working with another person—not to be worried about being wrong?

K: Well, um, I think it's important because you don't, if you're worried about being wrong, then you're not gonnna get anything done. You're gonna keep on going back to that problem and keep on having that come up . . . like, and, then asking the other person what they think. . . . And if you both agree on that thing, then it's gonna, it will probably be right. Cuz that's what two people think, and it's two against one. Probably, then, that would be the best guess to just go along with your idea that the other person thinks, if you agree with it.

E: So you think if two people agree on something, then it's more likely to be right.

K: Yeah.

E: What about the idea of agreeing? I think you both mentioned that it's important not to fight and to try and see the other person's point and to try to agree. Why do you think that's important?

K: Well, if you fight all the time, then you can't get anything done, and you're not, you, you just don't agree with anything they say. And, even if the person's right, you just don't want to agree. . . . You could agree, but you just don't want to.

E: You mean if you're fighting about it . . . that you wouldn't. Can you explain a little bit more what you mean?

K: Well, you just, like, you refuse to agree. You're just not going to. No matter what the person says, if you ask the teacher who's gonna be right, then they're gonna, you won't agree, so you have to see the other person's point and try to agree on things.

E: So, you think if you get into fighting about it that it would keep you from trying to see the other person's point.

K: Um, like when you're absolutely positive that you're right, and you know, like in math, for instance, you've done it on the calculator a few times and you're positively, absolutely sure that you're right. . . . And as the other person, you know, just sort of was thinking . . . playing around with the ruler, and, you know . . . typing numbers into the calculator and then just sort of came up with an idea that they're, you can, um, disagree with them. Uh, you can say, you know, that I've done this a few times on the calculator. . . . I've asked the teacher for help, and I think that we, that I'm right.

E: So you would, you would try to get some evidence that would support your idea. So, what do you think, M? Are there some times when it, it's OK to disagree?

M: Yeah. Well, um, um . . .

E: Can you give me an example of a time when it would be OK to disagree?

M: Well, yeah. I'd take K's example and then I'd probably also add to, and I'd also add and probably say to the person, "You've just been fiddling around," and they, and the, um, I'd have been, um, doing a lot of things . . . that will probably, so I'm, so I think I'm right.

E: What do you think are the qualities of a good problem-solving dyad or team?

M: Cooperation.

K: Well, understanding each other's point, like trying to see the other person's point and not just staying with your idea. . . . Like, be flexible. Don't always have to go with, like. . .

M: Whatever you came up with and you stay there, and you never know.

K: Yeah.

E: Anything else you can think of?

K: Getting along.

E: What, and what do you mean by that? In terms of, like, cooperating and getting along?

K: Getting along. Like, um, sort of trying to work together. . . . Like, just staying together and working together. Don't go off and do something yourself. . . . Like, you know, think sort of positively, like, you know, we're partners. We're supposed to be together. . . .

(Nastasi, 1993)

APPENDIX 3B

Worksheet for Collaborative Program Development

Participants:

Step 1. Define the problem.

Problem description:
Goal:

Step 2. Brainstorm solutions (number them 1, 2, 3, etc.; use back of sheet as needed).

Step 3. Consider and evaluate *each* solution.

#	Consequences?	Facilitators?	Inhibitors?

Step 4. Choose the "best" solution (based on evaluation in Step 3).

Step 5. Design a plan for implementation and evaluation of the solution.

Describe the plan for implementation (what? who? when? where?).

Describe the plan for evaluation.

Step 6. Implement plan and collect evaluation data.
  [Keep necessary records, based on plan of evaluation.]

Step 7. Evaluate the solution (support conclusions with data you collected).

To what extent is the plan being followed?

Is it successful?

Is it acceptable to all parties?

What revisions are needed?

Step 8. Review evaluation data on periodic basis and revise plan as needed.
  [Repeat problem solving process as needed.]

4

The ESCAPE Program

The ESCAPE program is a theoretically and empirically based curriculum designed to enhance generalizable coping skills of the high-risk population of COAs in kindergarten through grade 12. We specifically focus on developing self-efficacy, social interaction skills, and interpersonal problem solving. ESCAPE includes curricular content and instructional strategies that are typically part of existing school curriculum. We use literature, expressive arts, creative writing, films, group discussion, role playing, and cooperative learning. Thus, ESCAPE is designed to be integrated into existing academic programs. For example, activities that use literature are easily incorporated into language arts, and those related to group functioning and family dynamics are suitable to social studies. Cooperative learning may be applied across the curriculum. This program can be incorporated into existing drug education and social skills curricula. ESCAPE is best implemented as a collaborative effort between teachers and pupil support personnel (e.g., school psychologists, counselors, social workers). Although these activities may be modified for individual or small group application, they are intended for classroom application.

We identify specific objectives and activities for each target component of personal–social competence (self-efficacy, social interaction, interpersonal problem solving). The activities within each component build upon previous activities for that component. Although we address component areas separately, the program is designed as an integrated curriculum. This integration reflects the synergism of the three personal–social competence components, as we discussed in Chapter 1. Thus, activities focused on self-efficacy may also address objectives relevant to social interaction or interpersonal problem solving. For example, all collaborative (group) activities also provide opportunities for promoting social interaction, and we typically provide guidelines for facilitating the collaborative activity to achieve objectives relevant to both competence areas. Similarly, goal setting (a self-efficacy activity) requires applying problem-solving skills (cf. interpersonal problem-solving goals). Facilitators are advised to review the entire curriculum and coordinate activities across competence areas (e.g., incorporating activities across the three areas within one social studies unit). In addition, the needs of the participants may dictate such integration. For example, in implementing collaborative activities, it may be necessary to focus particular attention on promoting social skills development for some students. The program is designed for such modification. Facilitators should refer to Chapter 3 for more detailed information about specific instructional, assessment, and evaluation methods, and practical and ethical considerations. We also make reference throughout the curriculum to Tables 3.2 through 3.9 in Chapter 3, which are part of the materials for many of the activities. Furthermore, Chapters 5 and 6 provide additional resource materials to facilitate implementation and evaluation.

In this chapter, we present the goals, objectives, and activities of the ESCAPE program. For each goal, we delineate objectives and provide activities by grade levels (typically categorized as K–2, 3–5, 6–8, and 9–12). For each set of objectives, we provide (1) an activity, (2) a list of the necessary materials, and (3) one or more extensions. Some activities are intended for implementation over several sessions and are numbered as such. Extensions are designed to provide additional practice and/or generalization (e.g., across the curriculum and/or outside of the school setting). In some instances, extensions are consistent with and/or provide an introduction to subsequent activities relevant to goals within the same domain of competence.

SELF-EFFICACY

Goal 1. Enhancing Self-Perception

Grade Level: Kindergarten–Second

Objectives

1. Provide opportunities to develop healthy self-concept.
2. Provide social feedback to enhance sense of competence.
3. Provide models of self-concept.

Materials

Art materials (newsprint, construction paper, drawing paper, crayons, markers, paint, watercolors, fasteners).

Activity

Students draw, write, or tell (e.g., dictate a story) about some aspect of the *self* (e.g., about their social attributes). The aspects of self include, but are not limited to, physical, social, and cognitive attributes; gender, race, and ethnicity; talents, activities, hobbies, and other preferences. Encourage expression of ideas without regard for accuracy in mechanics (e.g., spelling and punctuation). Guide discussion of individual depictions, noting common and unique characteristics and encouraging students to recognize and appreciate the commonalties and differences within the group. The activity is repeated for different aspects of the self; students then compile these into a book about the self (e.g., "All About Me").

Extension

The book provides the basis for developing individual portfolios, to which students add other items such as additional depictions, work, awards, photographs, mementos. The purpose is to extend the depiction and recognition of self beyond the classroom setting to include home, family, peer group, community activities, and organizations. In addition, depictions provide a basis for early writing activities.

    Note: The activity and extension facilitate integration of language and creative arts curricula, and provide the basis for early social studies activities.

❖   ❖   ❖

Grade Level: Third–Fifth

Objectives

    1. Provide opportunities to develop healthy self-concept.
    2. Provide social feedback so as to enhance sense of competence.
    3. Provide opportunities for decision/choice making.
    4. Facilitate realistic goal setting.
    5. Facilitate task structuring (e.g., proximal goal setting, performance-contingent reward).
    6. Provide models of self-efficacy.

Materials

Story, art materials (newsprint, construction paper, drawing and writing paper, crayons, markers, paint, watercolors, fasteners), Table 3.5.

Suggested Story*

Isadora, R. (1976). *Max.* NY: Collier Books.

    *Detailed information concerning books and films is supplied in Chapter 5.

Activity

1. Read *Max* to the class. Discuss the story, using the suggested sequence in Table 3.5, and emphasize how Max discovered something new about himself. Next, students construct "pies" to depict the parts of the self, with sections of the pie proportional to students' perceptions of their competencies (i.e., What do you do best, next best, least best; with proportion of the pie corresponding to relative amount/level of each skill). Link the concept of proportions of the self to the mathematical construct of proportion. Guide discussion of individual depictions, noting common and unique characteristics and encouraging students to recognize and appreciate the commonalties and differences within the group. To facilitate social feedback, encourage students to identify other competencies they have noticed in peers.

2. To facilitate choice making and goal setting, ask each individual to determine whether the depicted amounts of the self (the pie) correspond to level of importance (i.e., How important is that skill to you? Would you like to change any aspect?). Each student then makes a new pie depicting a preferred set of competencies. Help students to identify a realistic goal related to preferred competencies. (Developing plans for goal attainment is an extension of this activity.)

Note: This activity facilitates integration of language arts, mathematics, health, and social studies curricula. In addition, goal setting extends the problem-solving processes typically used in mathematics to other academic and social competencies (e.g., selecting a goal for personal skill development is similar to defining the problem in mathematical problem solving).

Extension

From the preferred set of competencies, each student chooses one as a focus for developing an individual behavior change plan (e.g., for learning a new skill). With facilitation, students develop plans to get closer to identified goals (what do you need to learn or do, etc.). Focus on determining the steps to the goal, identifying and acquiring necessary resources, setting short- and long-term goals, and devising a plan for evaluation. Have students evaluate goal setting and planning, using the checklist for goal setting (Table 3.9). Journals also can be used for monitoring and evaluating progress toward the goal and generalization to other settings (e.g., use the checklist to guide journal writing).

Note: Consider implementing through collaborative problem solving, with two or more students with the same goal working together. Students with more advanced skills could provide scaffolding for their peers (within or across groups). In addition, goal setting and attainment might involve consultation with teachers of specific content areas, other pupil support personnel (e.g., psychologists, nurses, social workers, guidance counselors), and family and community resources.

❖   ❖   ❖

Grade Level: Sixth–Eighth

Objectives

1. Provide opportunities to develop healthy self-concept.
2. Provide social feedback so as to enhance sense of competence.
3. Provide opportunities for decision/choice making.
4. Facilitate realistic goal setting.
5. Facilitate task structuring (e.g., proximal goal setting, performance-contingent reward).
6. Provide models of self-efficacy.

Materials

Story, art materials (newsprint, construction paper, drawing and writing paper, crayons, markers, paint, watercolors, fasteners), VCR and monitor, Table 3.5.

Suggested Story

Lanning, S. (Producer), Rosemont, N. (Executive Producer), & Grint, A. (Director). (1987). *The Secret Garden.*

Activity

1. View the film, *The Secret Garden.* Discuss the story, using the suggested sequence in Table 3.5. Emphasize how the characters develop their competencies and encounter their limitations, in part through their interactions with others. Next, students construct "pies" to depict the parts of the self, with sections of the pie proportional to students' perceptions of their competencies (i.e., what do you do best, next best, least best; with proportion of the pie corresponding to relative amount of each skill). Link the concept of proportions of the self to the mathematical construct of proportion. Guide discussion of individual depictions, noting common and unique characteristics and encouraging students to recognize and appreciate the commonalties and differences within the group. To facilitate social feedback, encourage students to identify other competencies they have noticed in peers.

2. To facilitate choice making and goal setting, ask each individual to determine whether the depicted amounts correspond to level of importance (i.e., How important is that skill to you? Would you like to change any aspect?). Each student then makes a new pie depicting a preferred set of competencies. Help students to identify realistic goals related to preferred competencies. Group students with different goals and have the

students match their pies and discuss how they might help each other with respective goal attainment, thus facilitating social support and prosocial interaction. (Developing plans for goal attainment is an extension of this activity.)

Note: This activity facilitates the integration of language arts, social studies, health, and mathematics curricula. In addition, goal setting extends the problem-solving processes typically used in mathematics to other academic and social competencies (e.g., selecting a goal for personal skill development is similar to defining the problem in mathematical problem solving).

Extension

From the preferred set of competencies, each student chooses one as a focus for developing an individual behavior change plan (e.g., for learning a new skill). With facilitation, students develop plans to get closer to identified goals (what do you need to learn or do, etc.). Focus on determining the steps to the goal, identifying and acquiring necessary resources, setting short- and long-term goals, and devising a plan for evaluation. Have students evaluate goal setting and planning, using the checklist for goal setting (Table 3.9). Journals also can be used for monitoring and evaluating progress toward the goal and generalization to other settings (e.g., use the checklist to guide journal writing).

Note: Consider implementing through collaborative problem solving, with two or more students with different goals working together. Students with more advanced skills could provide scaffolding for their peers (within or across groups). In addition, goal setting and attainment might involve consultation with teachers of specific content areas, other pupil support personnel (e.g., psychologists, nurses, social workers, guidance counselors), and family and community resources.

❖   ❖   ❖

Grade Level: Ninth–Twelfth

Objectives

1. Provide opportunities to develop healthy self-concept.
2. Provide social feedback so as to enhance sense of competence.
3. Provide opportunities for decision/choice making.
4. Facilitate realistic goal setting.
5. Facilitate task structuring (e.g., proximal goal setting, performance-contingent reward).
6. Provide models of self-efficacy.

Materials

Autobiography or biography of historical or contemporary figures, materials for journal writing, materials for production of play or video and viewing of film (e.g., props, video camera, VCR, monitor), Tables 3.2, 3.3, 3.4, 3.5.

Suggested Stories

Haley, A. (1964). *Autobiography of Malcolm X.*
Musca, T. (Producer), & Menendez, R. (Director). (1988). *Stand and Deliver.*

See also the list of books and films in Chapter 5.

Activity

As part of social studies or language arts curriculum, select an autobiographical or biographical book or film about a figure of historical or cultural significance. Students read the book individually during designated class period or as homework, or view the film in class as a group. Discuss the story, using the suggested sequence in Table 3.5. Emphasize the characters' personal and work-related competencies, and efforts to define the self while moving toward adulthood. As reading/viewing and discussions proceed, the class generates themes, and writes and produces a series of skits depicting various personal, family, and/or peer issues that arise during adolescence. The activity is structured as a cooperative learning experience, with emphasis on individual accountability, interdependence, conflict resolution (i.e., resolving social as well as cognitive conflicts), and mutual construction of ideas. Facilitators could also use this as an opportunity to discuss strategies for group problem solving (see Tables 3.2, 3.3, 3.4). Variations of this activity could include small-group rather than whole-class discussion, art work with different media, or variations in the type of writing assignment.

Extensions

1. Students individually select and read autobiography or biography about figures of personal, historical, or cultural significance, and complete book reports on selected readings. Individually or in small groups, students perform dramatic presentations of respective stories.

2. As a homework assignment, students interview a variety of adults regarding their personal and work-related histories from adolescence through adulthood. Students in small groups develop interview questions and incorporate findings into written and oral accounts (e.g., biographies, news report, newsletter, magazine) to be distributed within the school

and/or community. Seek consultation and assistance from representatives of local news agencies; for example, invite reporters, editors, advertising agents, and/or illustrators to speak to the students.

3. Students write autobiographies of childhood or projected autobiographies through adulthood. This could be further extended to writing of peer's biographies. For example, students work in pairs, share personal histories, and write and cross-edit each other's biographies.

4. Each student develops an individual personal and career plan. With facilitation, students develop plans to get closer to identified goals (what do you need to learn or do, etc.). Focus on determining the steps to the goal, identifying and acquiring necessary resources, setting short- and long-term goals, and devising a plan for evaluation. Have students evaluate goal setting and planning, using the checklist for goal setting (Table 3.9). Use journals for monitoring and evaluating progress toward the goal and generalization to other settings (e.g., use the checklist to guide journal writing). Consider implementing through collaborative problem solving, with two or more students with different goals working together. Students with more advanced skills could provide scaffolding for their peers (within or across groups). In addition, goal setting and attainment might involve consultation with teachers of specific content areas, other pupil support personnel (e.g., psychologists, nurses, social workers, guidance counselors), and family and community resources (e.g., representatives from various careers as speakers and mentors).

Note: This activity and the extensions facilitate integration of English composition, literature, history, health, and electives or extracurricular activities (e.g., debate, speech, psychology, career clubs, yearbook staff, school newspaper staff).

Goal 2. Defining Self in Relation to Others (Fostering Interdependence)

Grade Level: Kindergarten–Fourth

Objectives

1. Provide opportunities to develop healthy self-concept.
2. Provide opportunities to identify common and unique characteristics within the group.
3. Provide opportunities to foster and discuss interdependence.

Materials

Newsprint, crayons or markers, scissors, metal brads, Tables 3.2, 3.3, and 3.4.

Activity

Small-group cooperative activity (maximum of 10 students per group). Students construct paper figures composed of tracings of body parts (e.g., head, legs, arms) from all group members, called "Frankenclass" (adapted from Smith, 1982). Depending on the class size, several figures may need to be constructed to ensure that each student contributes a body part. Facilitator guides (1) formation of groups to ensure heterogeneity and (2) decision making about who will be each body part, who will trace, and in which order. Next students individually color their respective body parts, sharing materials. Then the parts are assembled with brads. Facilitator continues to guide the students' interactions, including decision making, problem solving, conflict resolution, throughout the activity. Following the activity, facilitator guides group discussion of (1) the importance of the contribution of each member, (2) the importance of working toward a mutual goal, (3) ways to work together effectively, and (4) physical similarities and differences, using examples from situations that arose during the activity (see Tables 3.2, 3.3, 3.4). Make explicit the parallel between the diversity reflected in the Frankenclasses and the diversity in the group composition.

Note: This activity could be incorporated into the art curriculum and/or into a health unit related to body image.

Extension

In small groups (3 to 4 members), students construct collages on a common theme relevant to an academic unit. Then, the group collages are combined to form a class collage. Each group is directed to discuss orally or in writing the common and unique characteristics of their collage compared to the class collage. Guide group discussion of the importance of the contribution of each member to the small- and large-group products and processes (e.g., focus discussion of process on ways to work effectively toward a mutual goal; see Tables 3.2, 3.3, 3.4, 3.9). For older students, include a language arts activity in which individuals or small groups describe in writing their section of the collage (e.g., a composition accompanies each section of the collage).

❖   ❖   ❖

Grade Level: Fifth–Eighth

Objectives

1. Provide opportunities to develop healthy self-concept.
2. Provide opportunities to identify common and unique characteristics within the group.
3. Provide opportunities to foster and discuss interdependence.

4. Provide opportunities for decision/choice making.
5. Facilitate realistic goal setting.

Materials

Paper, pens, newsprint, markers, Table 4.1.

Activity

Students construct a class chart such as that depicted in Table 4.1 with categories of preferences as column headings and students' names as row headings. Students can generate alternative preference categories. Students record their individual preferences for each category on paper, and use these recordings to construct the class chart. Students individually write about and the facilitator guides discussion of the common and unique preferences of class members. Discussion might include the recip-

TABLE 4.1. Who Are We? (Grades 5–8)

Name	What I like to do at school	What I like to do at home	What I like to do with my family	What I like to do with my freinds	What I like to do by myself

Name	Foods I like	TV shows I like	Colors I like

rocal nature of individual and group identity; that is, the role of individual preferences in formation of groups and the influence of group membership on individual preferences (e.g., learning, recreational, political, religious, cultural, ethnic and racial preferences and groups, as well as cliques and gangs), particularly as related to students' experiences.

Note: This activity could be incorporated into the social studies curriculum or health curriculum focused on individual and group development.

Extensions

1. Using the categories, students in small groups (3 to 4 members) develop plans for accommodating all the preferences within the context of a given activity. For example, students plan a real or hypothetical meal for the class taking into consideration all of the food preferences listed in the chart. To extend this activity across the curriculum, have students consider nutritional standards (health) and cost (mathematics), compose announcements and/or menus (art), and arrange entertainment (music, dance, physical education). Following the planning activities, guide group discussion of the importance of the contribution of each member to the group products and processes (e.g., focus discussion of process on ways to work effectively toward a mutual goal; see Tables 3.2, 3.3, 3.4, 3.9).

2. Older students plan a school-sponsored recreation night for middle school students, taking into account factors such as (1) activity preferences of fifth through eighth graders, (2) school rules, (3) adult supervision, (4) costs, (5) advertisement, (6) refreshments, and (7) clean-up. This activity could be incorporated into language arts, mathematics, and science (e.g., constructing, implementing, and compiling data from a survey of student interests); creative arts (developing advertisement); health (planning refreshments); social studies (meeting social standards and responsibilities related to school rules, providing adult supervision, clean-up activities); and physical education (planning the recreational activities). Following the planning activities, guide group discussion of the importance of the contribution of each member to the group products and processes (e.g., focus discussion of process on ways to work effectively toward a mutual goal; see Tables 3.2, 3.3, 3.4, 3.9).

❖   ❖   ❖

Grade Level: Ninth–Twelfth

Objectives

1. Provide opportunities to develop healthy self-concept.
2. Provide opportunities to identify common and unique characteristics within the group.

3. Provide opportunities to foster and discuss interdependence.
4. Provide opportunities for decision/choice making.
5. Facilitate realistic goal setting.

Materials

Paper, pens, newsprint, markers, Table 4.2.

TABLE 4.2. What Do We Believe? (Grades 9–12)

Name	A friend is someone who . . .	A female friend is someone who . . .	A male friend is someone who . . .	A girl/boyfriend is someone who . . .

Name	Parents should . . .	Teachers should . . .	High school students should . . .	If I were principal I would . . .	If I were president I would . . .

Name	People who smoke are . . .	People who use alcohol are . . .	People who use other drugs are . . .	[Have students generate other category(ies)]

Activity

Students construct a class chart such as that depicted in Table 4.2 with categories of beliefs as column headings and students' names as row headings. Students can generate alternative belief categories. Students record their individual beliefs for each category on paper and use these to construct the class chart. Students individually write about and the facilitator guides discussion of the common and unique beliefs of class members. Discussion might include the reciprocal nature of individual and group identity; that is, the role of individual beliefs in formation of groups and the influence of group membership on individual beliefs (e.g., learning, recreational, political, religious, cultural, ethnic, and racial preferences and groups, as well as cliques and gangs), particularly as related to students' experiences.

Note: This activity could be incorporated into the social studies curriculum or health curriculum focused on individual and group development.

Extensions

1. Students in small groups (3 to 4 members) discuss current and/or historical real-life dilemmas related to the reciprocal influence of beliefs in the individual and group identity. For example, within the context of social studies, students discuss the role of beliefs in the formation of relationships within and across racial or ethnic groups, in the current society, and at various points throughout U. S. history. Students could be asked to develop plans for fostering peaceful functioning of a multicultural community. Following the small-group discussions, guide whole-class discussion of the importance of the contribution of each member to the group products and processes (e.g., focus discussion of process on ways to work effectively toward a mutual goal; see Tables 3.2, 3.3, 3.4, 3.9).

2. Integration across the curriculum could include reading relevant biographies and historical novels (literature), as well as writing and producing video or other dramatic presentations of the dilemmas and/or their solutions (art, drama, instructional technology, language arts, mathematics, home economics).

Goal 3. Recognizing and Exercising the Limits of Personal Control

Grade Level: Kindergarten–Second

Objectives

1. Provide opportunities for decision/choice making.
2. Facilitate realistic goal setting.

   3. Encourage development of coping strategies for handling difficulties.
   4. Ensure skill development to foster success.
   5. Facilitate task structuring through proximal goal setting.
   6. Provide models of effective goal setting and decision making.

Materials

Story, language and creative arts materials (drawing and writing paper, crayons, markers, paint, watercolors, fasteners), Tables 3.3, 3.4, 3.5, and 3.9.

Suggested Story

Bolliger-Savelli, A. (1974). *Miranda's Magic*.

Activity

Read *Miranda's Magic* to the class. Discuss the story, using the suggested sequence in Table 3.5, and emphasize how the children and adults worked together to turn the public square into a playground. Help students to (1) identify a group goal that requires collaborative effort, and (2) develop and implement a step-by-step plan for goal attainment, with consideration of developmental level, available resources, and curricular relevance. Have students evaluate collaborative goal setting and planning (use Tables 3.3, 3.4, 3.9 as guides). Journals also can be used for monitoring and evaluating progress toward the goal and generalization to other settings. Guide discussion of the similarities between this group project and the community project depicted in *Miranda's Magic*, emphasizing that community helped adults and children work together to accomplish a goal that was difficult for the children alone.

Extensions

   1. Students write, illustrate, and enact their own story about their collaborative project. Provide guidance and assistance as necessary. This activity is easily incorporated into language and creative arts curricula.
   2. As part of a social studies unit, students visit a community service agency that exemplifies working together to help other people; for example, fire department, police station, soup kitchen, community recreational center. Follow-up activities could include writing thank-you notes to the agency personnel and/or depicting experiences through art and/or writing.

❖   ❖   ❖

Grade Level: Third–Fifth

Objectives

1. Provide opportunities for decision/choice making.
2. Facilitate realistic goal setting.
3. Encourage development of coping strategies for handling difficulties.
4. Ensure skill development to foster success.
5. Facilitate task structuring through proximal goal setting.
6. Provide models of effective goal setting and decision making.

Materials

Story, notebook for journal writing, Tables 3.5 and 3.9.

Suggested Stories

Hoffman, M., & Binch, C. (1991). *Amazing Grace.*
Lopez, B. (1990). *Crow and Weasel.*

Activity

Read the story to the class. Discuss the story (using the suggested sequence in Table 3.5), emphasizing the importance of self-confidence, social support, realistic goal setting, and effort in accomplishing one's dreams or goals. Direct students to write in their journals about something they want to accomplish (i.e., their own dream/goal), and guide them in developing individual plans for accomplishing those dreams/goals. Focus on (1) clearly defining realistic short- and long-term goals, (2) identifying and procuring necessary material and social resources (e.g., supplies, reference material, assistance, information), (3) developing step-by-step plans, (4) self-assessing level of confidence, and (5) monitoring progress. Table 3.9 provides a self-evaluation checklist for goal-setting activities. Encourage collaboration among students with similar goals, and peer tutoring by students with more advanced skills. In addition, encourage students to seek assistance from other adults within the school, family, or community. Use journals as the means for monitoring progress toward the goal (e.g., students record daily/weekly progress, attainment of specific steps in narrative or chart form; use Table 3.9 as a guide).

    Note: This activity could be incorporated into language arts and social studies curricula.

Extensions

1. As part of language and creative arts curricula, students write and illustrate their own stories about something they accomplished. Encourage them to identify the factors (e.g., talent/skill, social support, confidence, effort) that contributed to success.

2. Have students read a biography about a key figure in history, science, mathematics, language, or creative arts, and discuss the factors that contributed to success. Students might also dramatize the individual's story.

3. Help students to identify members of their communities whose accomplishments relate to their own interests or goals, and write letters inviting the individuals to speak with the class. Assist the students in developing questions for the speakers related to identifying factors contributing to success. Following the presentation, students write essays or stories about the speakers' attainments. This activity could facilitate integration of several curricular areas (e.g., language arts, social studies, science, mathematics).

❖   ❖   ❖

Grade Level: Sixth–Eighth

Objectives

1. Provide opportunities for decision/choice making.
2. Facilitate realistic goal setting
3. Encourage development of coping strategies for handling difficulties.
4. Ensure skill development to foster success.
5. Facilitate task structuring through proximal goal setting.
6. Provide models of effective goal setting and decision making.

Materials

Story, notebook for journal writing, Tables 3.5, 3.8, and 3.9.

Suggested Story

Frank, A. (1952). *The Diary of a Young Girl*.

Activity

Students read *The Diary of a Young Girl* and discuss the story (using the suggested sequence in Table 3.5), emphasizing the theme of coping with the limits of personal control. Discuss factors that contribute to coping with and overcoming adversity; for example, talent or skill, social support, confidence, effort. Direct students to write in their journals about situations in which they encountered the limitations of personal control over external events, using the format depicted in Table 3.8. Focus on (1) clearly defining realistic short- and long-term goals, (2) identifying and procuring necessary material and social resources (e.g., supplies, reference material, assistance, information), (3) developing step-by-step plans, (4) self-assessing level of confidence, and (5) monitoring progress. Table 3.9 provides a self-evaluation checklist for goal-setting activities. Encourage collaboration among students with similar goals, and peer tutoring by students with more advanced skills. In addition, encourage students to seek assistance from other adults within the school, family, or community. Use journals as the means for monitoring progress toward the goal (e.g., students record daily/weekly progress, attainment of specific steps in narrative or chart form; use Table 3.9 as a guide).

Note: This activity could be incorporated into language arts and social studies curricula.

Extensions

1. As part of language and creative arts curricula, students write and illustrate their own stories about something they accomplished. Encourage them to identify the factors (e.g., talent/skill, social support, confidence, effort) that contributed to and/or interfered with their success.

2. Students research and write about the accomplishments of a key figure in history, science, mathematics, language, or creative arts, identifying the factors that contributed to success. Reports could also be presented orally or dramatically.

3. Students interview individuals within the community about accomplishments related to the student's interests or goals. Assist students in designing interview questions for identifying factors that facilitate or inhibit success. Students with similar interests could work collaboratively to develop questions. Have students practice interviews in pairs.

❖   ❖   ❖

Grade Level: Ninth–Twelfth

Objectives

1. Provide opportunities for decision/choice making.
2. Facilitate realistic goal setting.
3. Encourage development of coping strategies for handling difficulties.

4. Ensure skill development to foster success.
5. Facilitate task structuring through proximal goal setting.
6. Provide models of effective goal setting and decision making.

Materials

Story, notebook for journal writing, VCR and monitor, Tables 3.5 and 3.8.

Suggested Story

Katzka, G., (Producer), & Schlesinger, J. (Producer & Director). (1984). *The Falcon and the Snowman*.

Activity

Students view the film and discuss story themes (using the suggested sequence in Table 3.5), including (1) choices made by the characters and the consequences of their choices, and (2) how the characters recognized and exercised limits of personal control. Students then use the format depicted in Table 3.8 to write, from the character's perspective, about situations encountered by one of the story's characters. Guide group discussion of alternative choices and possible consequences. Students then write a story, poem, or essay about personal experiences that involved difficult choices or reaching the limits of personal control in interactions with authority figures. Using these personal stories, discuss factors that contribute to coping with and overcoming adversity; for example, talent or skill, social support, confidence, effort.

Note: This activity could be incorporated into language arts and social studies curricula.

Extensions

1. Students write in their journals about limitations of personal control over external events, using the format depicted in Table 3.8. Focus on (1) clearly defining realistic short- and long-term goals, (2) identifying and procuring necessary material and social resources (e.g., supplies, reference material, assistance, information), (3) developing step-by-step plans, (4) self-assessing level of confidence, and (5) monitoring progress. Table 3.9 provides a self-evaluation checklist for goal-setting activities. Encourage collaboration among students with similar goals, and peer tutoring by students with more advanced skills. In addition, encourage students to seek assistance from other adults within the school, family, or community. Use journals as the means for monitoring progress toward the goal (e.g., students record daily/weekly progress, attainment of specific steps in narrative or chart form; use Table 3.9 as a guide).

2. Students investigate career interests, establish tentative short- and

long-term goals, and develop plans related to career goals. Students interview individuals within the community about accomplishments related to the students' career interests. Assist students in designing interview questions for identifying factors that facilitate or inhibit success. Students with similar interests could work collaboratively to develop questions. Have students practice interviews in pairs.

3. As feasible, students participate in apprenticeship or mentorship programs related to career interests.

SOCIAL INTERACTION SKILLS

Goal 1. Caring for Self and Others

Grade Level: Kindergarten–Second

Objectives

1. Promote an understanding of the importance of prosocial behavior (reciprocal helping, caring, empathy).
2. Promote an understanding of the importance of caring for self.
3. Provide opportunities to apply prosocial interaction skills.
4. Foster a prosocial climate.
5. Provide models of prosocial behaviors.

Materials

Story, drawing and writing materials (drawing and writing paper, crayons, markers, paint, watercolors), ingredients for stone soup (stones, vegetables), Tables 3.3, 3.4, 3.5, and 3.9.

Suggested Story

McGovern, A. (1986). *Stone Soup.*

Activity

1. Read *Stone Soup* to the class. Discuss the story, using the suggested sequence in Table 3.5 and emphasizing depictions within the story of caring for self and others. Have the students draw and/or write stories from their own experiences about how people care for themselves and each other. Facilitate sharing of examples within the whole group. During discussions make explicit (1) the similarities in behaviors that reflect caring for self and others and (2) the reciprocal nature of caring for others.

2. Whole group makes stone soup, ensuring that all contribute in some way (e.g., supplies, effort), consistent with resources available to the individual. After eating the soup, students collaborate to write and/or draw

a story about their experiences of making stone soup. Guide students' interactions—including decision making, problem solving, and conflict resolution—throughout the activity. Following the activity, guide group discussion of (1) the importance of the contribution of each member, (2) the importance of working toward a mutual goal, (3) ways to work together effectively, and (4) ways to display caring for self and others. Use examples from situations that arose during the activity (use Tables 3.3, 3.4, 3.9 as guides).

Note: This activity could be incorporated into health, and language and creative arts curricula.

Extension

Students participate in dyadic or small-group cooperative activities applied to academic curricula. For example, students are instructed to work collaboratively on a mathematics problem-solving activity. Throughout the activity, guide students' interactions, including decision making, problem solving, and conflict resolution. Following the activity, guide group discussion of (1) the importance of the contribution of each member, (2) the importance of working toward a mutual goal, (3) ways to work together effectively, and (4) ways to display caring for self and others. Use examples from situations that arose during the activity.

❖   ❖   ❖

Grade Level: Third–Fifth

Objectives

1. Promote an understanding of the importance of prosocial behavior (reciprocal helping, caring, empathy).
2. Promote an understanding of the importance of caring for self.
3. Promote an understanding of the connection between caring for self and others.
4. Provide opportunities to apply prosocial interaction skills.
5. Foster a prosocial climate.
6. Provide models of prosocial behaviors.

Materials

Story, green stones, writing and drawing materials, Table 3.5.

Suggested Stories

Koci, M. (1987). *Sarah's Bear*.
Walker, A. (1991). *Finding the Green Stone*.
Williams, M. (1983). *The Velveteen Rabbit: Or How Toys Become Real*.

Activity

Read *Finding the Green Stone* to the class. Discuss the story, using the suggested sequence in Table 3.5 and emphasizing depictions within the story of caring for self and others. Have the students write and illustrate stories from their own experiences about how people care for themselves and each other. Facilitate sharing of examples within the whole group. As individual students share their stories, each is provided with a "green stone" as a reminder of caring for self. During discussions make explicit (1) the similarities in behaviors that reflect caring for self and others, (2) the reciprocal nature of caring for others, and (3) how caring for the self is reflected in part by valuing one's uniqueness.

Note: This activity could be incorporated into language and creative arts curricula.

Extension

Students participate in dyadic or small-group cooperative activities applied to academic curricula. For example, students are instructed to work collaboratively on a mathematics problem-solving activity. Throughout the activity, guide the students' interactions, including decision making, problem solving, and conflict resolution. Following the activity, guide group discussion of (1) the importance of the contribution of each member, (2) the importance of working toward a mutual goal, (3) ways to work together effectively, and (4) ways to display caring for self and others. Use examples from situations that arose during the activity (use Tables 3.3, 3.4, 3.9 as guides).

❖   ❖   ❖

Grade Level: Sixth–Eighth

Objectives

1. Promote an understanding of the importance of prosocial behavior (reciprocal helping, caring, empathy).
2. Promote an understanding of the importance of caring for self.
3. Promote an understanding of the connection between caring for self and others.
4. Provide opportunities to apply prosocial interaction skills.
5. Foster a prosocial climate.
6. Provide models of prosocial behaviors.

Materials

Story, VCR and monitor (if film is used), Table 3.5.

Suggested Stories

Elfand, M. (Producer), Moloney, M. (Exec. Producer), & Mulligan, R. (Director). (1988). *Clara's Heart.*
Silverstein, S. (1964). *The Giving Tree.*

Activity

View *Clara's Heart.* Discuss the story, using the suggested sequence in Table 3.5 and emphasizing depictions within the story of caring for self and others. Have students write and illustrate stories from their own experiences about how people care for themselves and each other. Facilitate sharing of examples within the whole group. During discussions, make explicit (1) the similarities in behaviors that reflect caring for self and others, (2) the reciprocal nature of caring for others, (3) how caring for the self is reflected in part by valuing one's uniqueness, and (4) how caring for self can complement as well as conflict with caring for others.

Note: This activity could be incorporated into language and creative arts curricula.

Extension

Students participate in dyadic or small-group cooperative activities applied to academic curricula. For example, students are instructed to work collaboratively on a mathematics problem–solving activity. Guide the students' interactions—including decision making, problem solving, and conflsiict resolution—throughout the activity. Following the activity, guide group discussion of (1) the importance of the contribution of each member, (2) the importance of working toward a mutual goal, (3) ways to work together effectively, and (4) ways to display caring for self and others. Use examples from situations that arose during the activity (use Tables 3.3, 3.4, 3.9 as guides).

❖   ❖   ❖

Grade Level: Ninth–Twelfth

Objective

1. Promote an understanding of the importance of prosocial behavior (reciprocal helping, caring, empathy).
2. Promote an understanding of the importance of caring for self.
3. Promote an understanding of the connection between caring for self and others.
4. Provide opportunities to apply prosocial interaction skills.

5. Foster a prosocial climate.
6. Provide models of prosocial behaviors.

Materials

Story (film), notebooks for journals, writing supplies, VCR and monitor, Table 3.5.

Suggested Story

Evans, B. A. (Producer), Gideon, R. (Producer), Schernman, A. (Producer), & Reiner, R. (Director). (1986). *Stand by Me.*

Activity

View the film, *Stand by Me.* Discuss the story, using the suggested sequence in Table 3.5 and emphasizing depictions within the story of caring for self and others. Have the students write and illustrate stories from their own experiences about how people care for themselves and each other. Facilitate sharing of examples within the whole group. During discussions, make explicit (1) the similarities in behaviors that reflect caring for self and others, (2) the reciprocal nature of caring for others, (3) how caring for the self is reflected in part by valuing one's uniqueness, and (4) how caring for self can complement as well as conflict with caring for others.

Note: This activity could be incorporated into life skills, and language and creative arts curricula.

Extensions

1. Students participate in dyadic or small-group cooperative activities applied to academic curricula. For example, students are instructed to work collaboratively on a mathematics problem-solving activity. Throughout the activity, guide students' interactions, including decision making, problem solving, and conflict resolution. Following the activity, guide group discussion of (1) the importance of the contribution of each member, (2) the importance of working toward a mutual goal, (3) ways to work together effectively, and (4) ways to display caring for self and others. Use examples from situations that arose during the activity (use Tables 3.3, 3.4, 3.9 as guides).

2. As part of history or social studies units, students identify examples of caring for self and others within current news media (e.g., newspaper, TV news, news magazines) or historical accounts. Students present examples in written or oral form.

3. As part of life skills or language arts activities, students identify examples of caring for self and others within daily life experiences, lit-

erature, popular media (e.g., TV shows, movies, magazines). Students present examples in written or oral form.

4. Students collaboratively produce a video designed to teach younger students about caring. The class writes and produces a series of skits depicting real-life examples of caring for self and others. Students record in their journals their reflections on the experience of working together, with emphasis on personal examples of caring. This activity could facilitate integration of several curricular areas (art, drama, instructional technology, language arts, mathematics, home economics, psychology, social studies).

5. Students review and critique young children's literature regarding the depiction of caring, compile a list of recommended books, and develop a series of lessons for implementation with early elementary students (see Tables 3.6 and 3.7). Students implement the lessons with young children in the school system, local preschool, or other community setting. This activity could facilitate integration of several curricular areas (language arts, home economics, psychology, social studies, child development).

Goal 2. Relating in the Private Sphere (Friends, Family, and Other Intimate Relationships)

Grade Level: Kindergarten–Second

Objectives

1. Promote an understanding of friendship.
2. Promote an understanding of family.
3. Provide models of prosocial behaviors in the private sphere.

FRIENDSHIP ACTIVITY

Materials

Story, language and creative arts materials (drawing and writing paper, crayons, markers, paint, watercolors, fasteners), Table 3.5.

Suggested Story

Hallinan, P. K. (1977). *That's What a Friend Is.*

Activity

Read *That's What a Friend Is* to the class. Discuss the story, using the suggested sequence in Table 3.5, and guide students to identify (1) the characteristics of a friend, with focus on actions that signify friendship; (2) the various types of friends (e.g., peers, adults, same- and cross-gender); and (3) examples of individuals they consider to be friends. Using students' descriptors, compose a group definition of "friend." Students write or draw a story about a friend. Guide sharing of stories, relating the students' stories to the group's definition and adding to the definition as needed.

Note: This activity could be incorporated into language and creative arts, health, and drug education curricula.

Extensions

1. Students write and/or draw stories about ways they display or might display caring toward friends. Guide sharing of stories, emphasizing the reciprocal nature of friendship and relating the students' descriptors to the group definition of friendship.

2. Students in small groups make "friendship" collages, with drawings or pictures from magazines depicting friendship. Throughout the activity, guide students' interactions, including decision making, problem solving, and conflict resolution. Following the activity, guide discussion of (1) the various depictions of friendship, (2) ways in which students displayed caring interactions and worked cooperatively during the activity, and (3) the importance of the contributions of each group member (use Tables 3.3 and 3.4 as guides).

FAMILY ACTIVITY

Materials

Language and creative arts materials (drawing and writing paper, crayons, markers, paint, watercolors, fasteners), story.

Suggested Story

Anglund, J. W. (1987). *All About My Family.*

Activity

Using *All About My Family* as a guide, have students write and/or illustrate books (e.g., using drawings, photographs) about their own families. Include pages for the following categories, encouraging students to include their own conceptions in any category: My family (with individual depictions of family members), Things I do with my family, Special days (family celebrations/holidays), My home, My extended family (depictions of grandparents, aunts, uncles, cousins, and other significant people). Use each page/section of the book as a stimulus for discussing and defining family, with focus on the diversity of definitions. Guide students to identify the characteristics of a family, the various types of families, and the various relationships within families (e.g., parent–child, child–sibling, sibling–parent, parent–parent, child–other adult/relative, parent–other adult/relative, child–pet, parent–pet). Discuss the ways in which family members show that they care for each other.

Note: This activity could be incorporated into social studies, language and creative arts, health, and drug education curricula.

Extensions

1. Read to the class children's stories (such as those listed below) that depict families and family relationships from various perspectives. Guide discussion, using the suggested sequence in Table 3.5, of how the characters or authors define family in written and pictorial form. Students then write and illustrate their own stories about their families, using the information from their family books. Guide sharing of their stories, with focus on diversity of family definition. Including stories about families from various cultures facilitates integration of social studies with language and creative arts. Suggested books follow:

Boegehold, B. (1985). *Daddy Doesn't Live Here Anymore.*
Collins, J. (1989). *My Father.*
dePaola, T. (1983). *The Legend of the Bluebonnet.*
Rylant, C. (1982). *When I Was Young in the Mountains.*
Seuling, B. (1985). *What Kind of Family Is This?*

2. Students write and/or illustrate stories about ways they display or might display caring to family members. Guide sharing of the stories, emphasizing the reciprocal nature of family relationships and the similarities and differences between relationships with friends and family members.

3. Students in small groups make "family" collages, with drawings or pictures from magazines depicting various types of families. Throughout the activity, guide students' interactions, including decision making, problem solving, and conflict resolution. Following the activity, guide discussion of (1) the various depictions of family, (2) ways in which students displayed caring interactions and worked cooperatively during the activity, and (3) the importance of the contributions of each group member (use Tables 3.3 and 3.4 as guides).

❖   ❖   ❖

Grade Level: Third–Fifth

Objectives

1. Promote an understanding of the role of prosocial behavior in developing and maintaining friendships.

2. Promote an understanding of the role of prosocial behavior in family relationships.

3. Promote an understanding of the behaviors that facilitate or interfere with establishing and maintaining relationships.

4. Provide opportunities to apply skills related to initiating and maintaining relationships.

5. Provide models of prosocial behaviors in the private sphere.

FRIENDSHIP ACTIVITY

Materials

Story, writing and drawing materials, Table 3.5.

Suggested Stories

Paterson, K. (1977). *Bridge to Terabithia*.
Viorst, J. (1974). *Rosie and Michael*.
Walker, A. (1988). *To Hell with Dying*.

Activity

Facilitator reads the story, *Rosie and Michael*, to the class. Focus discussion of the story on the topic of friendship, using the suggested sequence in Table 3.5 and the following questions as guides: What is a friend? How do you know if someone is your friend? What actions facilitate or interfere with establishing and maintaining friendship? How do friends show that they care about each other? In small groups, students develop stories about ways to establish and/or maintain friendships using specific situations from their own experiences. Small groups then role play the stories for the whole group. Encourage other students to generate and enact alternative behaviors to those depicted/enacted. Guide discussion about the depictions of caring and of behaviors that facilitate or interfere with establishing and maintaining friendships. Throughout the activity, guide students' interactions, including decision making, problem solving, and conflict resolution. Following the activity, guide discussion of the ways in which students displayed caring interactions and worked cooperatively during the activity, and the importance of the contributions of each member.

Note: This activity could be incorporated into social studies, language and creative arts, health, and drug education curricula.

Extensions

1. With guidance from the facilitator, students revise stories generated and practiced during the friendship activity. Revised stories are enacted and videotaped to provide examples to same-age or younger students of ways to facilitate friendship.

2. Students write and illustrate stories about ways they display or might display caring toward friends. Guide sharing of stories, emphasizing role of prosocial behavior in developing and maintaining friendships.

3. Students in small groups make "friendship" collages, with drawings or pictures from magazines depicting friendship. Throughout the activity, guide students' interactions, including decision making, problem solving, and conflict resolution. Following the activity, guide discussion of (1) the various depictions of friendship, (2) ways in which students displayed caring interactions and worked cooperatively during the activity, and (3) the importance of the contributions of each group member (use Tables 3.3 and 3.4 as guides).

4. Students select a "Group Friendship Goal," and list ways to achieve the goal that could be implemented within the school context. As a collaborative activity, students make a poster depicting the goal and the ways to achieve it; the poster can be used to cue students as needed. Throughout the activity, guide students' interactions, including decision making, problem solving, and conflict resolution. On a weekly basis, guide group discussion of ways they have engaged in or observed behaviors consistent with the goal, adding to the list as new ideas are generated.

FAMILY ACTIVITY

Materials

Story, writing and drawing materials, Tables 3.3, 3.4, and 3.5.

Suggested Story

Rylant, C. (1985). *The Relatives Came.*

Activity

Facilitator reads *The Relatives Came* to the class. Focus discussion of the story on the topic of family, using the suggested sequence in Table 3.5 and the following questions as guides: What is a family? What are the various types of families? What are the different types of relationships in families (e.g., parent–child, child–sibling, sibling–parent, parent–parent, child–other adult/relative, parent–other adult/relative, child–pet, parent–pet)? What actions facilitate or interfere with family relationships? How do family members show that they care about each other? In small groups (3 to 4 members), students develop stories about ways that family members help and care about each other. Small groups then role play the stories for the whole group. Encourage other students to generate and enact alternative behaviors to those depicted/enacted. Guide discussion about the depictions of caring and of behaviors that facilitate or interfere with family relationships. Throughout the activity, guide the students' interactions, including decision making, problem solving, and conflict resolution. Following the activity, guide discussion of the ways in which students displayed caring interactions and worked cooperatively during the activity, and the importance of the contributions of each member (use Tables 3.3 and 3.4 as guides).

Note: This activity could be incorporated into social studies, language and creative arts, health, and drug education curricula.

Extensions

1. With guidance from the facilitator, students revise stories generated and practiced during the family activity. Revised stories are enacted and videotaped to provide examples of ways that family members display caring. The videotape could be used for demonstration of the curriculum to parents (e.g., parent conferences, open house, parent–teacher organizations, school-sponsored family night).

2. Students write and illustrate stories about ways they display or might display caring toward family members. Guide sharing of stories, emphasizing the role of prosocial behavior in family relationships.

3. Students write and illustrate stories about experiences with extended family. Guide sharing of stories, emphasizing the role of prosocial behavior in family relationships. Variations of this activity include small-group rather than whole-class discussion, art work with different media, variation in the type of writing assignment, group composition of a story or play, and role playing of students' stories.

4. Students read stories (such as those listed below) that depict families and family relationships from various perspectives, and write book reports. Use book reports to facilitate discussion of how the characters or authors depict family in written and pictorial form. Students then write and illustrate their own stories or books about their families. Guide sharing of their stories, with focus on multiple definitions of family. Including stories about families from various cultures facilitates integration of social studies with language and creative arts. Suggested books follow:

MacLachlan, P. (1980). *Through Grandpa's Eyes.*
MacLachlan, P. (1985). *Sarah, Plain and Tall.*
Rosen, M. J. (Editor). (1992). *Home.*

5. Students in small groups make "families" collages, with drawings or pictures from magazines depicting families. Throughout the activity, guide students' interactions, including decision making, problem solving, and conflict resolution. Following the activity, guide discussion of (1) the various depictions of family, (2) ways in which students displayed caring

interactions and worked cooperatively during the activity, and (3) the importance of the contributions of each group member (use Tables 3.3 and 3.4 as guides).

6. Read to the class *The Pain and the Great One* (Blume, 1974). Using the suggested sequence in Table 3.5, discuss sibling relationships and the similarities and differences between friend and sibling relationships, with focus on behaviors that facilitate or interfere with these relationships. Questions to guide discussion include: How do you get along with your sisters and brothers? In what ways do you act the same and differently with your friends and your sisters and brothers?

❖   ❖   ❖

Grade Level: Sixth–Eighth

Objectives

1. Promote an understanding of the role of prosocial behavior in developing and maintaining friendships, with focus on students' personal experiences.

2. Promote an understanding of the role of prosocial behavior in family relationships, with focus on students' personal experiences.

3. Promote an understanding of the behaviors that facilitate or interfere with establishing and maintaining relationships, with focus on students' personal experiences.

4. Provide opportunities to apply and evaluate relationship skills.

5. Provide models of prosocial behaviors in the private sphere.

FRIENDSHIP ACTIVITY

Materials

Story, notebook for journal, video equipment (camera, VCR, monitor), Tables 3.3, 3.4, 3.5.

Suggested Stories

Blume, J. (1987). *Just as Long as We're Together.*
Schain, D. (Producer), Anderson, D. (Producer), Balsam, M. (Producer), & Van Wagenen, S. (Director). (1992). *Alan and Naomi.*

Activity

Students view the film *Alan and Naomi*; facilitator guides discussion, using the sequence suggested in Table 3.5, with focus on how friendships are developed and maintained. Have students write in their journals about ways they show caring in their friendships. As a group, students then identify behaviors that facilitate or hinder friendship formation and maintenance, and generate a list of situations related to friendships or other close relationships. Encourage students to consider various types of close relationships including those with same- and cross-gender peers and adults. Using this information, students write and produce a series of skits depicting situations related to friendships or other close relationships; when possible, have students videotape skits. Structure this activity as a cooperative learning experience, with emphasis on interdependence, mutual construction of ideas, conflict resolution, and individual accountability. Following the activity, discuss the collaborative process, with focus on evaluation of group problem solving, conflict resolution, and prosocial skills (see Tables 3.3 and 3.4).

Note: This activity could be incorporated into social studies, drama, language arts, health, and drug education curricula.

Extensions

1. Students select individual friendship goals using the list of behaviors that facilitate or hinder friendship formation and maintenance generated during the friendship activity. Students then generate plans for goal attainment. Focus on (1) clearly defining realistic short- and long-term goals, (2) identifying and procuring necessary material and social resources (e.g., supplies, reference material, assistance, information), (3) developing step-by-step plans, (4) self-assessing level of confidence, and (5) monitoring progress. Table 3.9 provides a self-evaluation checklist for goal-setting activities. Encourage collaboration among students with similar goals, and peer tutoring by students with more advanced skills. In addition, encourage students to seek assistance from other adults within the school, family, or community. Use journals as the means for monitoring progress toward the goal (e.g., students record daily/weekly progress, attainment of specific steps in narrative or chart form; use Table 3.9 as a guide). This activity could facilitate integration of language arts and health or drug education curricula.

2. As part of the language arts curricula, students select and read books that depict various types of close relationships (e.g., with same- and cross-gender peers and adults), and write book reports. Use book reports to facilitate discussion of how the characters or authors define close relationships and resolve dilemmas within those relationships. Students then write and illustrate their own stories or books about dilemmas in close relationships. Facilitate sharing of their stories, with focus on the diversity of definitions of relationships and the influence of interpersonal behaviors on developing and maintaining friendships.

FAMILY ACTIVITY

Materials

Story, notebook for journal, video equipment (camera, VCR, monitor), Tables 3.3, 3.4, and 3.5.

Suggested Stories

Burnett, F. H. (1911). *The Secret Garden*.
Caracciolo, J. M. (Producer), Friendly, D. T. (Producer), Grazer, B. (Producer), & Zieff, H. (Director). (1992). *My Girl*.
Dickens, C. (1838/1961). *Oliver Twist*.
Evans, B. A. (Producer), Gideon, R. (Producer), Schernman, A. (Producer), & Reiner, R. (Director). (1986). *Stand by Me*.
Lanning, S. (Producer), Rosemont, N. (Executive Producer), & Grint, A. (Director). (1987). *The Secret Garden*.
Smith, B. (1943). *A Tree Grows in Brooklyn*.

Activity

Students view the film, *The Secret Garden*; facilitator guides discussion, using the suggested sequence in Table 3.5, with focus on the following questions about family: What is a family? What are the various types of families? What are the different types of relationships in families (e.g., parent–child, child–sibling, sibling–parent, parent–parent, child–other adult/relative, parent–other adult/relative, child–pet, parent–pet)? What actions facilitate or interfere with family relationships? How do family members show that they care about each other? Have students write in their journals about ways that caring is displayed within their families. As a group, students then identify behaviors that facilitate or hinder family relationships, and generate a list of relevant family situations they have encountered. Encourage students to consider various types of family relationships. Using this information, students write and produce a series of skits depicting family situations; when possible, have students videotape skits. Structure this activity as a cooperative learning experience, with emphasis on interdependence, mutual construction of ideas, conflict resolution, and individual accountability. Following the activity, discuss the collaborative process with focus on evaluation of group problem solving, conflict resolution, and prosocial skills (see Tables 3.3 and 3.4).

Note: This activity could be incorporated into social studies, drama, language arts, health, and drug education curricula.

Extensions

1. Students keep journals regarding depictions of family life in popular media (e.g., newspapers, magazines, television, movies, books, music).

Use journals to discuss variations in family constellation, interactions, communication styles, and strategies for resolving family dilemmas.

2. As part of the language arts curricula, students select and read books that depict families and family relationships from various cultural perspectives, and write book reports. Use book reports to facilitate discussion of how the characters or authors depict family relationships and resolve dilemmas within those relationships. Students then write and illustrate their own stories or books about dilemmas in family relationships. Facilitate sharing of their stories, with focus on multiple definitions of family and the influence of interpersonal behaviors on developing and maintaining family relationships. Including stories about families from various cultures facilitates integration of social studies with language and creative arts.

3. Students interview peers and adults (e.g., parents, grandparents, extended family, neighbors, friends, teachers) regarding their own relationships with family and peers during their middle school years. Structure activity as a collaborative project to produce a magazine or newspaper issue about family and peer relationships during middle school years. Have students work collaboratively to develop interview questions, conduct interviews, and write magazine articles. Seek consultation and assistance from representatives of local news agencies; for example, invite reporters, editors, advertising agents, and/or illustrators to speak to the students. This activity could facilitate integration of several curricular areas (e.g., language and creative arts, social studies, health, and drug education). To extend to other curricular areas, students could compute costs of production (mathematics) and use age-appropriate desktop publishing programs (computer education). Throughout the activity, discuss the collaborative process, with focus on evaluation of group problem solving, conflict resolution, and prosocial skills (see Tables 3.3 and 3.4).

❖   ❖   ❖

Grade Level: Ninth–Twelfth

Objectives

1. Promote an understanding of the role of prosocial behavior in developing and maintaining friendships and other intimate relationships, with focus on students' personal experiences.

2. Promote an understanding of the role of prosocial behavior in family relationships, with focus on students' personal experiences.

3. Promote an understanding of the behaviors that facilitate or interfere with establishing and maintaining relationships, with focus on students' personal experiences.

4. Provide opportunities to apply and evaluate relationship skills.
5. Provide models of prosocial behaviors in the private sphere.

FRIENDSHIP ACTIVITY

Materials

Story, writing materials, video equipment (camera, VCR, monitor), Tables 3.3, 3.4, and 3.5.

Suggested Stories

Hughes, J. (Producer), Chinich, M. (Producer), Colby, R., (Producer), & Deutch, H. (Director). (1987). *Some Kind of Wonderful.*

Nicolaides, S. (Producer), & Singleton, J. (Director). (1991). *Boyz 'n the Hood.*

Tanem, N. (Producer), Hughes, J. (Producer), & Hughes, J. (Director). (1985). *Breakfast Club.*

Activity

Students view the film, *Some Kind of Wonderful*; facilitator guides discussion, using the suggested sequence in Table 3.5, with focus on how friendships and other intimate relationships are developed and maintained. Have students write in their journals about ways that caring is demonstrated in these types of relationships. Encourage students to consider close relationships with same- and cross-gender peers and adults. As a group, students then identify behaviors that facilitate or hinder relationship formation and maintenance, and generate a list of situations related to friendships or other intimate relationships during adolescence. Using this information, students write and produce a series of skits depicting situations related to friendships or other intimate relationships; when possible, have students videotape skits. Structure this activity as a cooperative learning experience, with emphasis on interdependence, mutual construction of ideas, conflict resolution, and individual accountability. Following the activity, discuss the collaborative process, with focus on evaluation of group problem solving, conflict resolution, and prosocial skills (see Tables 3.3 and 3.4).

Note: This activity could be incorporated into social studies, drama, language arts, health, drug education, and home economics curricula.

Extensions

1. Students select individual relationship goals, using the list of behaviors that facilitate or hinder relationship formation and maintenance generated during the friendship activity. Students then generate plans for goal attainment. Focus on (1) clearly defining realistic short- and long-

term goals, (2) identifying and procuring necessary material and social resources (e.g., supplies, reference material, assistance, information), (3) developing step-by-step plans, (4) self-assessing level of confidence, and (5) monitoring progress. Table 3.9 provides a self-evaluation checklist for goal-setting activities. Encourage collaboration among students with similar goals, and peer tutoring by students with more advanced skills. In addition, encourage students to seek assistance from other adults within the school, family, or community. Use journals as the means for monitoring progress toward the goal (e.g., students record daily/weekly progress, attainment of specific steps in narrative or chart form; use Table 3.9 as a guide). This activity could facilitate integration of language arts with health, drug education, or home economics curricula.

2. As part of the language arts curricula, students select and read books that depict friendships and other intimate relationships (e.g., with same- and cross-gender peers and adults), and write book reports. Use book reports to facilitate discussion of how the characters or authors depict intimate relationships and resolve dilemmas within those relationships. Students then write and illustrate their own stories or books about dilemmas in friendships and other intimate relationships. Facilitate sharing of their stories, with focus on the diversity of definitions of relationships and the influence of interpersonal behaviors on developing and maintaining intimate relationships.

3. Students maintain a journal regarding depictions of various types of intimate relationships in popular media (e.g., newspapers, magazines, television, movies, books, music). In their journals, students describe how the media depictions reflect and influence their own experiences in relationships, with focus on (1) caring in interpersonal interactions, (2) expectations about relationships, (3) communication patterns, and (4) strategies for resolving dilemmas. In small, cross-gender groups, students discuss how the popular media reflect and influence social norms about intimate relationships. Encourage students to consider discrepancies about social norms within their groups, and to discuss how these differences might influence their own relationships. Large-group discussion should focus on variations in social norms within the popular media and among students. Encourage discussion about how gender, race, ethnicity, family, religion, and other cultural factors influence social construction of norms. Throughout the activity, facilitate group monitoring of the collaborative process, with focus on evaluation of group problem solving, conflict resolution, and prosocial skills (see Tables 3.3 and 3.4).

4. As a class project, students review and critique young children's literature regarding the depiction of friendships, compile a list of recommended books, and develop a series of lessons about friendship for early elementary students (see Tables 3.6 and 3.7). In dyads, students implement the lessons with young children in the school system, local preschool,

or other community setting. Throughout the project, facilitate group monitoring of the collaborative process, with focus on evaluation of group problem solving, conflict resolution, and prosocial skills (see Tables 3.3 and 3.4). This activity could facilitate integration of several curricular areas (language arts, home economics, psychology, social studies, child development). As an extension of this project, students could write and illustrate children's books about friendship.

FAMILY ACTIVITY

Materials

Multimedia equipment and supplies, popular media (newspapers, magazines, television, movies, books, music), Table 3.6.

Activity

1. Students research the popular media and identify depictions of family relationships. Specifically, they provide detailed descriptions (e.g., giving examples) of the following: (1) definition of family, (2) types of family relationships, (3) interactions among family members, (4) behaviors that seem to facilitate or interfere with family relationships, (5) how caring is demonstrated within families, (6) explicit or implicit expectations about relationships, (7) communication patterns, and (8) strategies for resolving dilemmas. In addition, students critique the method of presentation (see Guidelines for Story Selection, Table 3.6).

2. As a class, students compile and summarize the data from their reviews. Using these data, they discuss how media depictions reflect and influence social norms about family. Encourage students to consider discrepancies about norms within the media and amongst themselves. Facilitate discussion about how gender, race, ethnicity, family, religion, and other cultural factors influence social construction of norms.

Extensions

1. Students produce multimedia productions about family, using both the data collected and their own experiences to guide their interpretations of family. The multiple meanings of family could be portrayed in a series of articles for the school or community newspaper; a film; posters; illustrated books of poetry, essays, short stories; art exhibits including photography, paintings, sculpture, drawings; a series of one-act plays; a musical production; or songs. These productions could be displayed or presented to the school and local community. In addition, students could report the results of their research in the school or community newspaper.

2. Students participate in planning, monitoring, and evaluating the

project described in Extension 1. For example, students in business and economics courses assist in fiscal management; that is, provide cost projections, solicit funds, monitor expenditures, and prepare a final financial report. Throughout the project, all students should maintain journals of their activities and monitor the collaborative process through self-evaluation of prosocial skills, collaborative problem solving, and conflict resolution (see Tables 3.3 and 3.9).

Note: These extensions facilitate integration across the school curriculum, including mathematics, business, language arts, creative arts, home economics, psychology, social studies, child development, computer education, instructional technology. They also provide opportunities for school–home–community collaboration. Family and other community members could be invited to share their expertise with the students. Local merchants could provide equipment and supplies or other financial support. Government offices, churches, libraries, museums, theaters, and other public agencies could display works or provide facilities for productions.

Goal 3. Relating in the Public Sphere

Grade Level: Kindergarten–Second

Objectives

1. Foster development of social interaction skills (e.g., initiation, cooperation, communication, reciprocity).

2. Provide opportunities to apply social interaction skills within public contexts.

3. Promote an understanding of the importance of rules.

4. Provide opportunities to participate in the formulation of rules within public contexts.

5. Foster a sense of community (e.g., within the classroom and school).

6. Promote a recognition of diversity.

7. Provide models of prosocial behaviors in the public sphere.

Materials

Stories, poster board, markers, art materials for collage (e.g., drawing paper, poster board, markers, paint, magazines, paste, scissors), Tables 3.3, 3.4, and 3.5.

Suggested Stories

Brown, B. & Krensky, S. (1983). *Perfect Pigs: An Introduction to Manners*. Demi. (1990). *The Empty Pot*.

Activity

1. Read *Perfect Pigs: An Introduction to Manners* to the class. Discuss the story, using the suggested sequence in Table 3.5; emphasize how rules facilitate social order and prosocial interactions, and guide behaviors. Ask students to state (1) the rules of the classroom, (2) the purpose of each rule, (3) the consequences for following or violating rules, and (4) what might happen if there were no classroom rules. Link classroom rules to school rules. Then, have students generate three to five rules for the cooperative activity to follow, with emphasis on how rules facilitate social order and prosocial interactions, and guide behavior. Record the rules on poster board for display during the activity.

2. Students in small groups make "rules" collages, with drawings or pictures from magazines depicting people following rules. Guide (1) formation of groups to ensure heterogeneity, (2) decision making about individual responsibilities and steps necessary for task completion, (3) sharing of materials, (4) communication among students, and (5) conflict resolution. Students then describe their collages, noting the rules depicted. Following the activity, guide group discussion of (1) the importance of the contribution of each member, (2) the importance of working toward a mutual goal, and (3) ways to work together effectively. Use situations from the activity as examples (use Tables 3.3 and 3.4 as guides). In addition, discuss the extent to which the students' rules facilitated effective social interaction and task completion. This activity could facilitate integration of art and social studies curricula.

3. Read to the class a story, such as *The Empty Pot*, that depicts social norms in a specific culture. Discuss the story, using the suggested sequence in Table 3.5. Facilitate discussion of (1) the implicit and explicit rules depicted in the story, and (2) comparison to rules/norms in their own neighborhoods. Help students to make explicit the similarities and differences between rules in students' neighborhoods and the school setting, and among the various neighborhoods represented. This activity could be integrated into curricula focused on cultural diversity.

Extensions

1. Students participate in dyadic or small-group cooperative activities applied to academic curricula. Have students generate three to five rules regarding cooperation, with emphasis on how the rules facilitate social order and prosocial interactions, and guide behavior. Guide (1) formation of groups to ensure heterogeneity, (2) decision making about individual responsibilities and steps necessary for task completion, (3) sharing of materials, (4) communication among students, and (5) conflict resolution. Follow the activity with group discussion of (1) the importance of the contribution of each member, (2) the importance of working toward a

mutual goal, and (3) ways to work together effectively. Use situations from the activity as examples (use Tables 3.3 and 3.4 as guides). In addition, discuss the extent to which the students' rules facilitated effective social interaction and task completion.

2. Invite senior citizens who represent the cultural diversity of the community (e.g., individuals from retirement communities, students' grandparents, volunteers from local community agencies) to participate in a storytelling program for early elementary students. Stories should focus on the customs of the respective cultures, with individuals sharing the influences of these customs on their childhood experiences. Prior to the events, students write invitations to and discuss social customs for interacting with their prospective guests. Subsequently, students write thank-you notes. Students can also assist in preparing and serving refreshments to their guests. This activity facilitates integration of language arts, social studies, and social skills curricula.

3. To promote generalization across situations, make explicit the social norms or rules of the multiple situations within the school setting. To extend this into the community, plan field trips to local government agencies that are involved in rule making or enforcement (e.g., courthouse, fire department, police department, mayor's office, environmental protection agency, recycling center). In addition, discuss behavioral expectations and rules appropriate to field trips.

❖   ❖   ❖

Grade Level: Third–Fifth

Objectives

1. Facilitate development of social interaction skills (e.g., initiation, cooperation, communication, reciprocity).

2. Provide opportunities to apply social interaction skills within public contexts.

3. Promote an understanding of the importance of rules.

4. Provide opportunities to participate in the formulation and application of rules within public contexts.

5. Foster a sense of community (e.g., within the classroom and school).

6. Promote a recognition of diversity.

7. Provide models of prosocial behaviors in the public sphere.

Materials

Literature and films (e.g., required readings from literature and social studies classes, student-selected books for book reports, popular films, film presentations of classic literature), writing materials, Tables 3.3 and 3.4.

Suggested Story

Rosen, M. (1992). *South and North, East and West: The Oxfam Book of Children's Stories*.

Activity

1. As part of the language arts and social studies curricula, students read selected literature or view films depicting various cultures and identify the customs, social norms, and rules of each culture. Facilitate class discussion of the variations in customs, norms, and rules across diverse cultures, with focus on (1) the reasons for cultural standards, (2) the manner in which such standards evolve, (3) the consequences for following or violating standards of conduct, and (4) what might happen if there were no rules.

2. As a class project, students identify and invite community leaders and government officials (e.g., from the justice system, fire department, police department, mayor's office, environmental protection agency, recycling center) representing various cultures to talk about (1) the reasons for rules, (2) how rules are made, (3) the consequences for following or violating rules, and (4) what might happen if there were no rules. Prior to the events, students write invitations to and discuss social customs for interacting with their prospective guests. Subsequently, students write thank-you notes. To extend this into the community, plan field trips to local agencies that are involved in rule making or enforcement. In addition, discuss behavioral expectations and rules appropriate to field trips.

3. Students write and illustrate "A Rule Book for Kids." In small groups, students develop sets of rules (i.e., customs, social norms, and explicit rules) for multiple settings—classroom, school, peer group, and neighborhood. To facilitate perspective taking, encourage students to think about what a newcomer to each setting would need to know. Encourage students to use relevant resources. For example, have them consult the school code of conduct; interview principals, teachers, and other students; and interview adults and peers in the neighborhood. Facilitate writing and practice of interview questions. This activity might be particularly appropriate to school districts that serve transient populations or are attempting to integrate diverse populations.

Note: In forming groups, have students generate three to five rules regarding cooperation, with emphasis on how the rules facilitate social order and prosocial interactions, and guide behavior. Guide (1) formation of groups to ensure heterogeneity, (2) decision making about individual responsibilities and steps necessary for task completion, (3) sharing of materials, (4) communication among students, and (5) conflict resolution. Follow the activity with group discussion of (1) the importance of the contribution of each member, (2) the importance of working toward a mutual goal, and (3) ways to work together effectively. Use situations from the activity as examples (use Tables 3.3 and 3.4 as guides). In addition, discuss the extent to which the students' rules facilitated effective social interaction and task completion. These activities facilitate integration of language and creative arts, social studies, social skills, health, and drug education curricula.

Extensions

1. As a class project, students identify and invite senior citizens who represent the cultural diversity of the community (e.g., individuals from retirement communities, students' grandparents, volunteers from local community agencies) to participate in a storytelling program for students. Stories should focus on the customs of the respective cultures, with individuals sharing the influences of these customs on their childhood experiences. Prior to the events, students write invitations to and discuss social customs for interacting with their prospective guests. Subsequently, students write thank-you notes. Students can also assist in preparing and serving refreshments to their guests. This activity facilitates integration of language arts, social studies, and social skills curricula.

2. Students participate in dyadic or small-group cooperative activities applied to academic curricula. Have students generate three to five rules regarding cooperation, with emphasis on how rules facilitate social order and prosocial interactions, and guide behavior. Guide (1) formation of groups to ensure heterogeneity, (2) decision making about individual responsibilities and steps necessary for task completion, (3) sharing of materials, (4) communication among students, and (5) conflict resolution. Follow the activity with group discussion of (1) the importance of the contribution of each member, (2) the importance of working toward a mutual goal, and (3) ways to work together effectively. Use situations from the activity as examples (use Tables 3.3 and 3.4 as guides). In addition, discuss the extent to which the students' rules facilitated effective social interaction and task completion.

❖   ❖   ❖

Grade Level: Sixth–Eighth

Objectives

1. Facilitate development of social interaction skills (e.g., initiation, cooperation, communication, reciprocity).

2. Provide opportunities to apply social interaction skills within public contexts.

3. Promote an understanding of the relevance of social norms to community functioning.

4. Provide opportunities for the social construction of norms within public contexts.

5. Foster a sense of community (e.g., within the classroom and school).

6. Promote a recognition of diversity.

7. Provide models of prosocial behaviors in the public sphere.

Materials

Literature and films (e.g., required readings from literature and social studies classes, student-selected books for book reports, popular films, film presentations of classic literature), notebooks for journals, writing materials, Tables 3.3 and 3.4.

Activity

1. As part of the language arts and social studies curricula, students read selected literature or view films depicting various cultures and write book reports with focus on the following points: (1) identifying the customs, social norms, and rules of each culture; (2) hypothesizing the reasons for cultural standards and the manner in which they evolved; (3) identifying the actual or potential consequences for following or violating standards of conduct; and (4) proposing what might happen if there were no rules within that culture. Facilitate class discussion of the book reports with focus on the common and unique customs, norms, and rules across diverse cultures. In their journals, students write about points (1) through (4) with regard to their own cultures. Facilitate class discussion of journal entries with focus on the common and unique aspects of student experiences.

2. As a class project, students identify and interview community leaders and government officials (e.g., from the justice system, fire department, police department, mayor's office, environmental protection agency, recycling center, human service agencies, advocacy groups) representing various cultures. In dyads, students develop interview questions that address points (1) through (4) in the first part of this activity, role play interviews, and conduct the actual interviews. Guide discussion of techniques, behavioral expectations, and rules for interviewing. Following the interviews, students write letters of appreciation to interviewees and discuss findings. In journals, students evaluate their application of social interaction skills to the interview and peer collaboration processes (see Tables 3.3 and 3.4).

3. Students write and illustrate a *code of conduct manual* for middle school students. In small groups, students develop codes of conduct (i.e., customs, social norms, and explicit rules) for multiple settings—classroom,

school, peer group, and neighborhood. To facilitate perspective taking, encourage students to think about what a newcomer to each setting would need to know. Encourage students to use relevant resources. For example, have them consult the school code of conduct; interview principals, teachers, and other students; and interview adults and peers in the neighborhood. Facilitate writing and practice of interview questions.

Note: In forming groups, have students generate rules regarding cooperation, with emphasis on how rules facilitate social order and prosocial interactions, and guide behavior. Guide (1) formation of groups to ensure heterogeneity, (2) decision making about individual responsibilities and steps necessary to complete tasks, (3) sharing of materials, (4) communication among students, and (5) conflict resolution. On a daily basis, students use journals to record self-evaluations of social interaction skills applied to the collaborative processes (see Tables 3.3 and 3.4). Follow the activity with group discussion of (1) the importance of the contribution of each member, (2) the importance of working toward a mutual goal, and (3) ways to work together effectively. Use situations from the activity as examples. In addition, discuss the extent to which the students' rules facilitated effective social interaction and task completion. These activities facilitate integration of language and creative arts, social studies, social skills, health, and drug education curricula.

Extensions

1. Students participate in dyadic or small-group cooperative activities applied to academic curricula. Have students generate rules regarding cooperation, with emphasis on how rules facilitate social order and prosocial interactions, and guide behavior. Guide (1) formation of groups to ensure heterogeneity, (2) decision making about individual responsibilities and steps necessary for task completion, (3) sharing of materials, (4) communication among students, and (5) conflict resolution. Students use journals to record self-evaluations of social interaction skills applied to the collaborative processes (see Tables 3.3 and 3.4). Follow the activity with group discussion of (1) the importance of the contribution of each member, (2) the importance of working toward a mutual goal, and (3) ways to work together effectively. Use situations from the activity as examples. In addition, discuss the extent to which the students' rules facilitated effective social interaction and task completion.

2. Students analyze the customs, social norms, or explicit rules in community-based social or political events (e.g., holiday celebrations, elections, town meetings), and depict the cultural standards in written (e.g., essay, poem, story, letter to the editor, news item) and/or pictorial form (e.g., cartoon, photograph, drawing). This extension facilitates integration of social studies, language and creative arts, and social skills curricula.

❖   ❖   ❖

Grade Level: Ninth–Twelfth

Objectives

1. Facilitate development of social interaction skills (e.g., initiation, cooperation, communication, reciprocity).
2. Provide opportunities to apply social interaction skills within public contexts.
3. Promote an understanding of the relevance of social norms to community functioning.
4. Provide opportunities for the social construction of norms within public contexts.
5. Foster a sense of community (e.g., within the classroom and school).
6. Promote a recognition of diversity.
7. Provide models of prosocial behaviors in the public sphere.

Materials

Literature and films (e.g., required readings from literature and social studies classes, student-selected books for book reports, popular films, film presentations of classic literature), notebooks for journals, writing materials, Tables 3.3 and 3.4.

Activity

1. As part of the language arts and social studies curricula, students read selected literature or view films depicting various cultures and write book reports with focus on the following points: (1) identifying the customs, social norms, and rules of each culture; (2) hypothesizing the reasons for cultural standards and the manner in which they evolved; (3) identifying the actual or potential consequences for following or violating standards of conduct; and (4) proposing what might happen if there were no formal standards of conduct within that culture. Facilitate class discussion of the book reports, with focus on the common and unique customs, norms, and rules across diverse cultures. In their journals, students write about points (1) through (4) with regard to their own cultures. Facilitate class discussion of journal entries, with focus on the common and unique aspects of student experiences.

2. As a class project, students identify and interview former and current community leaders and government officials (e.g., from the justice system, fire department, police department, mayor's office, environ-

mental protection agency, recycling center, human service agencies, advocacy groups) representing various cultures. Students conduct in-depth interviews designed to gather oral histories regarding cultural influences on the individual's role as a community leader, with focus on how customs, social norms, and rules (1) influenced personal and career development, (2) influenced values and behaviors as community leaders, and (3) were consistent with or conflicted with the values and behaviors of other leaders. In addition, interviews focus on the individual's contribution to current cultural standards. In small groups, students develop the in-depth interview questions, and they role play interviews. Individually, students conduct, tape-record, and transcribe the actual interviews. Following the interviews, students write letters of appreciation to interviewees. In small groups, students analyze the transcriptions and address the following questions: What were the common and unique customs, social norms, and rules that influenced the development, values, and behaviors of community leaders? How have these leaders influenced current cultural standards? How have customs, social norms, and rules within the culture changed over time? What are the possible reasons for existing cultural standards? How are cultural standards likely to change, considering the values and behaviors of current community leaders? What role might the students play in influencing future customs, social norms, and rules? Each group prepares a written summary of their findings. Findings and transcripts could be compiled and bound for addition to the holdings of the school or local library. (This activity could be linked to the interview activity related to conflict resolution described below).

Note: In forming groups, have students generate rules regarding cooperation, with emphasis on how rules facilitate social order and prosocial interactions, and guide behavior. Guide (1) formation of groups to ensure heterogeneity, (2) decision making about individual responsibilities and steps necessary for task completion, (3) sharing of materials, (4) communication among students, (5) conflict resolution, and (6) discussion of techniques, behavioral expectations, and rules for interviewing. Throughout the process, students evaluate their application of social interaction skills to the interview and peer collaboration processes in their journals (see Tables 3.3 and 3.4). Encourage students to reflect on how the information they gather interacts with their own values and perceptions of the culture. Follow the activity with group discussion of (1) the importance of the contribution of each member, (2) the importance of working toward a mutual goal, and (3) ways to work together effectively. Use situations from the activity as examples. In addition, discuss the extent to which the students' rules facilitated effective social interaction and task completion. These activities facilitate integration of language and creative arts, social studies, psychology, social skills, health, and drug education curricula.

Extensions

1. Students write and illustrate a *code of conduct manual* for high school students. In small groups, students develop codes of conduct (i.e., customs, social norms, and explicit rules) for multiple settings—classroom, school, peer group, neighborhood, and community. To facilitate perspective taking, encourage students to think about what a newcomer to each setting would need to know and how multiple perspectives might best be reflected. Encourage students to use relevant resources. For example, have them consult the school code of conduct; interview principals, teachers, and other students; and interview adults and peers in the neighborhood and community. In forming groups, have students generate rules regarding cooperation, with emphasis on how rules facilitate social order and prosocial interactions, and guide their behavior. Guide (1) formation of groups to ensure heterogeneity, (2) decision making about individual responsibilities and steps necessary for task completion, (3) sharing of materials, (4) communication among students, and (5) conflict resolution. On a daily basis, students use journals to record self-evaluations of social interaction skills applied to the collaborative processes (see Tables 3.3 and 3.4). Follow the activity with group discussion of (1) the importance of the contribution of each member, (2) the importance of working toward a mutual goal, and (3) ways to work together effectively. Use situations from the activity as examples. In addition, discuss the extent to which the students' rules facilitated effective social interaction and task completion.

2. Students participate in dyadic or small-group cooperative activities applied to academic curricula. Have students generate rules regarding cooperation, with emphasis on how rules facilitate social order and prosocial interactions, and guide behavior. Guide (1) formation of groups to ensure heterogeneity, (2) decision making about individual responsibilities and steps necessary for task completion, (3) sharing of materials, (4) communication between students, and (5) conflict resolution. Students use journals to record self-evaluations of social interaction skills applied to the collaborative processes (see Tables 3.3 and 3.4). Follow the activity with group discussion of (1) the importance of the contribution of each member, (2) the importance of working toward a mutual goal, and (3) ways to work together effectively. Use situations from the activity as examples. In addition, discuss the extent to which the students' rules facilitated effective social interaction and task completion.

INTERPERSONAL PROBLEM SOLVING

Activities in this section focus on teaching and facilitating the use of the steps of cognitive problem solving as applied to individual and collaborative situations (see Table 3.2 and Figure 4.1).

FIGURE 4.1. Steps of effective interpersonal and collaborative problem solving. The circle reflects the recursive nature of the problem-solving process.

Goal 1. Recognizing Feelings in Self and Others

Grade Level: Kindergarten–Second

Objectives

1. Facilitate recognition and expression of feelings.
2. Provide models of affective expression.

Materials

The *Moody Gang* (adapted from Carnevale & Rothenbuhler, 1982; and Nastasi, 1985), which consists of felt-board characters that can be used to depict different emotions (e.g., happy, sad, angry, afraid, yucky); and felt board. Facilitator needs to construct felt pieces prior to the activity. Pieces include heads, hair, mouths, eyes, eyebrows, tears, and other facial features necessary to depict a range of feelings. (Appendix 4A provides the pattern for constructing the *Moody Gang*.) The Moody Gang should be culturally diverse. Students might be involved in preparation of materials as part of the creative arts curriculum. Additional materials include mirror(s), poster board, and marker.

Activity

1. Present the Moody Gang, explaining that different emotions can be depicted using the felt pieces. Guide students to create different facial expressions with the felt pieces. For example, create a depiction of "happy"

and have students identify the feeling. Have students in turn create other depictions, using examples of all categories (happy, sad, angry, afraid, yucky). Create a series of depictions and have students identify the emotions. Using the mirror(s), have students imitate facial expressions depicting various emotions. Have students pantomime expressions that others then identify. Encourage students to provide their own labels for the various emotions. Refer to feelings as "pleasant" or "unpleasant" rather than "good" or "bad."

2. Using the students' descriptors of the facial expressions, guide the students in generating a feelings vocabulary. Record the vocabulary on a poster board for future reference. Encourage multiple terms for the same feeling, using categories such as (1) happy, sad, angry, afraid, yucky (cf. Smith, 1982); (2) pleasant, unpleasant; or (3) categories that the group identifies. Have students provide visual representations to match the feelings vocabulary (e.g., students' drawings, pictures from magazines, photographs).

Extensions

1. As a language arts activity, read to the class stories (such as those listed below) with a theme relevant to one or more feelings. Discuss the story, using the suggested sequence in Table 3.5, with a focus on identifying feelings and how they are expressed by the characters. Following discussion, direct students to draw pictures of similar experiences and/or write a description of the event (with assistance as needed; e.g., younger students could dictate). Facilitate storytelling as students present their drawings. A list of suggested books follows:

Brandenberg, A. (1984). *Feelings.*
Preston, E. M. (1969). *The Temper Tantrum Book.*
Richardson, J. (1988). *Bad Mood Bear.*

2. Students in small groups make "feelings" collages, with drawings or pictures from magazines depicting various types of feelings or multiple expressions of the same feeling (e.g., happy). Facilitator then guides discussion of the various depictions of feelings, asking questions such as the following: What is the feeling? How can you tell the person is feeling _____ [use the student's label]? What do you think happened? Tell me about a time when you felt _____. How do you let people know when you are feeling _____? Throughout the activity, guide students' interactions, including decision making, problem solving, and conflict resolution. Following the activity, guide discussion of (1) the feelings students experienced during the activity (using similar questioning), (2) ways in which students worked cooperatively during the activity, and (3) the importance of the contributions of each group member (use Tables 3.3 and 3.4 as guides).

FIGURE 4.2. Feelings tags depicting common emotions—(top row, left to right) happiness, sadness, anger; (bottom row, left to right) fright, yuckiness.

3. As a creative arts activity, have students make cardboard faces depicting various emotions, and attach yarn to make "feelings tags" (adapted from Smith, 1982). Use tags as stimuli in related activities to facilitate labeling or expression of feelings. (Figure 4.2 provides an example of feelings tags; these depictions also can be used as patterns for constructing tags.)

❖   ❖   ❖

Grade Level: Third–Eighth (with modifications as needed depending on developmental level)

Objectives

1. Facilitate recognition and expression of feelings.
2. Provide models of affective expression.

Materials

Newsprint or poster board, magazines, markers, glue or paste, feelings thermometer (Figure 4.3), notebooks for journals, Tables 3.3, 3.4, and 3.8.

Activity

1. Students in small groups are instructed to construct murals depicting feelings, using pictures or print from magazines. Facilitate class discussion of the depictions of feelings, with focus on (1) verbal and nonverbal

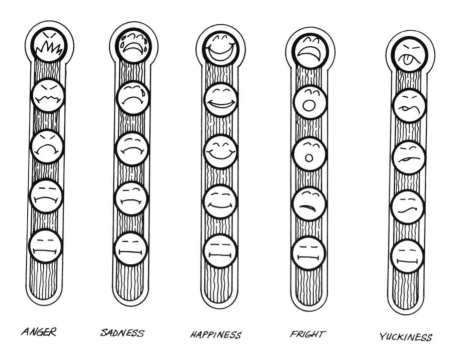

ANGER   SADNESS   HAPPINESS   FRIGHT   YUCKINESS

FIGURE 4.3. Feelings thermometers are used to gauge the intensity of five common emotions—anger, sadness, happiness, fright, yuckiness.

expression and (2) multiple ways to express the same feeling. In small groups, students generate feelings vocabulary lists. Facilitate integration of these lists into a class list, ensuring that a broad range of feelings is included. Throughout the activity, facilitate the students' interactions, including decision making, problem solving, and conflict resolution. Following the activity, guide group discussion of (1) the importance of the contribution of each member, (2) the importance of working toward a mutual goal, and (3) ways students worked together effectively. Use examples that arose during the activity (use Tables 3.3 and 3.4 as guides).

2. Introduce the feelings thermometer depicted in Figure 4.3, using anger as an example. The feelings thermometer provides a way for individuals to rate intensity of feelings. Discuss the red, white, and blue (R–W–B) anger styles, as described by Urbain (1982): (1) red (hostile) anger, "blow up, lose your temper"; (2) white (passive) anger, "don't say or do anything"; and (3) blue (assertive) anger, "keep your cool but say something to let the person know you are angry" (p. 35). Have students generate examples of these and their own styles for expressing anger.

3. Have students write in their journals about a time when they were angry (using questions from the first column in Table 3.8). Guide discussion of journal entries, with focus on (1) the different ways they expressed anger, (2) situations in which they felt angry, and (3) their evaluation of the outcomes.

4. Discuss the use of the feelings thermometer to rate intensity of a variety of feelings (e.g., happy, scared). Have students record in their journals experiences with different feelings, using the vocabulary list, thermometer, and questions in Table 3.8 as guides.

Extensions

1. As part of the language arts curriculum, have students read and discuss selected literature. Use the questions from Table 3.5 to facilitate the integration of the affective component of story into discussions and book reports. Focus on the different ways and situations in which feelings are expressed.

2. As a class project, students write and illustrate stories, poetry, or compositions about ways and situations in which their own feelings are expressed. Facilitate dissemination of products through oral readings and bound volumes.

Note: These activities and extensions can be incorporated into language and creative arts, health, and drug education curricula.

❖   ❖   ❖

Grade Level: Ninth–Twelfth

Objectives

1. Facilitate recognition and expression of feelings.
2. Provide models of affective expression.

Materials

Literature and films (e.g., required readings from literature classes, student-selected books for book reports, popular films, film presentations of classic literature), notebooks for journals.

Activity

As part of the language arts curriculum, students read selected literature or view films, and record in their journals descriptions of affective experiences of story characters as well as their own affective reactions to the stories. In small groups, students discuss their journal entries. Facilitate class discussion of the multiple ways in which feelings are depicted, expressed, and experienced. Include in the discussion verbal and nonverbal expression and external and internal indicators (e.g., clenched fists, tight stomach muscles). In small groups, students generate feelings vocabulary lists. Encourage them to consider a broad range of feelings. Facilitate integration of these lists into a class vocabulary list.

Extensions

1. As a class project, students review and critique young children's literature regarding the depiction of feelings, compile a list of recommended books, and develop a series of lessons for teaching young children about feelings (see Tables 3.6 and 3.7). In dyads, students implement the lessons with young children in the school system, local preschool, or other community setting. Structure this activity as a cooperative learning experience, with emphasis on interdependence, mutual construction of ideas, conflict resolution, and individual accountability. Encourage students to use their journals on a day-to-day basis to record their own affective reactions to stories and to project activities. These entries could be used to foster self-monitoring and reflection of their own and others' affective experiences, and to facilitate group monitoring of the collaborative process (use Tables 3.3, 3.4, and 3.8 as guides). This activity could facilitate integration of several curricular areas (language arts, home economics, psychology, social studies, child development). As an extension of this project, students could write and illustrate children's books about feelings.

2. Use language and creative arts activities to encourage depiction and expression of feelings; for example, through drawing, painting, sculpting, film production (visual arts); pantomime, plays, dance (dramatic arts); writing of poetry, prose, plays (language arts); musical composition or performance (musical arts). As a group cultural project, students could research, produce, and present portrayals of feelings through art. Products could be displayed in school and community settings. In a manner similar to the preceding extension, students could research, produce, and present artistic portrayals of feelings for younger audiences. Local artists might be invited to share their expertise with students.

Goal 2. Enhancing Intra- and Interpersonal Problem Solving (Alone and in Collaboration)

Grade Level: Kindergarten–Second

Objectives

1. Facilitate understanding of problem-solving strategies, with focus on feelings identification, problem identification, and alternative solution thinking.

2. Provide opportunities for application of problem-solving strategies.

3. Provide models of effective problem solving.

Materials

Story, art materials (newsprint, crayons, markers, tape), Tables 3.3, 3.4, 3.5, and 3.8.

Suggested Story

Viorst, J. (1972). *Alexander and the Terrible, Horrible, No Good, Very Bad Day.*

Activity

Read *Alexander and the Terrible, Horrible, No Good, Very Bad Day* to the class. Discuss the story, using the suggested sequence in Table 3.5, with emphasis on identifying Alexander's feelings and defining the problem and how he solved it. Link to lessons on feelings. Encourage students to discuss similar experiences. Have students draw and/or write stories from their own experiences about bad days, using Table 3.8. Facilitate sharing of personal stories within the whole group and incorporate into a class story, *We All Have Terrible, Horrible, No Good, Very Bad Days.* During discussions, help students to make explicit (1) feelings they experienced, (2) definition of the problem, (3) alternative strategies for solving the problem, and (4) anticipated or actual outcomes. Guide role playing of student-generated stories, encouraging other students to generate alternative problem-solving strategies. Younger students could make puppets to facilitate role playing. Throughout the activity, guide students' interactions, including decision making, problem solving, and conflict resolution. Following the activity, guide group discussion of ways to work together to solve problems using examples from the activity (use Tables 3.3 and 3.4 as guides).

Note: This activity could be incorporated into language and creative arts, health, social skills training, and drug education curricula.

Extensions

1. Students participate in dyadic or small-group cooperative activities applied to academic curricula. For example, students are instructed to work collaboratively on a science problem-solving activity. Throughout the activity, guide students' interactions, including decision making, problem-solving, and conflict resolution. Following the activity, facilitator guides group discussion of (1) the importance of the contribution of each member, (2) the importance of working toward a mutual goal, and (3) ways to work together effectively to solve problems. Use examples from the activity (use Tables 3.3 and 3.4 as guides). In addition, help students to make

explicit the similarities and differences between academic (e.g., science) problem solving and interpersonal problem solving.

2. To promote generalization, help students individually or as a group identify visual and/or verbal cues for the steps of problem solving (listed in Table 3.2). Use these cues to engage students in problem solving during academic activities, conflicts on the playground, and other situations in the school setting. Following such instances, facilitate discussion of problem solving, with focus on feelings, problem definition, strategies, and outcome.

❖　　❖　　❖

Grade Level: Third–Eighth (with modifications as needed depending on developmental level)

Objectives

1. Facilitate understanding of problem-solving strategies, with focus on feelings identification, problem identification, alternative solution thinking, means–end thinking, perspective taking, and implementation and evaluation of solutions.

2. Provide opportunities for application of problem-solving strategies.

3. Provide opportunities for evaluation of problem-solving strategies.

4. Provide models of effective problem solving.

Materials

Literature and films (e.g., required readings from literature classes, student-selected books for book reports, popular films, film presentations of classic literature), notebooks for journals, Tables 3.3, 3.4, 3.5, and 3.8.

Activity

1. As part of the language arts curriculum, students read selected literature or view films depicting problems experienced by same-age peers. Use the questions from Table 3.5 to facilitate a problem-solving analysis of the stories during class discussions and in book reports. Link to lessons on feelings.

2. In dyads, students rewrite the stories, proposing different outcomes and describing the steps the characters take to accomplish the new outcome. Facilitate sharing of stories with the whole group. Then guide reflection, discussion, and evaluation of the strategies dyads used to determine story content, integrate ideas, and resolve disagreements (use Tables 3.3 and 3.4 as guides).

3. Students write in their journals about personal experiences similar to those depicted in books or films, using the questions from Table 3.8 to do a problem-solving analysis. Facilitate sharing of examples within the whole group. During discussions, help students to make explicit (1) feelings they experienced, (2) definition of the problem, (3) strategies for solving the problem with specific focus on generating alternative strategies, and (4) outcome. In addition, discuss the influence of individual perspective on how students view and solve problems. Guide role playing of student-generated stories, encouraging other students to pose alternative perspectives of the problem definition and to generate alternative problem-solving strategies.

Note: Throughout the activity, guide students' interactions, particularly perspective taking, decision making, problem solving, and conflict resolution. Following the activity, guide group discussion of (1) the importance of the contribution of each member, (2) the importance of working toward a mutual goal, and (3) ways to work together effectively to solve problems. Use examples from the activity (use Tables 3.3 and 3.4 as guides). This activity could be incorporated into language and creative arts, health, social skills training, and drug education curricula.

Extensions

1. Students participate in dyadic or small-group cooperative activities applied to academic curricula. For example, students are instructed to work collaboratively on a science problem-solving activity that extends across several class periods. Throughout the activity, guide students' interactions, particularly perspective taking, decision making, problem-solving, and conflict resolution. Each day ask students to respond in their journals to a question about the academic and collaborative problem solving aspects of their work, and to evaluate their participation in the collaborative process (see Tables 3.3 and 3.4). Following the activity, guide group discussion of (1) the importance of the contribution of each member, (2) the importance of working toward a mutual goal, and (3) ways to work together effectively to solve problems, using examples from the activity. In addition, help students to make explicit the similarities and differences between academic (e.g., science) problem solving and interpersonal problem solving.

2. To promote generalization, have students describe in their journals academic or social situations in which they applied problem-solving skills, using the journal format (Table 3.8). Guide discussion and role playing of journal entries, with focus on feelings, problem definition, and strategies for actual and alternative outcomes. Regular use of journals facilitates self-monitoring and reflection on the effectiveness of problem-solving skills. Group discussion of journal entries can facilitate perspective

taking and provide opportunities for social feedback. Encourage students to develop visual or verbal cues for the application of problem solving as needed. This activity facilitates integration of language arts with health or drug education curricula.

❖   ❖   ❖

Grade Level: Ninth–Twelfth

Objectives

1. Facilitate understanding of problem-solving strategies, with focus on feelings identification, problem identification, alternative solution thinking, means–end thinking, perspective taking, causal thinking, consequential thinking, and implementation and evaluation of solutions.
2. Provide opportunities for application of problem-solving strategies.
3. Provide opportunities for evaluation of problem-solving strategies.
4. Provide models of effective problem solving.

Materials

Literature and films (e.g., required or student-selected readings for literature, history, health, psychology, personal development, and drug education courses; film presentations of classic literature and biographies; popular films), notebooks for journals, Tables 3.3, 3.4, and 3.5.

Activity

1. Students read selected literature or view films depicting problems experienced by same-age peers. Use the questions from Table 3.5 to facilitate a problem-solving analysis of the stories during class discussions and in book reports. Link to lessons on feelings.

2. Students engage in individual writing assignment. Give students the following instructions for rewriting the stories: (1) Propose how different perspectives, strategies, or situations lead to different outcomes for the characters. (2) Analyze cause–effect relationships among situations, feelings, thoughts, actions, and outcomes. (3) Discuss how decision making by individual characters requires consideration of perspectives, behaviors, and outcomes with respect to multiple characters. In dyads, students critique and edit each other's work. Encourage dyads to discuss and evaluate the strategies they used for providing informational feedback and social reinforcement (use Tables 3.3 and 3.4 as guides).

Note: These activities facilitate integration of literature, composition, history, health, psychology, personal development, and drug education courses.

Extensions

1. To promote generalization, have students write in their journals about personal problem-solving experiences, using the questions from Table 3.8 to facilitate explication of the problem-solving process, including (1) feelings identification, (2) problem identification, (3) alternative solution thinking, (4) means–end thinking, (5) perspective taking, (6) causal thinking, (7) consequential thinking, and (8) implementation and evaluation of solutions. Have students apply the problem-solving steps in a comparative analysis of actual and proposed (alternative) outcomes, with focus on (1) how different perspectives, strategies, or situations could lead to different outcomes and (2) the extent to which their decision making requires consideration of perspectives, behaviors, and outcomes with respect to other people. Regular use of journals facilitates self-monitoring and reflection on effectiveness of problem-solving skills. Encourage students to develop visual or verbal cues for the application of problem solving as needed.

2. Facilitate discussion of journal entries and role playing of student-generated stories, encouraging students to pose alternative perspectives with regard to analysis and application of the problem-solving process. Group discussion of journal entries and role playing of real-life experiences can facilitate perspective taking and provide opportunities for social feedback. Throughout the activity, guide students' interactions, particularly perspective taking, decision making, problem solving, and conflict resolution. Following the activity, have students evaluate the process of discussion and role playing, with focus on their individual contributions to the group process (see Tables 3.3 and 3.4). Journals and role playing activities can facilitate integration of language and creative arts with health, personal development, or drug education courses.

3. Students participate in dyadic or small-group cooperative activities applied to academic curricula. For example, students are instructed to work collaboratively across several class periods on a history project to rewrite a particular historical incident from multiple perspectives (e.g., the Emancipation Proclamation from the perspective of the U.S. President, an abolitionist, a feminist, a person of color, a slave owner, a slave, a journalist from South Africa). Each day students respond in their journals to a question about the academic and collaborative problem-solving aspects of their work, and evaluate their participation in the collaborative process (see Tables 3.3 and 3.4). Throughout the activity, guide students' interactions, particularly perspective taking, decision making, problem solving, and conflict resolution. Following the activity, guide group discussion of (1) the importance of the contribution of each member, (2) the importance of working toward a mutual goal, and (3) ways to work together effectively to solve problems, using examples from the activity.

In addition, help students to make explicit the similarities and differences between academic (e.g., science) problem solving and interpersonal problem solving.

Goal 3. Enhancing Intra- and Interpersonal Conflict Resolution

Grade Level: Kindergarten–Second

Objectives

1. Facilitate understanding of effective conflict resolution.
2. Foster an understanding of peaceful functioning of a diverse community.
3. Provide opportunities for application of conflict resolution strategies.
4. Provide models of effective conflict resolution.

Materials

Story, art materials for puppet making (e.g., paper lunch bags or socks, crayons, buttons, yarn, scissors, paste), Tables 3.2, 3.3, 3.4, and 3.5.

Suggested Story

Rose, D. L. (1990). *The People Who Hugged Trees.*

Activity

1. Read *The People Who Hugged Trees* to the class. Discuss the story, using the suggested sequence in Table 3.5, with emphasis on identifying the characters' feelings, the conflict from the multiple perspectives, and how the conflict was resolved. Help the students to consider how the various characters would evaluate the resolution. Encourage students to tell their own stories about similar experiences.

2. Select from the students' stories a conflict common to their experiences (e.g., when two groups of children want to play with the same equipment). Facilitate discussion and role play of the conflict and its resolution, using the steps of collaborative problem solving (see Table 3.2). Students make puppets to use in a role play. Guide students' interactions throughout the activity, helping them to choose roles and resolve their own conflicts. Following the activity, guide group discussion of how the students worked together and resolved their own conflicts (use Tables 3.3 and 3.4 as guides).

Note: This activity could be incorporated into language and creative arts, health, social studies, social skills training, and drug education curricula.

Extensions

1. Guide discussion and role play of conflicts between individuals or groups, drawn from current events, literature, or history. Use the steps of collaborative problem solving (Table 3.2).

2. To promote generalization, encourage students to engage in collaborative problem solving to resolve conflicts in the school setting. Following such instances, facilitate discussion of conflict resolution, with focus on feelings, definition of the conflict, strategies, and outcome (use Tables 3.2 and 3.3 as guides). Help the students to evaluate the resolution from the perspectives of those involved.

3. Within the science curriculum, apply the concept of conflict to discussions of relationships between human beings and the environment/ecology. Consider using stories such as *Just a Dream*, by Chris Van Allsburg (1990) to facilitate discussion.

4. Incorporate into the social studies curriculum the concept of the peaceful functioning of diverse communities. Read to the class *Sarah's Bear*, by Marta Koci (1987), and discuss the diverse community created by Sarah and the animals. In small groups, students construct mosaics of their own neighborhood communities. Guide formation of groups to ensure heterogeneity. Throughout the activity, guide students' interactions, including decision making, problem solving, and conflict resolution. Following the activity, guide group discussion of the collaborative process and how this relates to community functioning (use Tables 3.3 and 3.4 as guides). Help students to make explicit the diversity of ideas and/or communities and what they did to ensure that all aspects were represented in the final product.

❖   ❖   ❖

Grade Level: Third–Eighth (with modifications as needed depending on developmental level)

Objectives

1. Facilitate understanding of effective conflict resolution.

2. Foster an understanding of peaceful functioning of a diverse community.

3. Provide opportunities for application of conflict resolution strategies.

4. Provide opportunities for evaluation of conflict resolution strategies.

5. Provide models of effective conflict resolution.

Materials

Story, writing materials, notebook for journal, Tables 3.3, 3.4, 3.5, and 3.8.

Suggested Story

Scieszka, J. (1989). *The True Story of the 3 Little Pigs*.

Activity

1. Students tell the story of the three little pigs. Read *The True Story of the 3 Little Pigs* to the class. Discuss the story, using the suggested sequence in Table 3.5, with emphasis on identifying the characters' feelings, the conflict from the multiple perspectives, and how the conflict was resolved. Help the students to consider how the various characters would evaluate the resolution. Encourage students to discuss similar experiences.

2. Students in small groups write and illustrate a newspaper article for either the *Pigs Daily News* or the *Wolves Herald*, with a different ending depicting a peaceful resolution. Guide sharing of the stories, with focus on (1) diversity of perspectives in their depictions of the incident and (2) evaluation of the conflict resolution strategies. Throughout the activity, guide students' interactions, including decision making, problem solving, and conflict resolution. Following the activity, guide discussion of (1) the importance of the contribution of each member, (2) the importance of working toward a mutual goal, and (3) ways to work together effectively to resolve conflicts, using examples from the activity (use Tables 3.3 and 3.4 as guides).

3. To promote generalization, students describe in their journals academic or social situations in which they had interpersonal conflicts, using the journal format (Table 3.8). Facilitate discussion and role playing of journal entries, with focus on feelings, definition of the conflict, and strategies for actual and alternative outcomes. Regular use of journals facilitates self-monitoring and reflection on effectiveness of conflict resolution. Group discussion of journal entries can facilitate perspective taking and provide opportunities for social feedback.

Note: This activity could be incorporated into language and creative arts, social studies, health, social skills training, and drug education curricula.

Extensions

1. Guide discussion and role play of conflicts between individuals or groups, drawn from current events, literature, or history. Use the steps of collaborative problem solving (Table 3.2). This could also be incorporated into a writing assignment.

2. Encourage students to engage in collaborative problem solving to resolve conflicts in the school setting. Following such instances, facilitate discussion of conflict resolution with focus on feelings, definition of the conflict, strategies, and outcome (use Tables 3.2 and 3.3 as guides). Help the students to evaluate the resolution from the perspectives of those involved.

3. Within the science curriculum, apply the concept of conflict to discussions of relationships between human beings and the environment/ecology. As a writing assignment, students identify and evaluate such conflicts as depicted in their textbooks or popular media (network news, newspapers, magazines), using the steps of collaborative problem solving (Table 3.2) to describe what occurred. In small groups, students then discuss selected human–ecological conflicts and generate alternative resolutions using the steps of collaborative problem solving. Structure the activity as a simulation of peer mediation, with students choosing roles as "humans," "the ecology," and "mediator." The mediator is a neutral party who facilitates the negotiation process between the humans and the ecology, with focus on helping the parties to reach a mutually agreeable resolution. Guide students' interactions, including decision making, problem solving, conflict resolution, and mediation. Following the activity, students self-evaluate and discuss their participation in the collaborative process (see Tables 3.3 and 3.4). In whole-group discussion, focus on evaluation of strategies for resolving the conflicts that occurred during collaboration, comparing and contrasting those strategies with strategies generated for resolving human–ecological conflicts.

4. Incorporate into the social studies curriculum the concept of the peaceful functioning of diverse communities. Introduce to the class the book *Helping Out*, by George Ancona (1985), as an example of a photo essay. Guide discussion of helping and its importance to community functioning. In small groups, students construct collages, murals, or photo essays depicting helping in their own neighborhood or school communities. This could be combined with a language arts activity. Guide formation of groups to ensure heterogeneity. Throughout the activity, guide students' interactions, including decision making, problem solving, and conflict resolution. Following the activity, guide group discussion of the collaborative process and how it relates to community functioning (use Tables 3.3 and 3.4). Help students to make explicit the diversity of ideas

and/or communities and what they did to ensure that all aspects were represented in the final product.

❖   ❖   ❖

Grade Level: Ninth–Twelfth

Objectives

1. Facilitate understanding of effective conflict resolution.
2. Foster an understanding of peaceful functioning of a diverse community.
3. Provide opportunities for application of conflict resolution strategies.
4. Provide opportunities for evaluation of conflict resolution strategies.
5. Provide models of effective conflict resolution.

Materials

Story, writing materials, notebook for journal, Tables 3.2, 3.3, 3.4, 3.5, and 3.8.

Suggested Story

Scieszka, J. (1989). *The True Story of the 3 Little Pigs*.

Activity

1. Students tell the story of the three little pigs, then read the book, *The True Story of the 3 Little Pigs*. Discuss the story, using the suggested sequence in Table 3.5, with emphasis on identifying the characters' feelings, the conflict from the multiple perspectives, and how the conflict was resolved. Help the students to consider how the various characters would evaluate the resolution. Encourage students to discuss similar experiences.

2. As a class activity, retell and role-play two alternative resolutions to the conflict between the pigs and the wolf. In one alternative, add a mediator as a neutral party who facilitates the negotiation process between the pigs and the wolf. In the second, the pigs and the wolf interact directly to resolve the conflict without the aid of a mediator. In both instances, the objective is to reach a mutually agreeable resolution, using the steps of collaborative problem solving (see Table 3.2). Guide discussion of the two alternatives, with focus on (1) diversity of perspectives in depictions of the incident, (2) evaluation of conflict resolution strategies, (3) roadblocks to

effective conflict resolution, and (4) situations when mediation is necessary. Throughout the activity, guide students' interactions, including decision making, problem solving, and conflict resolution. Following the activity, students in their journals describe their participation in the collaborative process (see Tables 3.3 and 3.4), with focus on self-evaluation of strategies for resolving conflicts that occurred during collaboration, and comparing and contrasting those strategies with strategies generated for resolving the pigs–wolf conflict.

3. To promote generalization, students describe in their journals academic or social situations in which they had interpersonal conflicts, using the journal format (Table 3.8). Students apply the collaborative problem-solving steps in a comparative analysis of actual and proposed (alternative) outcomes, with focus on (1) how different perspectives, strategies, or situations could lead to different outcomes and (2) the extent to which their decision making requires consideration of perspectives, behaviors, and outcomes with respect to other people. Facilitate discussion and role playing of journal entries, with focus on feelings, definition of the conflict, and strategies for actual and alternative outcomes. Encourage students to pose alternative perspectives with regard to analysis and application of collaborative problem solving. Regular use of journals facilitates self-monitoring and reflection on effectiveness of conflict resolution. Group discussion of journal entries can facilitate perspective taking and provide opportunities for social feedback.

Note: This activity could be incorporated into history, language and creative arts, health, social skills training, and drug education curricula.

Extensions

1. Facilitate discussion and role play of conflicts between individuals or groups drawn from current events, literature, or history. Use the steps of collaborative problem solving (see Table 3.2). For example, students work collaboratively across several class periods to rewrite and role play a historical conflict, posing alternative resolutions with and without the aid of a mediator. In both instances, the objective is to reach a mutually agreeable resolution, using the steps of collaborative problem solving (Table 3.2). Guide discussion of the two alternatives, with focus on (1) diversity of perspectives in depictions of the incident, (2) evaluation of conflict resolution strategies, (3) roadblocks to effective conflict resolution, and (4) situations when mediation is necessary. Each day students respond in their journals to a question about the academic and collaborative problem-solving aspects of their work, and evaluate their participation in the collaborative process (see Tables 3.3 and 3.4). Throughout the activity, guide students' interactions, particularly perspective taking, decision making, problem solving, and conflict resolution. Following the activity, guide dis-

cussion of the collaborative process, with focus on self-evaluation of strategies for resolving conflicts that occurred during collaboration, and comparing and contrasting those strategies with strategies generated for resolving the historical conflict.

2. Encourage students to engage in collaborative problem solving to resolve conflicts in the school setting. Following such instances, facilitate discussion of conflict resolution, with focus on feelings, definition of the conflict, strategies, and outcome (use Tables 3.2 and 3.3 as guides). Help students to evaluate the resolution from the perspectives of those involved.

3. Within the science curriculum, apply the concept of conflict to discussions of relationships between human beings and the environment/ecology. As a writing assignment, students identify and evaluate such conflicts as depicted in their textbooks or popular media (network news, newspapers, magazines), using the steps of collaborative problem solving (Table 3.2) to describe what occurred. In small groups, students then discuss and role play selected human–ecological conflicts, posing alternative resolutions with and without the aid of a mediator. In both instances, the objective is to reach a mutually agreeable resolution, using the steps of collaborative problem solving (Table 3.2). Structure the activity as simulations of direct and mediated interactions between human beings and their ecology, with students choosing roles as "humans," "the ecology," and "mediator." The mediator is a neutral party who facilitates the negotiation process between the humans and the ecology, with focus on helping the parties to reach a mutually agreeable resolution. Guide students' interactions, including decision making, problem solving, conflict resolution, and mediation. Following the activity, students self-evaluate and discuss their participation in the collaborative process (see Tables 3.3 and 3.4). In whole-group discussion, focus on evaluation of strategies for resolving conflicts that occurred during collaboration, comparing and contrasting those strategies with strategies generated for resolving human–ecological conflicts.

4. Incorporate into the social studies curriculum the concept of the peaceful functioning of diverse communities. Use a film such as *Stand and Deliver* (Musca & Menendez, 1988) and the format for discussion of story (Table 3.5) to initiate discussion of ways to create a peacefully functioning community. As a class project, students create a model of a peacefully functioning community that could be applied within their own school.

5. To further extend this activity, students identify and interview community leaders about their own efforts to create peacefully functioning communities. In small groups, students develop interview questions and practice interviews through role plays. Individually, students conduct the interviews. Following the interviews, students write letters of appreciation to interviewees. In small groups, students address the following questions: What were the common and unique strategies used by community leaders to promote peaceful functioning? How effective are these strategies? What

roles have community members played in promoting peaceful functioning? What might schools do to facilitate peaceful communities? How do adolescents influence community functioning? What can they do to promote peaceful community functioning? Each group prepares a written summary of their interviews and conclusions. This activity could provide a base for developing school–community collaborative projects or could be linked to the interviews regarding relationships in the public sphere.

Note: Throughout the activity, guide students' interactions, including decision making, problem solving, conflict resolution, and mediation. Following the activity, guide discussion of the collaborative process, with focus on self-evaluation of strategies for creating peaceful functioning within their groups, and comparing and contrasting those strategies with strategies generated for promoting peaceful communities (use Tables 3.3 and 3.4 as guides).

Goal 4. Coping with Crises Related to Family Alcoholism

Activities in this section focus on teaching and facilitating the use of strategies for coping with family-oriented crises such as conflict, violence, abuse, death, divorce, and homelessness, with a specific focus on family alcoholism. The activities are applications and extensions of units on self-efficacy, social interaction skills, and interpersonal problem solving, and should be linked with drug education curricula. We recommend that they be implemented in collaboration with school or community mental health personnel and drug educators.

Grade Level: Kindergarten–Second

Objectives

    1. Encourage appropriate expression of feeling.
    2. Encourage social support by peer group.
    3. Foster climate of acceptance and caring.
    4. Explore strategies for coping with crisis.
    5. Provide models of effective coping.

Materials

Stories, drawing and writing materials, Table 3.5.

Suggested Stories

Goff, B. (1969). *Where Is Daddy?*
Paris, S. (1986). *Mommy and Daddy Are Fighting*.
Rosen, M. J. (Editor). (1992). *Home*.
Sanford, D. (1985). *It Must Hurt A Lot*.

Activity

Read to the class stories that depict family crises. Guide discussion, using the suggested sequence in Table 3.5, about how the characters coped with the crisis. Encourage students to draw and/or write a depiction of their own relevant experiences. Facilitate sharing of these experiences, helping students to make explicit (1) feelings they experienced, (2) definition of the problem, (3) alternative strategies for solving the problem, and (4) anticipated or actual outcomes. Link to units on self-efficacy, social interaction skills, and interpersonal problem solving by encouraging students to consider ways in which they have solved other types of problems, how they can seek and provide social support, and how they might display caring to others who are in crisis. From this discussion, generate a list of strategies and resources for coping with family-oriented crises. Generate another list of ways to help others in crisis. Within this context, introduce the role of school personnel as resources.

Extension

In conjunction with drug education curricula, present depictions of family alcoholism. For example, use *My Dad Loves Me, My Dad Has a Disease* by Claudia Black (1989), and the suggested sequence in Table 3.5, to discuss the characteristics of the family affected by alcohol. From this discussion, generate a list of strategies and resources for coping with family alcoholism. Generate another list of ways to help others in this situation. Within this context, reinforce the role of school personnel as resources.

❖　❖　❖

Grade Level: Third–Fifth

Objectives

1. Encourage appropriate expression of feeling.
2. Encourage social support by peer group.
3. Foster climate of acceptance and caring.
4. Explore strategies for coping with crisis.
5. Provide models of effective coping.

Materials

Stories, writing materials, notebooks for journals, Table 3.5.

Suggested Stories

Caracciolo, J. M., Friendly, D. T., Grazer, B. (Producers), & Zieff, H. (Director). (1992). *My Girl.*

Rosen, M. J. (Editor). (1992). *Home*.
Rylant, C. (1985). *A Blue-Eyed Daisy*.
Thomas, J. R. (1988). *Saying Good-Bye to Grandma*.

Activity

Students read or view stories that depict family crises. Guide discussion, using the suggested sequence in Table 3.5, about how the characters coped with the crisis. Encourage students to write a depiction of their own relevant experiences. Facilitate sharing of these experiences, helping students to make explicit (1) feelings they experienced, (2) definition of the problem, (3) alternative strategies for solving the problem, and (4) anticipated or actual outcomes. Link to units on self-efficacy, social interaction skills, and interpersonal problem solving by encouraging students to consider ways in which they have solved other types of problems, how they can seek and provide social support, and how they might display caring to others who are in crisis. From this discussion, generate a list of strategies and resources for coping with family-oriented crises. Generate another list of ways to help others in crisis. Within this context, introduce the role of school personnel as resources.

Extensions

1. In conjunction with drug education curricula, present depictions of family alcoholism. For example, use the educational film *Lots of Kids Like Us* (1983), and the suggested sequence in Table 3.5, to discuss the characteristics of the family affected by alcohol. From this discussion, generate a list of strategies and resources for coping with family alcoholism. Generate another list of ways to help others in this situation. Within this context, reinforce the role of school personnel as resources.

2. To promote generalization, have students describe in their journals family crises they have encountered, using the journal format (Table 3.8). Guide discussion and role playing of journal entries, with focus on feelings, problem definition, and strategies for actual and alternative outcomes. Regular use of journals facilitates reflection on and recording of effective coping. Group discussion of journal entries can facilitate empathy and provide opportunities for social support.

❖   ❖   ❖

Grade Level: Sixth–Eighth

Objectives

   1. Encourage appropriate expression of feeling.
   2. Encourage social support by peer group.

3. Foster climate of acceptance and caring.
4. Explore strategies for coping with crisis.
5. Provide models of effective coping.

Materials

Stories, writing materials, notebooks for journals, Table 3.5.

Suggested Stories

Blume, J. (1972). *It's Not the End of the World*.
Evans, B. A., Gideon, R., Schernman, A. (Producers), & Reiner, R. (Director). (1986). *Stand by Me*.
Hausman, M. (Producer), & Corr, E. (Director). (1986). *Desert Bloom*.
L'Engle, M. (1962). *A Wrinkle in Time*.
Shuler-Donner, L. (Producer), Donner, R. (Director), & Douglas, M., Bieber, R., Evans, D. M. (Exec. Producers). (1992). *Radio Flyer*.
Smith, B. (1943). *A Tree Grows in Brooklyn*.

Activity

Students read or view stories that depict family crises. Guide discussion, using the suggested sequence in Table 3.5, about how the characters coped with the crisis. Encourage students to write a depiction of their own relevant experiences. Facilitate sharing of these experiences, helping students to make explicit (1) feelings they experienced, (2) definition of the problem, (3) alternative strategies for solving the problem, and (4) anticipated or actual outcomes. Link to units on self-efficacy, social interaction skills, and interpersonal problem solving by encouraging students to consider ways in which they have solved other types of problems, how they can seek and provide social support, and how they might display caring to others who are in crisis. From this discussion, generate a list of strategies and resources for coping with family-oriented crises. Generate another list of ways to help others in crisis. Within this context, introduce the role of school personnel as resources.

Extensions

1. In conjunction with drug education curricula, present depictions of family alcoholism. For example, use the educational film *Soft Is the Heart of a Child* (1978), and the suggested sequence in Table 3.5, to discuss the characteristics of the family affected by alcohol. From this discussion, generate a list of strategies and resources for coping with family alcoholism. Generate another list of ways to help others in this situation. Within this context, reinforce the role of school personnel as resources.

2. To promote generalization, have students describe in their jour-

nals family crises they have encountered, using the journal format (Table 3.8). Guide discussion and role playing of journal entries with focus on feelings, problem definition, and strategies for actual and alternative outcomes. Regular use of journals facilitates reflection on and recording of effective coping. Group discussion of journal entries can facilitate empathy and provide opportunities for social support.

3. Students maintain journals regarding depictions of family alcoholism in popular media (e.g., newspapers, magazines, television, movies, books, music). Use journals to discuss depictions of roles and rules, interactions and communication styles, and strategies for coping with family alcoholism.

❖   ❖   ❖

Grade Level: Ninth–Twelfth

Objectives

1. Encourage appropriate expression of feeling.
2. Encourage social support by peer group.
3. Foster climate of acceptance and caring.
4. Explore strategies for coping with crisis.
5. Provide models of effective coping.

Materials

Stories, writing materials, notebooks for journals, Table 3.5.

Suggested Stories

Angelou, M. (1969). *I Know Why the Caged Bird Sings.*
Cormier, R. (1979). *After the First Death.*
Nicolaides, S. (Producer), & Singleton, J. (Director). (1991). *Boyz 'n the Hood.*
Nixon, J. L. (1984). *The Ghosts of Now.*
Tanem, N., Hughes, J. (Producers), & Hughes, J. (Director). (1985). *Breakfast Club.*

Activity

Students read or view stories that depict family crises. Guide discussion, using the suggested sequence in Table 3.5, about how the characters coped with the crisis. Encourage students to write a depiction of their own relevant experiences. Facilitate sharing of these experiences, helping students to make explicit (1) feelings they experienced, (2) definition of the problem, (3) alternative strategies for solving the problem, and (4) anticipated or actual outcomes. Link to units on self-efficacy, social interaction skills, and interpersonal problem solving by encouraging students to consider ways in which they have solved other types of problems, how they can seek and provide social support, and how they might display caring to others who are in crisis. From this discussion, generate a list of strategies and resources for coping with family-oriented crises. Generate another list of ways to help others in crisis. Within this context, introduce the role of school personnel as resources.

Extensions

1. In conjunction with drug education curricula, present depictions of family alcoholism. For example, use *Whiskey's Song*, by Mitzi Chandler (1987) and the suggested sequence in Table 3.5, to discuss the characteristics of the family affected by alcohol. From this discussion, generate a list of strategies and resources for coping with family alcoholism. Generate another list of ways to help others in this situation. Within this context, reinforce the role of school personnel as resources.

2. To promote generalization, have students describe in their journals family crises they have encountered, using the journal format (Table 3.8). Guide discussion and role playing of journal entries, with focus on feelings, problem definition, and strategies for actual and alternative outcomes. Regular use of journals facilitates reflection on and recording of effective coping. Group discussion of journal entries can facilitate empathy and provide opportunities for social support.

3. As a class project, students write and illustrate stories, poetry, or compositions that depict their understanding or experiences with family alcoholism. Facilitate dissemination of products through oral readings and bound volumes.

4. Students maintain journals regarding depictions of family alcoholism in popular media for same-age peers (e.g., newspapers, magazines, television, movies, books, music). Use journals to discuss depictions of roles and rules, interactions and communication styles, and strategies for coping with family alcoholism. In addition, students gather information from local agencies that provide services for adolescent COAs. As a group project, students produce educational materials (e.g., wallet-size information cards with phone numbers of resource agencies, posters, pamphlets, video) for their school, depicting coping strategies and resources for adolescents living in families affected by alcohol.

APPENDIX 4A

Pattern for Constructing the Moody Gang

The *Moody Gang* is a set of felt board characters used to depict different emotions (e.g., happy, sad, angry, afraid, yucky). Pieces include heads, hair, mouths, eyes, eyebrows, tears, and other facial features necessary to depict a range of feelings. Pattern pieces are made to scale and may be enlarged.

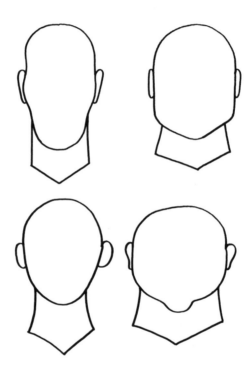

Moody Gang—Head Shapes

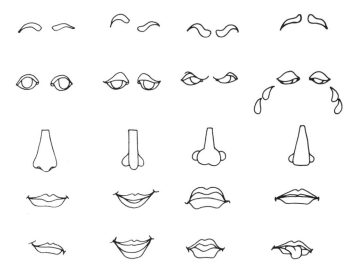

Moody Gang—Eyebrows, Eyes, Noses, Mouths

Moody Gang—Female Hair

Moody Gang—Male Hair

5

Annotated Bibliography
of Books and Films

This chapter provides an annotated list of books and films for use in the
ESCAPE curriculum. Annotations include developmental levels and relevant coping skills.

LITERATURE

Ancona, G. (1985). *Helping out*. New York: Houghton-Mifflin. [elementary–early
  adolescence; helping, caring, relationships, community]
Angelou, M. (1969). *I know why the caged bird sings*. New York: Bantam Books. Also
  available on film. [adolescence–adulthood; coping, family, crisis, sexual abuse]
Anglund, J. W. (1986). *All about me*. New York: Scholastic. [early elementary;
  self-concept, making friends]
Anglund, J. W. (1987). *All about my family*. New York: Scholastic. [early elementary;
  family]
Anthony, P. (1992). *Fractal mode*. New York: Ace Books. [adolescence; friendship,
  crisis, coping, conflict resolution, rules/norms]
Austen, J. (1959). *Pride and prejudice*. New York: Dell. (Original work published
  1813) [adolescence–adulthood; relationships, coping, social norms]
Black, C. (1989). *My dad loves me, my dad has a disease*. Minneapolis: Hazelden. (A
  workbook for COAs, ages 6–14) [elementary–early adolescence; family alco-
  holism]
Blume, J. (1972). *It's not the end of the world*. New York: Dell. [middle school–junior
  high; family relationships, coping with family crisis]
Blume, J. (1974). *The pain and the great one*. New York: Dell. [elementary–middle
  school; sibling/family relationships, self-esteem]
Blume, J. (1981). *Tiger eyes: A novel*. New York: Bradbury Press. [adolescence;
  coping with family crisis, family relationships, feelings]

Blume, J. (1987). *Just as long as we're together*. New York: Dell. [junior high; friendship, family relationships]

Boegehold, B. (1985). *Daddy doesn't live here anymore*. Racine, WI: Western. [early elementary; divorce, coping, family relationships]

Bolliger-Savelli, A. (1974). *Miranda's magic*. New York: Macmillan. [early elementary; problem solving, personal control]

Brandenberg, A. (1984). *Feelings*. New York: Mulberry Books. [elementary; feelings]

Brown, B., & Krensky, S. (1983). *Perfect pigs: An introduction to manners*. Boston: Little, Brown. [elementary; rules]

Bronte, C. (1848). *Jane Eyre*. New York: Bantam Books. [adolescence–adulthood; relationships, coping, social norms]

Bronte, E. (1939). *Wuthering Heights*. New York: Simon & Schuster. (Original work published 1847) [adolescence–adulthood; relationships, coping, social norms]

Buck, P. (1931). *The good earth*. New York: Simon & Schuster. [adolescence–adulthood; family, coping, self-efficacy]

Buffet, J., & Buffet, S. J. (1991). *Trouble dolls*. San Diego, CA: Harcourt, Brace, Jovanovich. [elementary; family relationships, problem solving, coping, feelings]

Burnett, F. H. (1911). *The secret garden*. New York: Harper Collins. [all ages; friendship, family]

Bulla, C. R. (1987). *The chalk box kid*. New York: Random House. [elementary; coping]

Buscaglia, L. (1982). *The fall of Freddie the leaf*. Thorofare, NJ: Slack. [all ages; feelings, coping, crisis]

Cervantes, M. (1957). *Don Quixote*. New York: Signet Classics. (Original work published 1605) [adolescence–adulthood; self-efficacy, self-concept, relationships, problem solving, goal setting]

Chandler, M. (1987). *Whiskey's song: An explicit story of surviving in an alcoholic home*. Pompano Beach, FL: Health Communications, Inc. (This is a book of poetry by an ACOA) [adolescence–adulthood; family alcoholism, self-efficacy, coping]

Cleary, B. (1975). *Ramona the brave*. New York: William Morrow & Co. [elementary; control, self-efficacy]

Cleary, B. (1977). *Ramona and her father*. New York: William Morrow. [elementary; family, coping]

Cleary, B. (1979). *Ramona and her mother*. New York: William Morrow. [elementary; family, coping]

Collins, J. (1989). *My father*. Boston: Little, Brown. [elementary; family relationships]

Cooper, J. F. (1957). *Last of the Mohicans*. New York: Simon & Schuster. Also available on film. [adolescence–adulthood; crisis, coping, self-efficacy, self-concept, relationships, community, conflict resolution, social norms]

Cormier, R. (1979). *After the first death*. New York: Dell. [high school; crisis, family, conflict resolution, social norms]

Demi. (1990). *The empty pot*. New York: Holt. [early elementary; rules, social norms, honesty]

dePaola, T. (1973). *Andy (that's my name)*. Englewood Cliffs, NJ: Prentice-Hall. [early elementary; relationships, self-efficacy] dePaola, T. (1973). *Nana upstairs and Nana downstairs*. New York: Putnam. [elementary; cross-generational family relationships, coping, crisis]

dePaola, T. (1983). *The legend of the bluebonnet*. New York: Putnam. [elementary; family, community, coping]

Dickens, C. (1961). *Oliver Twist*. New York: Signet Classics. (Original work published 1838) [adolescence–adulthood; coping, problem solving, family, relationships, community, social norms, self-efficacy]

Dickens, C. (1962). *David Copperfield*. New York: Signet Classics. (Original work published 1850) [adolescence–adulthood; coping, family, relationships, community, social norms, self-efficacy, self-concept]

DiGiovanni, K. (1986). *My house is different*. Center City, MN: Hazelden. [preschool–early elementary; COAs, 12-step recovery process, coping]

Dr. Seuss. (1990). *Oh, the places you'll go!* New York: Random House. [elementary–adulthood; self-efficacy, coping]

du Maurier, D. (1938). *Rebecca*. New York: Avon. Also available on film. [adolescence–adulthood; family, coping, perspective taking]

Durrell, A., & Sachs, M. (Eds.). (1990). *The big book for peace*. New York: Dutton. [elementary; conflict resolution]

Flournoy, V. (1985). *The patchwork quilt*. New York: Dial Books. [elementary; family relationships]

Fox, M. (1985). *Wilfrid Gordon McDonald Partridge*. Brooklyn, New York: Kane/Miller Books. [elementary; cross-generational relationships]

Frank, A. (1952). *The diary of a young girl*. New York: Simon & Schuster. [adolescence; coping, crisis, family, self-concept]

Gandhi, M. K. (1957). *Gandhi: An autobiography. The story of my experiments with truth*. Boston: Beacon Press. Also available on film. [adolescence–adulthood; community, peaceful conflict resolution, self-efficacy, caring]

Goff, B. (1969). *Where is daddy?* Boston: Beacon Press. [early elementary; divorce, coping, family relationships]

Goldberg, W. (1992). *Alice*. New York: Bantam Books. [all ages; problem solving, friendship, conflict resolution, self-concept, perspective taking]

Golding, W. (1959). *Lord of the flies*. New York: Putnam. Also available on film. [adolescence–adulthood; relationships, community, rules/norms, problem solving, coping, conflict resolution]

Gunther, D. (1949). *Death be not proud*. New York: Harper & Row. [adolescence; coping, crisis, family]

Guthrie, D. (1986). *Grandpa doesn't know it's me*. New York: Human Sciences Press. [elementary; cross-generational family relationships, caring, coping]

Hallinan, P. K. (1977). *That's what a friend is*. Chicago: Children's Press. [elementary; friendship]

Haley, A. (1964). *Autobiography of Malcolm X*. New York: Ballantine Books. [adolescence–adulthood; self-concept, self-efficacy, conflict resolution, social norms, relationships, family, community]

Hamilton, V. (1974). *M. C. Higgins, the great*. New York: Macmillan. [middle school; coping, self-efficacy]

Hansberry, L. (1958). *A raisin in the sun*. New York: Signet Classics. Also available on film. [all ages; family relationships, community, decision making, self-efficacy]

Hendershot, J. (1987). *In coal country*. New York: Alfred A. Knopf. [elementary; family, coping]

Hinton, S. E. (1967). *The outsiders*. New York: Dell. [adolescence; coping, relationships]

Hinton, S. E. (1971). *That was then, this is now*. New York: Dell. Also available on film. [adolescence; relationships, coping, decision making, problem solving]

Hoffman, M., & Binch, C. (1991). *Amazing Grace*. New York: Dial Books. [elementary; self-efficacy]

Isadora, R. (1976). *Max*. New York: Collier Books. [elementary; self-concept]

Koci, M. (1987). *Sarah's bear*. Natick, MA: Picture Book Studio. [elementary; friendship, caring]

Lee, H. (1961). *To kill a mockingbird*. Philadelphia: J. B. Lippincott. Also available on film. [adolescence–adulthood; friendship, community, self-efficacy, decision making, conflict resolution, social norms]

L'Engle, M. (1962). *A wrinkle in time*. New York: Farrar Straus Giroux. [adolescence; family, caring, relationships, problem solving, coping]

Lewis, C. S. (1950–56). *The chronicles of Narnia*. New York: Macmillan. [middle school–adulthood; relationships, conflict resolution, self-efficacy, self-concept, decision making]

Lopez, B. (1990). *Crow and weasel*. San Francisco: North Point Press. [elementary; friendship, problem solving, self-efficacy, coping]

MacLachlan, P. (1980). *Through grandpa's eyes*. New York: Harper Collins. [elementary; family relationships, perspective taking]

MacLachlan, P. (1985). *Sarah, plain and tall*. New York: Harper & Row. Also available on film. [elementary; family relationships, coping with crisis]

Mayer, M. (1968). *There's a nightmare in my closet*. New York: Dial Books. [early elementary; feelings, coping]

Mayer, M. (1983). *I was so mad*. New York: Western. [early elementary; feelings]

McGovern, A. (1986). *Stone soup*. New York: Scholastic. [preschool–early elementary; caring, community]

Morrison, T. (1970). *The bluest eye*. New York: Simon & Schuster. [adolescence–adulthood; family alcoholism, social norms, problem solving, sexual abuse, crisis, coping, relationships]

Nixon, J. L. (1984). *The ghosts of now*. New York: Dell. [adolescence; family alcoholism, denial, coping, feelings, problem solving, conflict resolution]

O'Brien, R. C. (1971). *Mrs. Frisby and the rats of NIMH*. New York: Macmillan. [early adolescence; cooperation, problem solving]

O'Dell, S. (1960). *Island of the blue dolphins*. New York: Dell. [elementary–middle school; self-efficacy, problem solving]

Paris, S. (1986). *Mommy and Daddy are fighting*. Seattle: Seal Press. [elementary; parental/family conflict; best used in context of therapeutic relationship]

Paterson, K. (1977). *Bridge to Terabithia*. New York: Thomas Y. Crowell. [middle school; crisis, coping, friendship, caring, feelings, family, self-efficacy]

Pfeffer, S. B. (1980). *Just between us*. New York: Dell. [middle school; friendship, problem solving, family]

Pinkney, G. J. (1992). *Back home*. New York: Dial Books. [elementary; family relationships, cross-generational relationships, family history]

Polacco, P. (1988). *The keeping quilt*. New York: Simon & Schuster. [early elementary; family]

Potok, C. (1967). *The chosen*. New York: Random House. [adolescence; coping, family, relationships, problem solving, conflict resolution]

Preston, E. M. (1969). *The temper tantrum book*. Cedar Grove, NJ: Puffin Books. [early elementary; mood management]

Ransom, C. F. (1988). *My sister the meanie*. New York: Scholastic. [middle school; sibling relationships, coping]

Richardson, J. (1988). *Bad mood bear*. New York: Barron's. [early elementary; mood management]

Ringgold, F. (1992). *Aunt Harriet's underground railroad in the sky*. New York: Crown. [elementary; coping, goal setting, community]

Rodriguez, L. J. (1993). *Always running. La vida loca: Gang days in L.A.* Willimantic, CT: Curbstone Press. [adolescence–adulthood; coping, self-efficacy, drugs, gangs, violence, family, peers, community]

Rose, D. L. (1990). *The people who hugged trees*. Niwot, CO: Rinehart. [elementary; problem solving, caring, social norms]

Rosen, M. (Ed.). (1992). *South and North, East and West: The Oxfam book of children's stories*. Cambridge, MA: Candlewick. [all ages; international collection of 25 stories representing diverse cultural heritages]

Rosen, M. J. (Ed.). (1992). *Home*. New York: Harper Collins. [all ages; 30 distinguished authors and illustrators of children's books provide definitions of home]

Ross, T. (1989). *I want a cat*. New York: Farrar Straus Giroux. [early elementary; problem solving, family]

Rylant, C. (1982). *When I was young in the mountains*. New York: Dutton. [elementary; family]

Rylant, C. (1985). *A blue-eyed daisy*. New York: Bradbury Press. [elementary; family, friendship, coping, family alcoholism]

Rylant, C. (1985). *The relatives came*. New York: Bradbury Press. [elementary; family, problem solving]

Sanford, D. (1985). *It must hurt alot*. Portland, OR: Multnomah. [elementary; feelings, coping, crisis, friendship]

Saint-Exupéry, A., de. (1943). *The little prince*. San Diego, CA: Harcourt Brace Jovanovich. [all ages; feelings, choices, responsibility, roles, caring, relationships, self-discovery]

Scieszka, J. (1989). *The true story of the 3 little pigs*. New York: Viking. [all ages; perspective taking]

Sendak, M. (1963). *Where the wild things are*. New York: Harper Collins. [elementary; feelings, coping]

Seuling, B. (1985). *What kind of family is this?* Racine, WI: Western. [early elementary; family relationships, stepfamilies, coping]

Silverstein, S. (1964). *The giving tree*. New York: Harper & Row. [elementary–adulthood; caring, relationships]

Smith, B. (1943). *A tree grows in Brooklyn*. Philadelphia: Blakiston. Also available on film. [adolescence; family alcoholism, family relationships, crisis, coping]

Stevenson, J. (1986). *When I was nine*. New York: Greenwillow Books. [elementary; family relationships, cross-generational relationships, perspective taking]

Stinson, K. (1984). *Mom and Dad don't live together anymore*. Toronto: Annick Press. [early elementary; family relationships, coping, crisis]

Thomas, J. R. (1988). *Saying good-bye to grandma*. New York: Houghton-Mifflin. [elementary; feelings, coping, family, crisis]

Udry, J. M. (1966). *What Mary Jo shared*. New York: Scholastic. [early elementary; family relationships, community]

Van Allsburg, C. (1990). *Just a dream*. Boston: Houghton-Mifflin. [elementary; human–ecology relationship, conflict]

Viorst, J. (1969). *I'll fix Anthony*. New York: Macmillan. [elementary; family, sibling relationships, coping, problem solving]

Viorst, J. (1971). *The tenth good thing about Barney*. New York: Macmillan. [elementary; coping, crisis, feelings]

Viorst, J. (1972). *Alexander and the terrible, horrible, no good, very bad day*. New York: Macmillan. [elementary; mood management, coping]

Viorst, J. (1974). *Rosie and Michael*. New York: Macmillan. [elementary; friendship]

Viorst, J. (1988). *The goodbye book*. New York: Macmillan. [elementary; family relationships, communication, feelings, coping]

Waber, B. (1972). *Ira sleeps over*. Boston: Houghton-Mifflin. [elementary; friendship, feelings, decision making, coping]

Walker, A. (1982). *The color purple*. New York: Simon & Schuster. Also available on film. [late adolescence–adulthood; family relationships, coping]

Walker, A. (1988). *To hell with dying*. San Diego, CA: Harcourt Brace Jovanovich. [elementary; relationships, feelings]

Walker, A. (1991). *Finding the green stone*. San Diego, CA: Harcourt, Brace, Jovanovich. [elementary; self-esteem, caring, relationships, boundaries]

White, E. B. (1952). *Charlotte's web*. New York: Harper & Row. [elementary; caring, relationships, problem solving, self-concept]

Wilhelm, H. (1985). *I'll always love you*. New York: Crown. [elementary; feelings, coping, crisis]

Williams, M. (1983). *The velveteen rabbit: Or how toys become real*. New York: Holt, Rinehart, & Winston. [elementary–adulthood; caring, relationships, self-esteem]

Winthrop, E. (1977). *That's mine!* New York: Holiday House. [early elementary; cooperation]

Wright, R. (1989). *Black boy*. New York: Harper Collins. [adolescence–adulthood; coping, family, relationships, social norms, self-efficacy, conflict resolution]

Zolotow, C. (1968). *My friend John*. New York: Harper Collins. [early elementary; friendship]

Zolotow, C. (1969). *The hating book*. New York: Harper Collins. [elementary; friendship, communication]

FILMS

Popular Films

(available through local video stores)

Caracciolo, J. M. (Producer), Friendly, D. T. (Producer), Grazer, B. (Producer), & Zieff, H. (Director). (1992). *My girl*. [Film]. Columbia Pictures. [elementary–high school; friendship, family]

Christiansen, R. W. (Producer), Rosenbery, R. (Producer), & Korty, J. (Director). *Autobiography of Miss Jane Pittman*. [Film]. Tomorrow Entertainment. Based on the novel by Ernest J. Gaines. [middle school–adulthood; self-efficacy, crisis, coping, relationships, community, conflict resolution]

Di Novi, D. (Producer), Burton, T. (Producer & Director), Hoshimoto, R. (Executive Producer). (1990). *Edward Scissorhands*. [Film]. CBS/Fox. [adolescence–adulthood; social norms, self-efficacy, self-concept, coping, goal setting, problem solving, relationships, family, peer relationships, community]

Elfand, M. (Producer), Moloney, M. (Executive Producer), & Mulligan, R. (Director). (1988). *Clara's heart*. [Film]. Warner Bros. Based on the novel by Joseph Olshan. [adolescence; caring, relationships, family]

Evans, B. A. (Producer), Gideon, R. (Producer), Schernman, A. (Producer), & Reiner, R. (Director). (1986). *Stand by me*. [Film]. RCA/Columbia Pictures. Based on the novella by Stephen King. [junior–senior high school; friendship, family, alcoholism]

Haft, S. (Producer), Witt, P. J. (Producer), Thomas, T. (Producer), & Weir, P. (Director). (1989). *Dead poets society*. [Film]. Touchstone Home Video. [adolescence–adulthood; coping, community, relationships, rules/norms, self-efficacy, crisis]

Hausman, M. (Producer), & Corr, E. (Director). (1986). *Desert bloom*. [Film]. RCA/Columbia Pictures. [junior high–adult; family alcoholism]

Hughes, J. (Producer), Chinich, M. (Producer), Colby, R. (Producer), & Deutch, H. (Director). (1987). *Some kind of wonderful*. [Film]. Paramount Pictures. [adolescence; peer and family relationships]

Jaffe, S. R. (Producer), Lansing, S. (Producer), Rissner, D. (Executive Producer), & Mandel, R. (Director). (1992). *School ties*. [Film]. Paramount Pictures. [adolescence–adulthood; prejudice, peer relationships, family relationships, problem solving, coping, rules, self-esteem, self-efficacy]

Jordan, G. (Producer & Director), Self, W. (Executive Producer), & Close, G. (Executive Producer). (1990). *Sarah, plain and tall*. [Film]. Hallmark Hall of Fame (Republic Pictures Home Video). Based on the book by Patricia MacLachlan. [all ages; family relationships, coping with crisis]

Katzka, G., (Producer), & Schlesinger, J. (Producer & Director). (1984). *The falcon and the snowman*. [Film]. Orion Pictures. Based on the book by Robert Lindsey. [high school–young adult; drug abuse, peer relationships, choices, decision making]

Lanning, S. (Producer), Rosemont, N. (Executive Producer), & Grint, A. (Director). (1987) *The secret garden*. [Film]. Hallmark Hall of Fame (Republic Pictures). Based on the novel by Frances Hodgson Burnett. [all ages; friendship, family]

Lighton, L. D. (Producer), & Kazan, E. (Director). (1945). *A tree grows in Brooklyn*. [Film, B&W]. Based the book by Betty Smith. [all ages; family alcoholism, family relationships, crisis, coping]

Losey, J. (Director). (1948). *The boy with the green hair*. [Film]. King of Video. [all ages, coping, self-efficacy, conflict resolution]

Musca, T. (Producer), & Menendez, R. (Director). (1988). *Stand and deliver*. [Film]. Warner Bros. [adolescence–adulthood (teachers); alternatives]

Nicolaides, S. (Producer), & Singleton, J. (Director). (1991). *Boyz 'n the hood*. [Film]. Columbia Pictures. [adolescence; family, alcohol use]

Pacula, A. (Producer), & Mulligan, R. (Director). (1962). *To kill a mockingbird.* [Film]. MCA Home Video. Based on the novel by Harper Lee. [adolescence–adulthood; friendship, community, self-efficacy, decision making, conflict resolution, social norms]

Schain, D. (Producer), Anderson, D. (Producer), Balsam, M. (Producer), & Van Wagenen, S. (Director). (1992). *Alan & Naomi.* [Film]. Columbia Pictures. Based on the novel by Myron Levoy. [middle school–adulthood; friendship]

Shuler-Donner, L. (Producer); Donner, R. (Director); Douglas, M., Bieber, R., & Evans, D. M. (Executive Producers). (1992). *Radio flyer.* [Film]. Columbia Pictures. [adolescence–adulthood; family, alcoholism, child abuse, sibling relationships]

Singh, A. (Producer), & Roodt, D. J. (Director). (1992). *Sarafina!* [Film]. Miramax. Based on a play by Mbongeni Ngema. [adolescence–adulthood; conflict, community, family, diversity, relationships, self-efficacy]

Tanem, N. (Producer), & Hughes, J. (Producer, Director). (1985). *Breakfast club.* [Film]. Universal City Studios. [junior–senior high school; peer and family relationships, substance use]

Yank, J. (Producer), Steakley, W. B. (Producer), Stone, O. (Executive Producer), Spielberg, M. (Co-Executive Producer), Gilber, B. (Co-Executive Producer), & Anderson, S. (Director). (1992). *South Central.* [Film]. Warner Bros. Based on the novel, *Crips,* by Donald Bakeer. [adolescence–adulthood; decision making, self-efficacy, family, peers, community, drugs, gangs, prison, rules/norms, parental substance abuse]

Educational Films and Audiotapes

Alateen tells it like it is. (1987). [Film]. New York: Al-Anon Family Group Headquarters. 16 minutes. Also available in audiocassette. Produced by COAs who are members of Alateen. [adolescence; family alcoholism, Alateen]

Alcoholism, the family disease. (1982). [Audiotape]. New York: Al-Anon Family Group Headquarters. 60 minutes. Also available in written form. Presents personal stories from members of families affected by alcohol. [late adolescence–adulthood; family alcoholism, Al-Anon]

Lots of kids like us. (1983). [Film]. MTI Productions. 28 minutes. Available through school district film libraries. [elementary–junior high; family alcoholism]

Roddy, P. (Executive Producer), Jennings, P. (Senior Editor), Jackson, B. (Senior Producer), & Goodman, R. (Director). (1992). *Prejudice: Answering children's questions.* [Film]. ABC News. 75 minutes. Available from MPI Home Video Department, ABC, 15825 Rob Roy Drive, Oak Forest, IL 60457. [elementary–adulthood; perspective taking, conflict resolution, community, social relationships]

Soft is the heart of a child. (1978). [Film]. 28 minutes. Available through school district film libraries. [all ages; family alcoholism]

What's "drunk," Mama? (1990). [Audiotape]. New York: Al-Anon Family Group Headquarters. 24 minutes. Also available in written form. Stories told by children from families affected by alcohol. [elementary–adulthood; family alcoholism, coping, Al-Anon]

6

Resource Materials

This chapter provides resources for professionals to facilitate the design, implementation, and evaluation of school-based programs for COAs. The first section includes annotated bibliographies of selected intervention programs and assessment instruments. The second section is a more extensive bibliography covering several topics: (1) alcoholism and other substance abuse, (2) family alcoholism and COAs, (3) general intervention strategies, (4) observational and qualitative methods, and (5) general assessment and program evaluation methods. The final section includes resource lists of support groups, clearinghouses, and organizations.

ANNOTATED BIBLIOGRAPHY OF INTERVENTION PROGRAMS

This section provides a list of selected programs that contain activities consistent with the goals and objectives of the ESCAPE program. The programs are designed for use with small groups or entire classrooms. Many activities can be easily incorporated into classroom routines. Some programs and activities are specifically designed for teacher use, whereas others require collaboration of the teacher and school psychologist, social worker, or counselor. We include programs focused specifically on drug education and family alcoholism, and more generally on social and coping skills.

Drug Education and Family Alcoholism Programs

Children Are People (CAP)

This agency provides training, manuals, and curricular materials for implementing chemical abuse prevention programs for children ages 5–12 (designed specifically for children of alcoholics). The *Support Group* is an 8-week program (16 sessions, two meetings per week). Session topics include Goal Setting, Feelings, Defenses, Chemical Dependency, Risks and Choices, Families, Specialness, and Parent–Child Communication. The *Curriculum* is an 8-week program for children in Grades K–6, designed for classroom implementation. Target issues include self-esteem, peer pressure, problem solving, coping, and chemicals. Contact: Children Are People, Inc. (Chemical Abuse Prevention Programs), 493 Selby Ave., St. Paul, MN 55102; (612) 490-9257.

Discovery Kit: Positive Connections for Kids

The Office for Substance Abuse Prevention (1992) produced this cross-cultural drug prevention program for individuals aged 10–15; designed for school- or community-based implementation. Foci are education about alcohol and family alcoholism, and promotion of personal–social competence of at-risk children, particularly COAs. Goals include the prevention of alcohol abuse, and the enhancement of resiliency, sense of connectedness, self-esteem, and coping and problem-solving skills. Program materials include leader's guide, manual, posters, worksheets, videotape, audiotape, and stories. Multicultural content depicts the experiences of African American, Caucasian, Hispanic American, and Native American children and families. Leader's guide presents activities in lesson format, with suggestions for integration into existing school curricula (language arts, mathematics, social studies, health/physical education). Also provides suggestions for involving families and extending to community. Publisher: U.S. Department of Health and Human Services (DHHS Publication No. ADM 92-1866). Contact: National Clearinghouse for Alcohol and Drug Information.

Here's Looking at You, 2000

This kindergarten through grade 12 comprehensive multimedia curriculum is designed to be used as part of a broader health curriculum. Risk reduction, resistance strategies, drug information, making friends, and bonding are curriculum foci. Studies of earlier versions of this curriculum indicate improved knowledge about alcohol, positive effect on decision-making, and reduction in teenage drinking. Contact: Roberts, Fitzmahan

& Associates, 131 California Ave. S.W., Seattle, WA 93136-2599; (206) 824-2907.

Project Charlie (Chemical Abuse Resolution Lies in Education)

This drug abuse prevention program for elementary school children (K–6) is designed to prevent drug abuse and enhance social competence and self-esteem. Provides curricular activities and guidelines for structuring classroom climate. Contact: Project Charlie, 5701 Normandale Rd., Edina, MN 55424; (612) 830-1432.

Project DARE (Drug Abuse Resistance Education)

This kindergarten through grade 8 curriculum focuses on social influences, refusal skills, risk reduction, decision making, self-esteem, and drug information. Program implemented as collaborative effort between schools and police department. Positive effects for academic achievement reported in evaluation study. Contact: DARE Program, LAPD (Stop 439), 150 North Los Angeles St., Los Angeles, CA 90012, (213) 485-4856, or your local police department.

General Social and Coping Skills Programs

I Can Problem Solve: An Interpersonal Cognitive Problem-Solving Program

Program developed by M. B. Shure (1992) for teaching interpersonal cognitive problem-solving skills to students in preschool through intermediate elementary grades, based on extensive research by the author and her colleagues. Designed for use by classroom teachers. Contains formal lessons for introducing and teaching concepts and skills, as well as suggestions for application to daily classroom interactions and integration into academic curricula. Available in separate volumes by grade levels: preschool, kindergarten–primary, intermediate elementary. Publisher: Research Press, Champaign, IL.

Peer Mediation: Conflict Resolution in the Schools

Developed by F. Shrumpf, D. Crawford, and H. C. Usadel (1991), program is designed to teach middle- and high-school students peer mediation skills for facilitating conflict resolution through communication and problem solving. Goals include promoting a schoolwide peer mediation approach to conflict resolution. Provides guidelines and materials for program planning, peer-mediator training (in a 2-day workshop format), and program implementation (with ongoing consultation and mediator self-evaluation). The training model has a cognitive–behavioral focus and uses such methods as demonstration, role play, discussion, and engagement in and evaluation of cooperative interactions. Manual provides descriptive data regarding success. The program, Common Ground, was first implemented in Urbana, Illinois at the middle school level and resulted in successful resolution of 95% of over 500 peer-mediated conflicts in a 3-year period. Appropriate for middle school and high school. Includes program guide and student manual. Publisher: Research Press, Champaign, IL.

Skillstreaming: Teaching Prosocial Skills

Goldstein, A. P. (1988). *The prepare curriculum: Teaching prosocial competencies.* [junior high and high school]

Goldstein, A. P., Glick, B., Reiner, S., Zimmerman, B., & Coultry, T. M. (1987). *Aggression replacement training: A comprehensive intervention for aggressive youth.* [adolescents]

Goldstein, A. P., & Huff, C. R. (Eds.). (1993). *The gang intervention handbook.*

Goldstein, A. P., Reagles, K. W., & Amann, L. L. (1990). *Refusal skills: Preventing drug use in adolescents.*

Goldstein, A. P., Sprafkin, R. P., Gershaw, N. J., & Klein, P. (1980). *Skillstreaming the adolescent: A structured approach to teaching prosocial skills.*

McGinnis, E., & Goldstein, A. P. (1984). *Skillstreaming the elementary school child: A guide for teaching prosocial skills.*

McGinnis, E., & Goldstein, A. P. (1990). *Skillstreaming in early childhood: Teaching prosocial skills to the preschool and kindergarten child.*

Skillstreaming is a theoretically and empirically based psychoeducational, behavioral approach to teaching prosocial skills and is based on extensive research by Goldstein and his colleagues. This approach uses techniques of modeling, role play, performance feedback, and transfer training. Target skill areas include surviving in the classroom, making friends, dealing with feelings, dealing with stress, finding alternatives to aggression, planning, handling group pressure, and negotiating. The program texts provide structured lessons for teaching target skills, assessment tools for preassessment and evaluation, and reproducible program materials. Skillstreaming is appropriate for preschool through high school students and can be applied at primary, secondary, and tertiary levels of intervention. *Refusal Skills* describes the application of Skillstreaming to the prevention of substance abuse among adolescents. Publisher: Research Press, Champaign, IL.

Social Skills Intervention Guide: Practical Strategies for Social Skills Training

Developed by S. N. Elliott and F. M. Gresham (1991), the intervention component of the *Social Skills Rating System* (SSRS; see the assessment component description on page 242) provides treatment techniques for enhancing 43 social skills in five domains deemed important by parents and teachers—Cooperation, Assertion, Responsibility, Empathy, and Self-Control (CARES). Designed for students in grades 1 through 10 who have specific social skills deficits. Links intervention to assessment using the SSRS. The intervention program has a strong social learning theory base and uses intervention methods such as modeling, rehearsing, coaching, reinforcing, and contracting. Attention is given also to teaching social problem solving and fostering generalization. Designed for use with individuals or small groups. For each skill, the manual provides a step-by-step guide for teaching, practice, and generalization. Encourages parental involvement (e.g., use of home notes for generalization). Publisher: American Guidance Service, Circle Pines, MN.

Thinking, Feeling, Behaving: An Emotional Education Curriculum

Developed by A. Vernon (1989), this program is based on the principles of rational–emotive therapy, focuses on self-acceptance, feelings, beliefs and behavior, problem solving/decision making, and interpersonal relationships. Available in two versions—for children and adolescents. Each version includes 90 field-tested activities, arranged by grade level, that are appropriate for small-group or classroom-based application. Knowledge and skills are taught using a variety of methods, including didactic presentation, discussion, stories, games, role play, writing assignments, and art activities. Publisher: Research Press, Champaign, IL.

ANNOTATED BIBLIOGRAPHY OF ASSESSMENT INSTRUMENTS

This section provides a list of selected self-report measures and teacher- and parent-rating scales for assessing personal–social competence, and a commonly used screening measure to facilitate identification of COAs, *The Children of Alcoholics Screening Test* (CAST). We review both commercially published, norm-referenced instruments and empirically validated research instruments. Professionals with relevant training and experience (e.g., school psychologists) should be responsible for final selection, administration, and interpretation of these measures.

Behavior Assessment System for Children (BASC)

The BASC, developed by C. R. Reynolds and R. W. Kamphaus (1992), is a multidimensional approach to assessing behavior and self-perceptions of individuals ages 4–18 (self-report, 8–18). Includes self-report, parent and teacher ratings, structured developmental history, and systematic classroom observation. Designed for program evaluation, research, and diagnosis consistent with psychiatric and special education classification systems. Standardized on a national sample of over 10,000 children, which is representative of the U.S. Census on race/ethnicity, gender, and parent education. Clinical norms are based on individuals receiving services in school and clinic settings for emotional or behavioral problems. Hand- and computer-scoring are available. Psychometric properties support use of the BASC for clinical diagnosis. Internal consistency indices are high—.80 to .90 for teacher and parent ratings, .80 for self-report. Test–retest reliability indices range from .70 to low .90s across all measures. Moderate to high correlations with other behavior rating scales support construct validity of the teacher, parent, and self-report forms. Factor analytic procedures were used to develop and confirm composite scale structure. Available from: American Guidance Service, Circle Pines, MN.

The Children of Alcoholics Screening Test (CAST)

CAST, developed by J. W. Jones (1983), is a 30-item self-report inventory, with a yes–no response format, for school-age through adulthood. Designed as a clinical and research tool to identify COAs and to measure feelings, attitudes, and perceptions regarding parental drinking behavior. Item content includes emotional distress associated with parents' alcohol use/misuse, perception of parental discord as alcohol related, attempts to control parental drinking, attempts to escape alcoholism, exposure to family violence associated with drinking, tendency to view parents as alcoholics, and desire for assistance. The manual provides evidence of split-half reliability (Spearman Brown coefficient of .98), face validity (based on judgments of counselors and adult COAs), and discriminant validity (differentiates between individuals known to have an alcoholic parent and those for whom parental nonalcoholism was presumed but unsubstantiated). Based on validity studies with latency-age children and adolescents, the author provides criteria for cutoff scores: 0–1, non-COAs; 2–5, COPDs; 6 or higher, COAs. A score of 6 identified 100% of COAs accurately, but also identified 23% false positives (in the nonalcoholic group). The results of one study of 494 adolescents suggest the need for different cutoff criteria for males and females; males scored significantly lower than females (Dinning & Berk, 1989). This study also provided evidence of strong internal consistency of the CAST (with coefficients in the mid-.90s), and of significant relationships between CAST scores and family environment measures. That is, high CAST scores were correlated with high family conflict, low family cohesion, and low family support. The measure is most appropriate for clinical and research purposes related to identifying children who have concerns about parental drinking. Caution should be exercised in using the CAST as a diagnostic tool. For additional information, see reviews by Hart (1989) and Schinke (1989). Chicago: Camelot Unlimited.

Child Behavior Checklist (CBCL), Teacher Report Form (TRF), Youth Self-Report (YSR)

Achenbach, T. M. (1991). *Manual for the Child Behavior Checklist/4–18 and 1991 Profile.*
Achenbach, T. M. (1991). *Manual for the Teacher's Report Form and 1991 Profile.*
Achenbach, T. M. (1991). *Manual for the Youth Self-Report and 1991 Profile.*

These measures provide parallel scales for gathering data from teachers, parents, and students (self-report). Scales are standardized, norm-referenced measures of behavior problems (internalizing and externalizing) and competencies for individuals aged 4–18 (CBCL, 4–18; TRF, 5–18; YSR, 11–18). Manuals provide norms based on age and sex. Norms for competence scales are based on a subset of a national sample of individuals without handicaps; the standardization sample was selected to be representative of the contiguous United States with regard to socioeconomic status (SES), ethnicity, region, and urban–suburban–rural residence. Norms for the behavior problem scales are based on a sample of clinically referred children, representing a broad distribution of SES, ethnic, and demographic characteristics in the Southern, Eastern, and Midwestern regions of the United States. Psychometric properties support the use of these scales for clinical diagnosis. Test–retest reliability is high for teacher and parent reports (.87–.92 for competence and problem scales) and adequate for self-report (.65–.82). Interrater agreement is adequate (CBCL, .65–.76; TRF, .54–.60) but verifies the importance of multiple raters. Content and criterion-related validity, and cutoff criteria for identifying the clinical range are supported by discrimination between referred and non-referred samples. Scales may be hand- or computer-scored. Available from the author: Thomas M. Achenbach, Department of Psychiatry, University of Vermont, Burlington, VT 05401.

Pictorial Scale of Perceived Competence and Social Acceptance for Young Children

A self-report measure, developed by S. Harter and R. Pike (1984a,b), for young children in preschool through grade 2 (separate versions—P–K and

1–2); 24-item Likert-type scale; to be administered individually. Items are presented in pictorial format, with oral descriptions of depicted skill or activity (separate versions for females and males, with gender-specific pictures). Assesses children's judgments on four scales regarding their competence (cognitive, physical) and social acceptance (peer, maternal). Factor analytic procedures confirm the two-factor structure—General Competence (cognitive and physical competence scales) and Social Acceptance (peer and maternal acceptance scales). Internal consistency estimates for specific scales across grade levels range from .50 to .85, with subscale intercorrelations ranging from .00 to .80. Research supports convergent, discriminant, and predictive validity; additional information regarding scale development and psychometric properties is available in a separate publication (Harter & Pike, 1984a). Available from the author: Susan Harter, Department of Psychology, University of Denver, Denver, CO 80208

Self-Perception Profile for Adolescents

A self-report measure, developed by S. Harter (1988), for adolescents in grades 8–12; 45-item Likert-type scale; individual or group administration. Assesses adolescents' judgments of their competencies in eight domains (scholastic, social, athletic, physical, behavioral, job, romantic, friendship) and of their overall (global) self-worth. Internal consistency estimates for specific scales across several samples range from .74 to .91, with subscale intercorrelations ranging from .02 to .73. Factor analytic techniques confirm the proposed delineation of subscales. Administration of the scale in two formats (perceived competence and importance ratings) permits calculation of competence–importance discrepancy scores. Available from the author: Susan Harter, Department of Psychology, University of Denver, Denver, CO 80208

Self-Perception Profile for Children

A self-report measure developed by S. Harter (1985a), for youth in grades 3–8 with a 36-item Likert-type scale; individual or group administration. Assesses children's judgments of their competencies in five domains (scholastic, social, athletic, physical, behavioral) and overall (global) self-worth. Internal consistency estimates for specific scales across several samples range from .71 to .86, with subscale intercorrelations ranging from .01 to .73. Factor analytic techniques confirm the proposed delineation of subscales. Administration of the scale in two formats (perceived competence and importance ratings) permits calculation of competence–importance discrepancy scores. Manual also provides a parallel teacher scale for rating students' actual behavior in relevant domains. Research confirms comparability of factor patterns for teacher and student (self-report) ratings, with congruence (of factor loadings) coefficients ranging from .90 to .97 for elementary grades and .72 to .88 for junior high (Harter, 1982). Available from the author: Susan Harter, Department of Psychology, University of Denver, Denver, CO 80208

Social Skills Rating System (SSRS)

Developed by F. M. Gresham and S. N. Elliott (1990), the assessment component of the SSRS provides parallel scales for gathering data from teachers, parents, and students (self-report) and for comparing ratings using a standard frame of reference (consistent standardization sample). Scales are standardized, norm-referenced measures of social competence and behavior problems for students in grades kindergarten through 12 (self-report, grades 3–12), in three domains—Social Skills (Cooperation, Assertion, Responsibility, Empathy, Self-Control), Problem Behaviors (Externalizing, Internalizing, Hyperactivity), and Academic Competence. These scales provide competence and importance ratings for identifying targets for intervention (see the intervention component of the SSRS, *Social Skills Intervention Guide*, described in the preceding section). Standardized on national sample of 4,170 children, 1,027 parents, and 259 teachers, 17% of the sample were classified as handicapped and receiving special education services in resource or self-contained classrooms. Norms are based on age and sex; additional norms are available for teacher ratings of elementary special education students. Internal consistency is strong (alpha coefficients, .73–.95 for major scales across forms and levels). Test–retest reliability is good to excellent for teacher and parent forms (.48–.93) and adequate for self-report (.52–.66). Criterion-related and construct validity are supported by such indices as moderate to strong correlations with other social–behavioral measures, convergent validity (e.g., moderate cross-informant correlations), and discriminant validity (e.g., differentiation of handicapped from nonhandicapped). Importance ratings contribute to social validity of the scales. Available from: American Guidance Service, Circle Pines, MN.

Structured Pediatric Psychosocial Interview (SPPI)

This standardized, norm-referenced, structured (20–30 minute) interview technique, developed by T. E. Webb and C. A. Van Devere (1985, 1990), for ages 5–19, with individual administration. Assesses expressions of life concerns and affective distress. Yields measures of interpersonal sensitivity, relating style, perceptions of causality, and state of arousal. Standardized on a group of 1,015 children and adolescents in Northeastern Ohio. Sample demographics included (1) diverse socioeconomic backgrounds, living in urban, suburban, and small town communities; (2) racial/ethnic representation and parental occupation similar to proportions in the United States; (3) 31% from single-parent families, of which 25% were due to separation or divorce, and 6% were due to death. Validation studies conducted with clinic and public school samples provide evidence of psychometric adequacy. Major scales—Feeling, Thinking, Relating, and Impetuosity—were developed using structural modeling and factor analytic procedures, and were cross-validated across age groups and separate clinical populations. Evidence of reliability is provided by high interrater agreement regarding scoring ($r = .90$), moderate levels of long-term stability (12–24 months, rs range .37–.40), and high internal consistency indices for three of the major scales (.70–.93; Impetuosity, .43–.48). The Thinking, Feeling, and Impetuosity scales were found to distinguish between maladjusted (clinic) and nonreferred (public school) samples; the Relating scale is more likely to reflect responses to transient stress. Correlations of the SPPI scales with measures of intelligence and achievement range from .02 to .22. A software program provides normative scoring and a narrative interpretation of the individual's responses. Publisher: Fourier, P. O. Box 80125, Akron, OH 44308; (615) 664-3552.

BIBLIOGRAPHY

Alcoholism and Other Substance Abuse

Glantz, M., & Pickens, R. (Eds.). (1992). *Vulnerability to drug abuse*. Washington, DC: American Psychological Association.
Goode, E. (1992). *Drugs in American society* (4th ed.). New York: McGraw-Hill.
Goodwin, D. W. (1988). *Is alcoholism hereditary?* New York: Ballantine Books.
Fingarette, H. (1988). *Heavy drinking: The myth of alcoholism as a disease*. Berkeley, CA: University of California Press.
Johnson, V. E. (1980). *I'll quit tomorrow* (rev. ed.). San Francisco: Harper & Row.
Kinney, J., & Leaton, G. (1987). *Loosening the grip: A handbook of alcohol information* (3rd ed.). St. Louis: Times Mirror/Mosby.

Family Alcoholism and COAs

Ackerman, J. (1978). *Children of alcoholics: A guide for parents, educators, and therapists* (2nd ed.) New York: Simon & Schuster.
Beattie, M. (1987). *Codependent no more: How to stop controlling others and start caring for yourself*. New York: Harper & Row (for Hazelden).
Black, C. (1981). *It will never happen to me*. Denver: M. A. C.
Black, C. (1985). *Repeat after me*. Denver: M. A. C.

Bowden, J. D., & Gravitz, H. L. (l988). *Genesis: Spirituality in recovery from childhood traumas*. Pompano Beach, FL: Health Communications.

Cork, M. (1969). *The forgotten child*. Toronto: Alcohol and Drug Addiction Research Foundation.

Deutsch, C. (1982). *Broken bottles, broken dreams: Understanding and helping the children of alcoholics*. New York: Teacher's College Press.

Gravitz, H. L., & Bowden, J. D. (1985). *Guide to recovery: A book for adult children of alcoholics*. Holmes Beach, FL: Learning Publications.

Hastings, J. M., & Typpo, M. H. (1984). *An elephant in the living room: The children's book*. Minneapolis: CompCare.

O'Gorman, P., & Oliver-Diaz, P. (1987). *Breaking the cycle of addiction: A parent's guide to raising healthy kids*. Pompano Beach, FL: Health Communications.

Sexias, J. S., & Youcha, G. (1985). *Children of alcoholism: A survivor's manual*. New York: Harper & Row.

Sher, K. J. (1991). *Children of alcoholics: A critical appraisal of theory and research*. Chicago: University of Chicago Press.

Steinglass, P., Bennett, L. A., Wolin, S. J., & Reiss, D. (1987). *The alcoholic family*. New York: Basic Books.

Typpo, M. H., & Hastings, J. M. (1984). *An elephant in the living room: A leader's guide for helping children of alcoholics*. Minneapolis: CompCare.

Wegscheider, S. (198l). *Another chance: Hope and health for the alcoholic family*. Palo Alto, CA: Science and Behavior Books.

Woititz, J. (1983). *Adult children of alcoholics*. Hollywood, FL: Health Communications.

Woititz, J. (1985). *Struggle for intimacy*. Pompano Beach, FL: Health Communications.

Woititz, J. G., & Garner, A. (1990). *Life-skills for adult children*. Deerfield Beach, FL: Health Communications.

General Intervention Strategies

Bernard, M. E., & Joyce, M. R. (1984). *Rational–emotive therapy with children and adolescents*. New York: Wiley.

Cartledge, G., & Milburn, J. F. (Eds.). (1986). *Teaching social skills to children: Innovative approaches*. (2nd ed.). New York: Pergamon Press.

Fluegelman, A. (Ed.) (1976). *New games book*. New York: Doubleday.

Friend, M., & Cook, L. (1992). *Interactions: Collaboration skills for school professionals*. New York: Longman.

Gumaer, J. (1984). *Counseling and therapy for children*. New York: Free Press.

Hernandez, H. (1989). *Multicultural education: A teacher's guide to content and process*. New York: Macmillan.

Ivey, A. E. (1986). *Developmental therapy: Theory into practice*. San Francisco: Jossey-Bass.

Johnson, D. W., & Johnson, R. (1991). *Teaching students to be peacemakers*. Edina, MN: Interaction Book.

Noddings, N. (1992). *The challenge to care in schools: An alternative approach to education*. New York: Teacher's College Press.

Oaklander, V. (1988). *Windows to our children.* Highland, New York: Center for Gestalt Development.

Price, R. H., Cowen, E. L., Lorion, R. P., & Ramos-McKay, J. (Eds.). (1988). *14 ounces of prevention.* Washington, DC: American Psychological Association.

Stoner, G., Shinn, M. R., & Walker, H. M. (Eds.). (1991). *Interventions for achievement and behavior problems.* Silver Spring, MD: National Association of School Psychologists.

Observational and Qualitative Methods

Bakeman, R., & Gottman, J. M. (1986). *Observing interaction: An introduction to sequential analysis.* New York: Cambridge University Press.

Miles, M. B., & Huberman, A. M. (1984). *Qualitative data analysis: A sourcebook of new methods.* Beverly Hills, CA: Sage.

Spradley, J. P. (1979). *The ethnographic interview.* New York: Holt, Rinehart, & Winston.

Spradley, J. P. (1980). *Participant observation.* New York: Holt, Rinehart, & Winston.

Stewart, D. W., & Shamdasani, P. N. (1990). *Focus groups: Theory and practice.* Newbury Park, CA: Sage.

Van Manen, M. (1990). *Researching lived experience: Human science for an action sensitive pedagogy.* Albany, NY: State University of New York Press.

General Assessment and Program Evaluation Methods

Cook, T. D., & Campbell, D. T. (1979). *Quasi-experimentation: Design and analysis issues for field settings.* Boston: Houghton-Mifflin.

Grotevant, H. D., & Carlson, C. I. (1989). *Family assessment: A guide to methods and measures.* New York: Guilford Press.

Kadzin, A. E. (1982). *Single-case research designs: Methods for clinical and applied settings.* New York: Oxford University Press.

Knoff, H. M. (Ed.). (1986). *The assessment of child and adolescent personality.* New York: Guilford Press.

Linney, J. A., & Wandersman, A. (1991). *Prevention Plus III: Assessing alcohol and other drug prevention programs at the school and community level.* (DHHS Publication No. ADM 91-1817). Washington, DC: U.S. Department of Health and Human Services.

Posavac, E. J., & Carey, R. G. (1985). *Program evaluation: Methods and case studies* (2nd ed.). Englewood Cliffs, NJ: Prentice-Hall.

Reynolds, C. R., & Kamphaus, R. W. (Eds.). (1990). *Handbook of psychological and educational assessment of children: Personality, behavior, and context.* New York: Guilford Press.

Sattler, J. (1988). *Assessment of children* (3rd ed.). San Diego, CA: Jerome M. Sattler.

Shapiro, E. S., & Kratochwill, T. R. (Eds.). (1988). *Behavioral assessment in schools: Conceptual foundations and practical applications.* New York: Guilford Press.

RESOURCE LISTS

Support Groups

Adult Children of Alcoholics
P. O. Box 3216
Torrance, CA 90510
(310) 534-1815; also check local telephone listings

Al-Anon/Alateen Family Groups
World Service Office
P. O. Box 862, Midtown Station
New York, NY 10018-0862
(212) 302-7240; (800) 356-9996;
    also check local telephone listings
Nationwide Group Meeting Information: (800) 344-2666 (USA);
    (800) 443-4525 (Canada)

Alcoholics Anonymous (AA)
AA World Services
475 Riverside Dr.
New York, NY 10027
(212) 870-3400; also check local
    telephone listings

Program Information and Materials: *Clearinghouses and Organizations*

Center for Substance Abuse Prevention (CSAP)
(formerly, Office of Substance Abuse
    Prevention [OSAP]; clearinghouse,
    National Clearinghouse for Alcohol
    and Drug Information [NCADI]
5600 Fishers Lane
Rockwall II Building
Rockville, MD 20857
(301) 443-0365

Children of Alcoholics Foundation,
    Inc.
P. O. Box 4185
Grand Central Station
New York, NY 10163
(212) 754-0656

National Association for Children of
    Alcoholics (NACOA)
11426 Rockville Pike, Suite 100
Rockvile, MD 20847
(301) 468-0985

National Association for Perinatal Addiction Research and Education
    (NAPARE)
(Information clearinghouse; conducts
    professional education seminars)
11 E. Hubbard St., Suite 200
Chicago, IL 60611
(312) 541-1272

National Clearinghouse for Alcohol
    and Drug Information (NCADI)
    (CSAP's clearinghouse)
P. O. Box 2345
Rockville, MD 20847
(301) 468-2600; (800) 729-6686

National Institute on Alcohol Abuse
    and Alcoholism (NIAAA)
5600 Fishers Lane, Room 16C-14
Rockville, MD 20857
(301) 443-3860

National Institute on Drug Abuse (NIDA)
Community and Professional Education Branch
5600 Fishers Lane, Room 10A-54
Rockville, MD 20857
(301) 443-6245

U. S. Department of Education Alcohol and Drug Abuse Education Program
Oversight Staff, Office of the Secretary
400 Maryland Avenue, SW
Room 1073, MS 6411
Washington, DC 20202
(202) 401-3030

References

Achenbach, T. M. (1991a). *Manual for the Youth Self-Report and 1991 profile*. Burlington, VT: University of Vermont, Department of Psychiatry.

Achenbach, T. M. (1991b). *Manual for the Child Behavior Checklist/4–18 and 1991 profile*. Burlington, VT: University of Vermont, Department of Psychiatry.

Achenbach, T. M. (1991c). *Manual for the Teacher's Report Form and 1991 profile*. Burlington, VT: University of Vermont, Department of Psychiatry.

Alexander, B. K. (1990). The empirical and theoretical bases for an adaptive model of addiction. *Journal of Drug Issues, 20*(1), 37–65.

American Psychiatric Association. (1982). *Diagnostic and statistical manual of mental disorders* (3rd ed.). Washington, D. C.: American Psychiatric Association.

American Psychiatric Association. (1987). *Diagnostic and statistical manual of mental disorders* (3rd, rev. ed.). Washington, DC: American Psychiatric Association.

American Psychological Association. (1992). Ethical principles of psychologists and code of conduct. *American Psychologist, 47*(12), 1597–1628.

American Psychological Association. (1993). Guidelines for providers of psychological services to ethnic, linguistic, and culturally diverse populations. *American Psychologist, 48*(1), 45–48.

Anthenelli, R. M., & Schuckit, M. A. (1990–91). Genetic studies of alcoholism. *International Journal of the Addictions, 25*(1A), 81–94.

Anthony, E. J., & Cohler, B. J. (Eds.). (1987). *The invulnerable child*. New York: Guilford Press.

Applebee, A. N. (1978). *The child's concept of story: Ages two to seventeen*. Chicago: University of Chicago Press.

Baer, P. E., McLaughlin, R. J., Burnside, M. A., & Pokorny, A. D. (1988). Alcohol use and psychosocial outcome of two preventive classroom programs with seventh and tenth graders. *Journal of Drug Education, 18*(3), 171–184.

Bakeman, R., & Gottman, J. M. (1986). *Observing interaction: An introduction to sequential analysis*. New York: Cambridge University Press.

Ballard, M., & Cummings, E. M. (1990). Response to adults' angry behavior in children of alcoholic and nonalcoholic parents. *Journal of Genetic Psychology*, *151*(2), 195–209.

Bandura, A. (1977). *Social learning theory*. Englewood Cliffs, NJ: Prentice-Hall.

Bandura, A. (1982). Self-efficacy mechanism in human agency. *American Psychologist*, *37*, 122–147.

Bandura, A. (1986). *Social foundations of thought and action: A social cognitive theory*. Englewood Cliffs, NJ: Prentice-Hall.

Bangert-Drowns, R. L. (1988). The effects of school-based substance abuse education—A meta-analysis. *Journal of Drug Education*, *18*(3), 243–265.

Barnard, C. P., & Spoentgen, P. A. (1986). Children of alcoholics: Characteristics and treatment. *Alcoholism Treatment Quarterly*, *3*(4), 47–64.

Bearison, D. J. (1982). New directions in studies of social interaction and cognitive growth. In F. C. Serafica (Ed.), *Social-cognitive development in context* (pp. 199–221). New York: Guilford Press.

Bearison, D. J., Magzamen, S., & Filardo, E. K. (1986). Socio–cognitive conflict and cognitive growth in young children. *Merrill-Palmer Quarterly*, *32*, 51–72.

Berger, P. L., & Luckman, T. (1966). *The social construction of reality: A treatise in the sociology of knowledge*. Garden City, New York: Doubleday.

Berkowitz, A., & Perkins, H. W. (1988). Personality characteristics of children of alcoholics. *Journal of Consulting and Clinical Psychology*, *56*(2), 206–209.

Bernard, M. E., & Joyce, M. R. (1984). *Rational-emotive therapy with children and adolescents: Theory, treatment strategies, preventative methods*. New York: Wiley.

Berndt, T. J. (1981). Effects of friendship on prosocial intentions and behavior. *Child Development*, *52*, 636–643.

Berndt, T. J., & Perry, T. B. (1986). Children's perceptions of friendships as supportive relationships. *Developmental Psychology*, *22*, 640–648.

Bettelheim, B. (1977). *The uses of enchantment: The meaning and importance of fairy tales*. New York: Vintage Books.

Black, C. (1981). *It will never happen to me!* Denver: M. A. C.

Bolton, R. (1979). *People skills*. New York: Simon & Schuster.

Botvin, G. J., Baker, E., Botvin, E. M., Filazzola, A. D., & Millman, R. B. (1984). Prevention of alcohol misuse through the development of personal and social competence: A pilot study. *Journal of Studies on Alcohol*, *45*(6), 550–552.

Botvin, G. J., Baker, E., Filazzola, A. D., & Botvin, E. M. (1990). A cognitive–behavioral approach to substance abuse prevention: One-year follow-up. *Addictive Behaviors*, *15*(1), 47–63.

Botvin, G. J., Baker, E., Renick, N. L., Filazzola, A. D., & Botvin, E. M. (1984). A cognitive–behavioral approach to substance abuse prevention. *Addictive Behaviors*, *9*, 137–147.

Botvin, G. J., & Wills, T. A. (1985). Personal and social skills training: Cognitive–behavioral approaches to substance abuse prevention. In C. S. Bell & R. Battjes (Eds.), *Prevention research: Deterring drug abuse among children and adolescents* (NIDA Research Monograph Series, No. 63; DHHS Publication No. ADM 85–1334, pp. 8–49). Rockville, MD: National Institute on Drug Abuse.

Brenner, A. (1984). *Helping children cope with stress*. Lexington, MA: Lexington Books.

Bronfenbrenner, U. (1989). Ecological systems theory. In R. Vasta (Ed.), *Annals of Child Development*, (Vol. 6, pp. 187–249). Greenwich, CT: JAI Press.

Brown, S. (1985). *Treating the alcoholic: A developmental model of recovery.* New York: Wiley

Brown, S. (1988). *Treating adult children of alcoholics: A developmental perspective.* New York: Wiley.

Bruner, J., & Haste, H. (Eds.). (1987). *Making sense: The child's construction of the world.* London: Methuen.

Calder, P., & Kostyniuk, A. (1989). Personality profiles of children of alcoholics. *Professional Psychology: Research and Practice, 20*(6), 417–418.

Camp, B. W., & Bash, M. A. S. (1985). *Think Aloud: Increasing social and cognitive skills—A problem-solving program for children.* Champaign, IL: Research Press.

Campione, J. C., & Brown, A. L. (1987). Linking dynamic assessment with school achievement. In C. S. Lidz (Ed.), *Dynamic assessment: An interactional approach to evaluating learning potential* (pp. 82–115). New York: Guilford Press.

Caplan, M., Weissberg, R. P., Grober, J. S., Sivo, P. J., Grady, K., & Jacoby, C. (1992). Social competence promotion with inner-city and suburban young adolescents: Effects on social adjustment and alcohol use. *Journal of Consulting and Clinical Psychology, 60*(1), 56–63.

Carnevale, L., & Rothenbuhler, C. (1982). *Cooperation–helping: A handbook of ideas to foster prosocial behavior in the classroom.* Kent, OH: Kent State University.

Caudill, B. D., Kantor, G. K., & Ungerleider, S. (1990). Project Impact: A national study of high school substance abuse intervention training. *Journal of Alcohol and Drug Education, 35*(2), 61–74.

Chipperfield, B., & Vogel-Sprott, M. (1988). Family history of problem drinking among young male social drinkers: Modeling effects on alcohol consumption. *Journal of Abnormal Psychology, 97*(4), 423–428.

Clair, D., & Genest, M. (1987). Variables associated with the adjustment of offspring of alcoholic fathers. *Journal of Studies on Alcohol, 48*(4), 345–355.

Clements, D. H. (1990). Metacomponential development in a Logo programming environment. *Journal of Educational Psychology, 82,* 141–149.

Clements, D. H., & Nastasi, B. K. (1988). Social and cognitive interactions in educational computer environments. *American Educational Research Journal, 25,* 87–106.

Clements, D. H., & Nastasi, B. K. (1990). Dynamic approach to measurement of children's metacomponential functioning. *Intelligence, 14,* 109–125.

Clements, D. H., & Nastasi, B. K. (1992). Computers and early childhood education. In M. Gettinger, S. N. Elliott, & T. R. Kratochwill (Ed.), *Preschool and early childhood treatment directions* (pp. 187–246). Hillsdale, NJ: Erlbaum.

Clements, D. H., & Nastasi, B. K. (1993). Electronic media and early childhood education. In B. Spodek (Ed.), *Handbook of research on the education of young children* (pp. 251–275). New York: Macmillan.

Colby, A., & Damon, W. (1992). *Some do care: Contemporary lives of moral commitment.* New York: Free Press.

Coles, C. D., & Platzman, K. A. (1992). Fetal alcohol effects in preschool children: Research, prevention, and intervention. In Office of Substance Abuse Prevention (Ed.), *Identifying the needs of drug-affected children: Public policy issues* (OSAP Prevention Monograph No. 11, DHHS Publication No. ADM 92–1814, pp. 59–86). Washington, DC: U. S. Department of Health and Human Services.

Copeland, A. P., & White, K. M. (1991). *Studying families*. Newbury Park, CA: Sage.

Cummins, J. (1986). Empowering minority students: A framework for intervention. *Harvard Educational Review, 56*(1), 18–36.

Damon, W. (1983). The nature of social–cognitive change in the developing child. In W. S. Overton (Ed.), *The relationship between social and cognitive development* (pp. 103–141). Hillsdale, NJ: Erlbaum.

Delapenha, L. (1992, Winter). New challenges for changing times. *School Safety*, pp. 11–13.

DeZolt, D. M. (1992). *Themes, age, and gender differences in children's stories about caring*. Unpublished dissertation, Kent State University, Kent, OH.

DeZolt, D. M., & Nastasi, B. K. (1991, February). Working with alcoholic families: Identification. *School Psychology in Illinois, 12*(4), 8–9.

DiCicco, L., Davis, R., & Orenstein, A. (1984). Identifying the children of alcoholic parents from survey responses. *Journal of Alcohol and Drug Education, 30*(1), 1–17.

Dielman, T. E., Shope, J. T., Butchart, A. T., & Campanelli, P. C. (1986). Prevention of adolescent alcohol misuse: An elementary school program. *Journal of Pediatric Psychology, 11*(2), 259–282.

Dinning, W. D., & Berk, L. A. (1989). The Children of Alcoholics Screening Test: Relationship to sex, family environment, and social adjustment in adolescents. *Journal of Clinical Psychology, 45*(2), 335–339.

Doise, W., & Mugny, G. (1979). Individual and collective conflicts of centrations in cognitive development. *European Journal of Social Psychology, 9*, 105–108.

Doise, W., & Mugny, G. (1984). *The social development of the intellect*. New York: Pergamon Press.

Donenberg, G. R., & Hoffman, L. W. (1988). Gender differences in moral development. *Sex Roles, 18*, 701–717.

Drake, R. E., & Vaillant, G. E. (1988). Predicting alcoholism and personality disorder in a 33–year longitudinal study of children of alcoholics. *British Journal of Addiction, 83*, 799–807.

Drew, N. (1987). *Learning the skills of peacemaking*. Rolling Hills Estates, CA: Jalmar Press.

Drugs and Drug Abuse Education Newsletter. (1990a, February). *XXI*(2).

Drugs and Drug Abuse Education Newsletter. (1990b, December). *XXI*(12).

Durlak, J. A. (1983). Social problem-solving as a primary prevention strategy. In R. D. Felner, L. A. Jason, J. N. Moritsugu, & S. S. Farber (Eds.), *Preventive psychology: Theory, research and practice* (pp. 31–48). New York: Pergamon Press.

Duryea, E. J. (1983). Utilizing tenets of inoculation theory to develop and evaluate a preventive alcohol education intervention. *Journal of School Health, 53*(4), 250–256.

Duryea, E. J. (1985). Student compliance in risky alcohol situations. *Journal of Alcohol and Drug Education, 30*(2), 44–50.

Duryea, E. J., Mohr, P., Newman, I. M., Martin, G. L., & Egwaoje, E. (1984). Six-month follow-up results of a preventive alcohol education intervention. *Drug Education, 14*(2), 97–104.

Duryea, E. J., & Okwumabua, J. O. (1988). Effects of a preventive alcohol education program after three years. *Journal of Drug Education, 18*(1), 23–31.

Dusenbury, L., Botvin, G. J., & James-Ortiz, S. (1990). The primary prevention of adolescent substance abuse through the promotion of personal and social competence. *Prevention in Human Services, 7*(1), 201–224.

Eisenberg, N., Cameron, E., Tryon, K., & Dodez, R. (1981). Socialization of prosocial behavior in the preschool classroom. *Developmental Psychology, 17,* 773–782.

Eisenberg, N., Miller, P. A., Shell, R., McNalley, S., & Shea, C. (1991). Prosocial development in adolescence: A longitudinal study. *Developmental Psychology, 27*(5), 849–857.

Eisenberg, N., Pasternack, J., Cameron, E., & Tryon, K. (1984). The relation of quantity and mode of prosocial behavior to moral cognitions and social style. *Child Development, 55,* 1479–1485.

Eisenberg, N., & Shell, R. (1986). Prosocial moral judgment and behavior in children: The mediating role of cost. *Personality and Social Psychology Bulletin, 12,* 426–433.

Eisenberg-Berg, N. (1979). Development of children's prosocial moral judgment. *Developmental Psychology, 15,* 128–137.

Eisenberg-Berg, N., & Hand, M. (1979). The relationship of preschoolers' reasoning about prosocial moral conflicts to prosocial behavior. *Child Development, 50,* 356–363.

Elias, M. J. (1987). Establishing enduring prevention programs: Advancing the legacy of Swampscott. *American Journal of Community Psychology, 15,* 539–553.

Elias, M. J., & Branden, L. R. (1988). Primary prevention of behavioral and emotional problems in school-aged populations. *School Psychology Review, 17,* 581–592.

Ellickson, P. L., & Bell, R. M. (1990). Drug prevention in junior high: A multi-site longitudinal test. *Science, 247,* 1299–1305.

Elliott, S. N., Witt, J. C., & Kratochwill, T. R. (1991). Selecting, implementing, and evaluating classroom interventions. In G. Stoner, M. R. Shinn, & H. M. Walker (Eds.), *Interventions for achievement and behavior problems* (pp. 99–136). Silver Spring, MD: National Association of School Psychologists.

Emihovich, C., & Miller, G. E. (1988). Talking to the turtle: A discourse analysis of Logo instruction. *Discourse Processes, 11,* 183–201.

Eron, L. (1986). Interventions to mitigate the psychological effects of media violence on behavior. *Journal of Social Issues, 42,* 155–169.

Felner, R. D., & Adan, A. M. (1988). The School Transitional Environment Project: An ecological intervention and evaluation. In R. H. Price, E. L. Cowen, R. P. Lorion, & J. Ramos-McKay (Eds.), *14 ounces of prevention: A casebook for practitioners* (pp. 111–122). Washington, DC: American Psychological Association.

Fisher, G. L., Jenkins, S. J., Harrison, T. C., & Jesch, K. (1992). Characteristics of adult children of alcoholics. *Journal of Substance Abuse, 4,* 27–34.

Forman, E. A., & Cazden, C. B. (1985). Exploring Vygotskian perspectives in education: The cognitive value of peer interaction. In J. V. Wertsch (Ed.), *Culture, communication, and cognition: Vygotskian perspectives* (pp. 323–347). New York: Cambridge University Press.

Friend, M., & Cook, L. (1992). *Interactions: Collaboration skills for school professionals.* New York: Longman.

Frisby, C. L. (1992). Issues and problems in the influence of culture on the psychoeducational needs of African-American children. *School Psychology Review*, *21*(4), 532–551.

Fry, P. S., & Addington, J. (1984). Comparison of social problem solving of children from open and traditional classrooms: A two-year longitudinal study. *Journal of Educational Psychology*, *76*(1), 318–329.

Garbarino, J., Dubrow, N., Kostelny, K., & Pardo, C. (1992). *Children in danger: Coping with the consequences of community violence.* San Francisco: Jossey-Bass.

Garrod, A., Beal, C., & Shin, P. (1990). The development of moral orientation in elementary school children. *Sex Roles*, *22*, 13–27.

Gersick, K. E., Grady, K., & Snow, D. L. (1988). Social–cognitive skill development with sixth graders and its initial impact on substance use. *Journal of Drug Education*, *18*(1), 55–70.

Gesten, E. L., & Weissberg, R. P. (1986). Social problem-solving training with children: A guide to effective practice. *Special Services in the Schools*, *2*(4), 19–38.

Gilchrist, L. D., Schinke, S. P., Trimble, J. E., & Cvetkovich, G. T. (1987). Skills enhancement to prevent substance abuse among American Indian adolescents. *International Journal of the Addictions*, *22*(9), 869–879.

Gilligan, C. (1982). *In a different voice: Psychological theory and women's development.* Cambridge, MA: Harvard University Press.

Giroux, H. A. (1988). Literacy and the pedagogy of voice and political empowerment. *Educational Theory*, *38*(1), 61–75.

Goldstein, A. P. (1988). *The Prepare Curriculum: Teaching prosocial competencies.* Champaign, IL: Research Press.

Goldstein, A. P., Reagles, K. W., & Amann, L. L. (1990). *Refusal skills: Preventing drug use in adolescents.* Champaign, IL: Research Press.

Goode, E. (1992). *Drugs in American society* (4th ed.). New York: McGraw-Hill.

Goodwin, D. W. (1988). *Is alcoholism hereditary?* New York: Ballantine Books.

Gordon, C. J., & Macinnis, D. (1993). Using journals as a window on students' thinking in mathematics. *Language Arts*, *70*(1), 37–43.

Graman, T. (1988). Education for humanization: Applying Paulo Freire's pedagogy to learning a second language. *Harvard Educational Review*, *58*(4), 433–448.

Graves, N. B., & Graves, T. D. (1985). Creating a cooperative learning environment: An ecological approach. In R. Slavin, S. Sharan, S. Kagan, R. H. Lazarowitz, C. Webb, & R. Schmuck (Eds.), *Learning to cooperate, cooperating to learn* (pp. 403–436). New York: Plenum Press.

Gresham, F. M. (1989). Assessment of treatment integrity in school consultation and prereferral intervention. *School Psychology Review*, *18*(1), 37–50.

Gresham, F. M., & Elliott, S. N. (1990). *Social Skills Rating System Manual.* Circle Pines, MN: American Guidance System.

Griffith, D. R. (1992). Prenatal exposure to cocaine and other drugs: Developmental and educational prognoses. *Phi Delta Kappan*, *74*(1), 30–34.

Gross, J., & McCaul, M. E. (1990–91). A comparison of drug use and adjustment in urban adolescent children of substance abusers. *International Journal of the Addictions*, *25*(4A), 495–511.

Grotevant, H. D., & Carlson, C. I. (1989). *Family assessment: A guide to methods and measures.* New York: Guilford Press.

Gumaer, J. (1984). *Counseling and therapy for children*. New York: Free Press.

Hansen, W. B., Graham, J. W., Wolkenstein, B. H., Lundy, B. Z., Pearson, J., Flay, B. R., & Johnson, C. A. (1988). Differential impact of three alcohol prevention curricula on hypothesized mediating variables. *Journal of Drug Education, 18*(2), 143–153.

Hansen, W. B., Johnson, C. A., Flay, B. R., Graham, J. W., & Sobel, J. (1988). Affective and social influences approaches to the prevention of multiple substance abuse among seventh grade students: Results from Project SMART. *Preventive Medicine, 17*, 135–154.

Hansen, W. B., Malotte, C. K., & Fielding, J. E. (1988). Evaluation of a tobacco and alcohol abuse prevention curriculum for adolescents. *Health Education Quarterly, 15*(1), 93–114.

Harford, T. C. (1992). Family history of alcoholism in the United States: Prevalence and demographic characteristics. *British Journal of Addiction, 87*, 931–935.

Hart, S. (1989). Review of the Children of Alcoholics Screening Test. In J. C. Conoley & J. J. Kramer (Eds.), *The Tenth Mental Measurements Yearbook* (pp. 157–158). Lincoln, NE: Buros Institute of Mental Measurements.

Harter, S. (1978). Effectance motivation reconsidered: Toward a developmental model. *Human Development, 21*, 34–64.

Harter, S. (1980). *A Scale of Intrinsic versus Extrinsic Orientation in the Classroom: Manual*. Denver: University of Denver.

Harter, S. (1982). The perceived competence scale for children. *Child Development, 53*, 87–97.

Harter, S. (1985a). *Manual for the Self-Perception Profile for Children*. Denver: University of Denver.

Harter, S. (1985b). *Manual for the Social Support Scale for Children*. Denver: University of Denver.

Harter, S. (1987). The determinants and mediational role of global self-worth in children. In N. Eisenberg (Ed.), *Contemporary topics in developmental psychology* (pp. 219–242). New York: Wiley.

Harter, S. (1988). *Manual for the Self-Perception Profile for Adolescents*. Denver: University of Denver.

Harter, S. (1990a). Causes, correlates, and the functional role of global self-worth: A life-span perspective. In R. J. Sternberg & J. Kolligan (Eds.), *Competence considered* (pp. 67–97). New Haven, CT: Yale University Press.

Harter, S. (1990b). Processes underlying adolescent self-concept formation. In R. Montemayor, G. R. Adams, & T. P. Gullotta (Eds.), *From childhood to adolescence: A transitional period?* (pp. 205–239). Newbury Park, CA: Sage.

Harter, S. (1990c). Self and identity development. In S. S. Feldman & G. R. Elliott (Eds.), *At the threshold: The developing adolescent* (pp. 352–387). Cambridge, MA: Harvard University Press.

Harter, S., & Marold, D. B. (1991). A model of determinants and mediational role of self-worth: Implications for adolescent depression and suicidal ideation. In J. Strauss & G. R. Goethals (Eds.), *The self: Interdisciplinary approaches* (pp. 66–92). New York: Springer-Verlag.

Harter, S., & Pike, R. (1984a). The pictorial scale of perceived competence and social acceptance for young children. *Child Development, 55*, 1962–1982.

Harter, S., & Pike, R. (1984b). *Procedural manual to accompany the Pictorial Scale of Perceived Competence and Social Acceptance for Young Children.* Denver: University of Denver.

Harter, S., Whitesell, N. R., & Kowalski, P. (1992). Individual differences in the effects of educational transitions on young adolescents' perceptions of competence and motivational orientation. *American Educational Research Journal, 29*(4), 777–808.

Hawkins, J. D., Catalano, R. F., & Miller, J. Y. (1992). Risk and protective factors for alcohol and other drug problems in adolescence and early adulthood: Implications for substance abuse prevention. *Psychological Bulletin, 112*(1), 64–105.

Helm, V. M. (1986). *What educators should know about copyright.* Bloomington, IN: Phi Delta Kappa Educational Foundation.

Hipple, M. L. (1985). Journal writing in kindergarten. *Language Arts, 62*(3), 255–261.

Hoffman, M. L. (1982). Development of prosocial motivation: Empathy and guilt. In N. Eisenberg (Ed.), *The development of prosocial behavior* (pp. 281–313). New York: Academic Press.

Horgan, C., Rosenbach, M., Ostby, E., & Butrica, B. (1991). Targeting special populations with drug abuse problems: Pregnant women. *NIDA Drug Abuse Services Research Series, 1,* 123–144.

Howard, G. S. (1991). Culture tales: A narrative approach to thinking, cross-cultural psychology, and psychotherapy. *American Psychologist, 46*(3), 187–197.

Huesmann, L. R. (1986). Psychological processes promoting the relation between exposure to media violence and aggressive behavior by the viewer. *Journal of Social Issues, 42,* 125–139.

Huesmann, L. R., & Malamuth, N. M. (1986). Media violence and antisocial behavior: An overview. *Journal of Social Issues, 42,* 1–6.

Jackson, J. K. (1954). The adjustment of the family to the crisis of alcoholism. *Quarterly Journal of Studies on Alcohol, 15,* 562–586.

Jarmas, A. L., & Kazak, A. E. (1992). Young adult children of alcoholic fathers: Depressive experiences, coping styles, and family systems. *Journal of Consulting and Clinical Psychology, 60*(2), 244–251.

Jellinek, E. M. (1960). *The disease concept of alcoholism.* New Haven, CT: United Printing Services.

Johnson, D. J., & Cole, C. K. (1992, Winter) Extraordinary care for extraordinary children. *School Safety,* pp. 7–9.

Johnson, D. W. (1981). Constructive peer relationships, social development, and cooperative learning experiences: Implications for the prevention of drug abuse. In S. Eiseman, J. A. Wingard, & G. J. Huba (Eds.), *Drug abuse: Foundation for a psychosocial approach* (pp. 24–41). Farmingdale, New York: Baywood.

Johnson, D. W., & Johnson, R. (1987). *Creative conflict.* Edina, MN: Interaction Book.

Johnson, D. W., & Johnson, R. (1989). *Cooperation and competition: Theory and research.* Edina, MN: Interaction Book.

Johnson, D. W., Johnson, R., Dudley, B., & Acikgoz, K. (1991). *Peer mediation: Effects of conflict resolution training on elementary school students.* Minneapolis: Cooperative Learning Center.

Johnson, D. W., & Johnson, R. T. (1983). The socialization and achievement crisis: Are cooperative learning experiences the solution? *Applied Social Psychology Annual, 4,* 119–164.

Johnson, D. W., & Johnson, R. T. (1985). Classroom conflict: controversy versus debate in learning groups. *American Educational Research Journal, 22,* 237–256.

Johnson, D. W., Johnson, R. T., & Dudley, B. (1991). *Effects of peer mediation on elementary school students.* Minneapolis: Cooperative Learning Center.

Johnson, D. W., Johnson, R. T., Dudley, B., & Burnett, R. (1991). *Peer mediation of student conflicts: A self-discipline school program.* Minneapolis: Cooperative Learning Center.

Johnson, D. W., Johnson, R. T., & Maruyama, G. (1983). Interdependence and interpersonal attraction among heterogeneous and homogeneous individuals: A theoretical formulation and meta-analysis of the research. *Review of Educational Research, 53,* 5–54.

Johnson, D. W., Johnson, R. T., Pierson, W. T., & Lyons, V. (1985). Controversy versus concurrence seeking in multi-grade and single-grade learning groups. *Journal of Research in Science Teaching, 22,* 835–848.

Johnson, D. W., Johnson, R. T., Roy, P., & Zaidman, B. (1985). Oral interaction in cooperative learning groups: Speaking, listening, and the nature of statements made by high-, medium-, and low-achieving students. *Journal of Psychology, 119,* 303–321.

Johnson, D. W., Johnson, R. T., & Scott, L. (1978). The effects of cooperative and individualized instruction on student attitudes and achievement. *Journal of Social Psychology, 104,* 207–216.

Johnson, D. W., Maruyama, G., Johnson, R. T., Nelson, D., & Skon, L. (1981). Effects of cooperative, competitive, and individualistic goal structures on achievement: A meta-analysis. *Psychological Bulletin, 89,* 47–62.

Johnson, J. L., Boney, T. Y., & Brown, B. S. (1990–91). Evidence of depressive symptoms in children of substance abusers. *International Journal of the Addictions, 25*(4A), 465–479.

Johnson, J. L., & Rolf, J. E. (1988). Cognitive functioning in children from alcoholic and nonalcoholic families. *British Journal of Addiction, 83,* 849–857.

Johnson, R. T., Brooker, C., Stutzman, J., Hultman, D., & Johnson, D. W. (1985). The effects of controversy, concurrence seeking, and individualistic learning on achievement and attitude change. *Journal of Research in Science Teaching, 22,* 197–205.

Johnson, R. T., Johnson, D. W., & Stanne, M. B. (1985). Effects of cooperative, competitive, and individualistic goal structures on computer-assisted instruction. *Journal of Educational Psychology, 77,* 668–677.

Johnson, V. E. (1980). *I'll quit tomorrow* (rev. ed.). San Francisco: Harper & Row.

Johnston, D. K. (1988). Adolescents' solutions to dilemmas in fables: Two moral orientations—two problem solving strategies. In C. C. Gilligan, J. V. Ward, J. M. Taylor, & B. Bardige (Eds.), *Mapping the moral domain* (pp. 49–71). Cambridge, MA: Harvard University Press.

Jones, D. C., & Houts, R. (1992). Parental drinking, parent–child communication, and social skills in young adults. *Journal of Studies on Alcohol, 53*(1), 48–56.

Jones, J. W. (1981). *The Children of Alcoholics Screening Test (CAST).* Chicago: Family Recovery Press.

Kehle, T. J., & Gonzales, F. (1991). Self-modeling for children's emotional and social concerns. In P. W. Dowrick (Ed.), *Practical guide to using video in the behavioral sciences* (pp. 244–255). New York: Wiley.

Kehle, T. J., & Nastasi, B. K. (1993, April). *Things to avoid when implementing intervention programs in school systems.* Paper presented at the meeting of the National Association of School Psychologists, Washington, DC.

Kim, S. (1988). A short- and long-term evaluation of *Here's Looking at You* alcohol education program. *Journal of Drug Education, 18*(3), 235–242.

Kinney, J., & Leaton, G. (1987). *Loosening the grip: A handbook of alcohol information.* St. Louis, MO: Mosby.

Knoblauch, D. L., & Bowers, N. D. (1989). A therapeutic conceptualization of adult children of alcoholics. *Journal of College Student Psychotherapy, 4*(1), 37–52.

Knoff, H. M. (Ed.). (1986). *The assessment of child and adolescent personality.* New York: Guilford Press.

Kreidler, W. J. (1984). *Creative conflict resolution.* Glenview, IL: Scott, Foresman.

Ladd, G. W., Lange, G., & Stremmel, A. (1983). Personal and situational influences on children's helping behavior: Factors that mediate compliant helping. *Child Development, 54*, 488–501.

Lazarus, R. S., & Folkman, S. (1984). *Stress, appraisal, and coping.* New York: Springer.

Lecca, P. J., & Watts, T. D. (1993). *Preschoolers and substance abuse: Strategies for prevention and intervention.* New York: Haworth Press.

Lindow, J. A., Wilkinson, L. C., & Peterson, P. L. (1985). Antecedents and consequences of verbal disagreements during small-group learning. *Journal of Educational Psychology, 77*, 658–667.

Lochman, J. E. (1992). Cognitive–behavioral intervention with aggressive boys: Three-year follow-up and preventive effects. *Journal of Consulting and Clinical Psychology, 60*(3), 426–432.

Lofland, J., & Lofland, L. H. (1984). *Analyzing social settings: A guide to qualitative observation and analysis.* Belmont, CA: Wadsworth.

Manning, D. T., Balson, P. M., & Xenakis, S. (1986). The prevalence of Type A personality in the children of alcoholics. *Alcoholism: Clinical and Experimental Research, 10*(2), 184–189.

Marton, J. P., & Acker, L. E. (1981). Television provoked aggression: Effects of gentle, affection-like training prior to exposure. *Child Study Journal, 12*, 27–43.

McGinnis, E., & Goldstein, A. P. (1990). *Skillstreaming in early childhood: Teaching prosocial skills to the preschool and kindergarten child.* Champaign, IL: Research Press.

Messer, B., & Harter, S. (1986). *The adult self-perception profile.* Unpublished manuscript, University of Denver, CO.

Midlarsky, E., & Hannah, M. E. (1985). Competence, reticence, and helping by children and adolescents. *Developmental Psychology, 21*, 534–541.

Morse, R. M., & Falvin, D. K. (1992). The definition of alcoholism. *Journal of the American Medical Association, 268*(2), 1012–1014.

Moss, P. A. (1992). Shifting conceptions of validity in educational measurement:

Implications for performance assessment. *Review of Educational Research,* *62*(3), 229–258.

Nastasi, B. K. (1985). *Coping for kids: A preventive intervention program for kindergarten-aged children.* Kent OH: Kent State University.

Nastasi, B. K. (1993). [Ethnographic study of collaborative interactions in an interactive video mathematics educational environment]. Unpublished raw data.

Nastasi, B. K., Bingham, A., & Clements, D. H. (1993, April). *Study of social processes in cooperative learning environments: The qualitative–quantitative mix.* Paper presented at the meeting of the American Educational Research Association, Atlanta, GA.

Nastasi, B. K., & Clements, D. H. (1991). Research on cooperative learning: Implications for practice. *School Psychology Review, 20,* 110–131.

Nastasi, B. K., & Clements, D. H. (1992). Social–cognitive behaviors and higher-order thinking in educational computer environments. *Learning and Instruction, 2,* 215–238.

Nastasi, B. K., & Clements, D. H. (1993). Motivational and social outcomes of cooperative computer education environments. *Journal of Computing in Childhood Education, 4*(1), 15–43.

Nastasi, B. K., & Clements, D. H. (in press). Effectance motivation, perceived scholastic competence, and higher-order thinking in two cooperative computer environments. *Journal of Educational Computing Research.*

Nastasi, B. K., Clements, D. H., & Battista, M. T. (1990). Social–cognitive interactions, motivation, and cognitive growth in Logo programming and CAI problem-solving environments. *Journal of Educational Psychology, 82,* 150–158.

Nastasi, B. K., & DeZolt, D. M. (1991, March). Curriculum-based interventions for children of alcoholics. *Communiqué, 19*(6), 12–13.

National Association of School Psychologists. (1992). *Professional conduct manual.* Silver Spring, MD: National Association of School Psychologists.

National Education Goals Panel. (1992). *The national education goals report: Building a nation of learners.* Washington, DC: U.S. Government Printing Office.

National Institute on Alcohol Abuse and Alcoholism. (1987). *Sixth special report to the U. S. Congress on alcohol and health.* (DHHS Publication No. ADM 87–1519). Washington, DC: U.S. Government Printing Office.

National Institute on Alcohol Abuse and Alcoholism. (1990a, April). Screening for alcoholism. *Alcohol Alert,* pp. 1–4.

National Institute on Alcohol Abuse and Alcoholism. (1990b, July). Children of alcoholics: Are they different? *Alcohol Alert,* pp. 1–4.

National Institute on Alcohol Abuse and Alcoholism. (1991a, July). Fetal Alcohol Syndrome. *Alcohol Alert,* pp. 1–4.

National Institute on Alcohol Abuse and Alcoholism. (1991b, October). Alcoholism and co-occurring disorders. *Alcohol Alert,* pp. 1–4.

Neemann, J., & Harter, S. (1986). *Manual for the Self-Perception Profile for College Students.* Denver: University of Denver.

Nelson-Le Gall, S. (1992). Children's instrumental help-seeking: Its role in the social acquisition and construction of knowledge. In R. Hertz-Lazarowitz & N.

Miller (Eds.), *Interaction in cooperative groups: The theoretical anatomy of group learning* (pp. 49–70). Cambridge, England: Cambridge University Press.

Newman, I. M., Anderson, C. S., & Farrell, K. A. (1992). Role rehearsal and efficacy: Two 15–month evaluations of a ninth-grade alcohol education program. *Journal of Drug Education*, 22(1), 55–67.

Noddings, N. (1984). *Caring*. Berkeley, CA: University of California Press.

Oden, S. (1986). Developing social skills instruction for peer interaction and relationships. In G. Cartledge & J. F. Milburn (Eds.), *Teaching social skills to children: Innovative approaches* (2nd ed., pp. 246–269). New York: Pergamon Press.

Office of Substance Abuse Prevention. (1992). *Identifying the needs of drug-affected children: Public policy issues* (OSAP Prevention Monograph No. 11, DHHS Publication No. ADM 92–1814). U. S. Department of Health and Human Services.

Parker, G. R., Cowen, E. L., Work, W. C., & Wyman, P. A. (1990). Test correlates of stress resilience among urban school children. *Journal of Primary Prevention*, 11(1), 19–35.

Parsons, R. D., & Meyers, J. (1984). *Developing consultation skills*. San Francisco: Jossey-Bass.

Pease, B. B., & Hurlbert, D. F. (1988). A comparative study of the attitudes of alcoholic veterans and nonalcoholic veterans toward child rearing practices and family life. *Journal of Drug Education*, 18(2), 125–134.

Pellegrini, D. S., & Urbain, E. S. (1985). An evaluation of interpersonal cognitive problem solving with children. *Journal of Child Psychology and Psychiatry*, 26(1), 17–41.

Pentz, M. A. (1985). Social competence and self-efficacy as determinants of substance abuse in adolescence. In S. Shiffman & T. A. Wills (Eds.), *Coping and substance use* (pp. 117–142). Orlando, FL: Academic Press.

Perkins, H. W., & Berkowitz, A. D. (1991). Collegiate COAs and alcohol abuse: Problem drinking in relation to assessments of parent and grandparent alcoholism. *Journal of Counseling and Development*, 69, 237–240.

Perlmutter, M., Behrend, S., Kuo, F., & Muller, A. (1986). *Social influence on children's problem solving at a computer*. Unpublished manuscript, University of Michigan, Ann Arbor.

Peterson, L. (1983). The role of donor competence, donor age, and peer presence on helping in an emergency. *Developmental Psychology*, 21, 534–541.

Peterson, P. L., Wilkinson, L. C., Spinelli, F., & Swing, S. R. (1984). Merging the process-product and the sociolinguistic paradigms: Research on small-group processes. In P. L. Peterson, L. C. Wilkinson, & M. Hallihan (Eds.), *The social context of instruction* (pp. 126–152). Orlando, FL: Academic Press.

Phelps, L., & Grabowski, J. A. (1992). Fetal Alcohol Syndrome: Diagnostic features and psychoeducational risk factors. *School Psychology Quarterly*, 7(2), 112–128.

Pokay, P., & Blumenfeld, P. C. (1990). Predicting achievement early and late in the semester: The role of motivation and use of learning strategies. *Journal of Educational Psychology*, 82(1), 41–50.

President's Commission on Mental Health. (1978). *Report to the President from the President's Commission on Mental Health*. Washington, DC: U.S. Government Printing Office.

Radke-Yarrow, M., Zahn-Waxler, C., & Chapman, M. (1983). Children's prosocial dispositions and behavior. In P. H. Mussen & E. M. Hetherington (Eds.), *Handbook of child psychology: Socialization, personality, and social development* (pp. 469–545). New York: Wiley.

Rappaport, J. (1987). Terms of empowerment/exemplars of prevention: Toward a theory for community psychology. *American Journal of Community Psychology, 15*(2), 121–144.

Reich, W., Earls, F., & Powell, J. (1988). A comparison of the home and social environments of children of alcoholic and non-alcoholic parents. *British Journal of Addiction, 83,* 831–839.

Reynolds, C. R., & Kamphaus, R. W. (Eds.). (1990). *Handbook of psychological and educational assessment of children: Personality, behavior, and context.* New York: Guilford Press.

Reynolds, C. R., & Kamphaus, R. W. (1992). *Behavior Assessment System for Children (BASC) Manual.* Circle Pines, MN: American Guidance Service.

Rhodes, J. E., & Jason, L. A. (1988). *Preventing substance abuse among children and adolescents.* New York: Pergamon Press.

Riel, M. (1985). The Computer Chronicles Newswire: A functional learning environment for acquiring literacy skills. *Journal of Educational Computing Research, 1,* 317–337.

Robinson, B. E. (1989). *Working with children of alcoholics: The practitioner's handbook.* Lexington, MA: Lexington Books.

Rogoff, B. (1990). *Apprenticeship in thinking: Cognitive development in social context.* New York: Oxford University Press.

Room, R. (1992). The impossible dream? Routes to reducing alcohol problems in a temperance culture. *Journal of Substance Abuse, 4,* 91–106.

Roosa, M. W., Beals, J., Sandler, I. N., & Pillow, D. R. (1990). The role of risk and protective factors in predicting symptomatology in adolescent self-identified children of alcoholic parents. *American Journal of Community Psychology, 18*(5), 725–741.

Roosa, M. W., Gensheimer, L. K., Ayers, T. S., & Short, J. L. (1990). Development of a school-based prevention program for children in alcoholic families. *Journal of Primary Prevention, 11*(2), 119–141.

Roosa, M. W., Gensheimer, L. K., Short, J. L., Ayers, T. S., & Shell, R. (1989). A preventive intervention for children in alcoholic families: Results of a pilot study. *Family Relations, 38,* 295–300.

Roosa, M. W., Sandler, I. N., Beals, J., & Short, J. L. (1988). Risk status of adolescent children of problem-drinking parents. *American Journal of Community Psychology, 16*(2), 225–239.

Roosa, M. W., Sandler, I. N., Gehring, M., Beals, J., & Cappo, L. (1988). The Children of Alcoholics Life-Events Schedule: A stress scale for children of alcohol-abusing parents. *Journal of Studies on Alcohol, 49*(5), 422–429.

Rotheram-Borus, M. J. (1988). Assertiveness training with children. In R. H. Price, E. L. Cowen, R. P. Lorion, & J. Ramos-McKay (Eds.), *14 ounces of prevention: A casebook for practitioners* (pp. 83–97). Washington, DC: American Psychological Association.

Rutter, M. (1979). Protective factors in children's responses to stress and disadvantage. In M. W. Kent & J. E. Rolf (Eds.), *Primary prevention of psychopathol-*

ogy. Volume III: Social competence in children (pp. 49–74). Hanover, NH: University Press of New England.

Rychtarik, R. G., Fairbank, J. A., Allen, C. M., Foy, D. W., & Drabman, R. S. (1983). Alcohol use in television programming: Effects on children's behavior. *Addictive Behaviors, 8,* 19–22.

Sanjek, R. (Ed.). (1990). *Fieldnotes: The making of anthropology.* Ithaca, New York: Cornell University Press.

Sarvela, P. D., Pope, D. J., Odylana, J., & Bajracharya, S. M. (1990). Drinking, drug use, and driving among rural Midwestern youth. *Journal of School Health, 60,* 215–219.

Schank, R. C. (1990). *Tell me a story: A new look at real and artificial memory.* New York: Charles Scribner.

Schinke, S. P. (1989). Review of the Children of Alcoholics Screening Test. In J. C. Conoley & J. J. Kramer (Eds.), *The Tenth Mental Measurements Yearbook* (pp. 158–159). Lincoln, NE: Buros Institute of Mental Measurements.

Schinke, S. P., Botvin, G. J., Trimble, J. E., Orlandi, M. A., Gilchrist, L. D., & Locklear, V. S. (1988). Preventing substance abuse among American-Indian adolescents: A bicultural competence skills approach. *Journal of Counseling Psychology, 35*(1), 87–90.

Schinke, S. P., Botvin, G. J., & Orlandi, M. A. (1991). *Substance abuse in children and adolescents: Evaluation and intervention.* Newbury Park, CA: Sage.

Schunk, D. H. (1983). Developing children's self-efficacy and skills: The roles of social comparative information and goal setting. *Contemporary Educational Psychology, 8,* 76–86.

Schunk, D. H. (1989a). Self-efficacy and achievement behaviors. *Educational Psychology Review, 1*(3), 173–208.

Schunk, D. H. (1989b). Social cognitive theory and self-regulated learning. In B. J. Zimmerman & D. H. Schunk (Eds.), *Self-regulated learning and academic achievement: Theory, research, and practice* (pp. 83–110). New York: Springer-Verlag.

Schunk, D. H. (1990a). Goal setting and self-efficacy during self-regulated learning. *Educational Psychologist, 25*(1), 71–86.

Schunk, D. H. (1990b). Self-concept and school achievement. In C. Rogers & P. Kutnick (Eds.), *The social psychology of the primary school* (pp. 70–91). London: Rutledge.

Schunk, D. H. (1991). Goal setting and self-evaluation: A social–cognitive perspective on self-regulation. In M. L. Maehr & P. R. Pintrich (Eds.), *Advances in motivation and achievement* (pp. 85–113). Greenwich, CT: JAI Press.

Schunk, D. H., & Rice, M. J. (1991). Learning goals and progress feedback during reading comprehension instruction. *Journal of Reading Behavior, 23*(3), 351–364.

Selzer, M. L. (1971). The Michigan Alcoholism Screening Test: The quest for a new diagnostic instrument. *American Journal of Psychiatry, 127,* 1653–1658.

Selzer, M. L., Vinokur, A., & Van Rooijen, L. (1975). A self-administered Short Michigan Alcoholism Screening Test (SMAST). *Journal of Studies on Alcohol, 36,* 117–126.

Severson, H., & Zoref, L. (1991). Prevention and early interventions for addictive behaviors: Health promotion in the schools. In G. Stoner, M. R. Shinn,

& H. M. Walker (Eds.), *Interventions for achievement and behavior problems* (pp. 539–557). Silver Spring, MD: National Association of School Psychologists.

Shapiro, E. S. (1989). *Academic skills problems: Direct assessment and intervention.* New York: Guilford Press.

Shapiro, E. S., & Kratochwill, T. R. (Eds.). (1988). *Behavioral assessment in schools.* New York: Guilford Press.

Shepherd, T. R., & Koberstein, J. (1989). Books, puppetry, and sharing: Teaching preschool children to share. *Psychology in the Schools, 26,* 311–316.

Sher, K. J., & Descutner, C. (1986). Reports of parental alcoholism: Reliability across siblings. *Addictive Behaviors, 11,* 25–30.

Shinn, M. R. (Ed.). (1989). *Curriculum-based measurement: Assessing special children.* New York: Guilford Press.

Shrumpf, F., Crawford, D., & Usadel, H. C. (1991). *Peer mediation: Conflict resolution in the schools.* Champaign, IL: Research Press.

Shure, M. B. (1992). *I Can Problem Solve: An interpersonal cognitive problem-solving program.* Champaign, IL: Research Press.

Shure, M. B., & Spivack, G. (1988). Interpersonal cognitive problem solving. In R. H. Price, E. L. Cowen, R. P. Lorion, & J. Ramos-McKay (Eds.), *14 ounces of prevention: A casebook for practitioners* (pp. 69–82). Washington, DC: American Psychological Association.

Skinner, E. A., Wellborn, J. G., & Connell, J. P. (1990). What it takes to do well in school and whether I've got it: A process model of perceived control and children's engagement and achievement in school. *Journal of Educational Psychology, 82*(1), 22–31.

Slavin, R. E. (1980). Cooperative learning. *Review of Educational Research, 50,* 315–342.

Slavin, R. E. (1986). Cooperative learning: Engineering social psychology in the classroom. In R. S. Feldman (Ed.), *The social psychology of education: Current research and theory* (pp. 153–171). Cambridge, England: Cambridge University Press.

Slavin, R. E., Sharan, S., Kagan, S., Lazarowitz, R. H., Webb, C., & Schmuck, R. (Eds.). (1985). *Learning to cooperate, cooperating to learn.* New York: Plenum Press.

Slavkin, S. L., Heimberg, R. G., Winning, C. D., & McCaffrey, R. J. (1992). Personal and parental problem drinking: Effects on problem-solving performance and self-appraisal. *Addictive Behaviors, 17,* 191–199.

Smith, C. A. (1982). *Promoting the social development of young children.* Palo Alto, CA: Mayfield.

Smith, K. A., Peterson, R. P., Johnson, D. W., & Johnson, R. T. (1986). The effects of controversy and concurrence seeking on effective decision making. *Journal of Social Psychology, 126,* 237–248.

Snow, D. L., Tebes, J. K., Arthur, M. W., & Tapasak, R. C. (1992). Two-year follow-up of a social–cognitive intervention to prevent substance use. *Journal of Drug Education, 22*(2), 101–114.

Solomon, D., Watson, M. S., Delucchi, K. L., Schaps, E., & Battistich, V. (1988). Enhancing children's prosocial behavior in the classroom. *American Educational Research Journal, 25*(4), 527–554.

Spivack, G., Platt, J., & Shure, M. (1976). *The problem-solving approach to adjustment.* San Francisco: Jossey-Bass.

Spivack, G., & Shure, M. (1974). *Social adjustment of young children: A cognitive approach to solving real-life problems.* San Francisco: Jossey-Bass.

Spradley, J. P. (1979). *The ethnographic interview.* New York: Holt, Rinehart, & Winston.

Spradley, J. P. (1980). *Participant observation.* New York: Holt, Rinehart, & Winston.

Steinglass, P., Bennett, L. A., Wolin, S. J., & Reiss, D. (1987). *The alcoholic family.* New York: Basic Books.

Stern, R., Kendall, A., & Eberhard, P. (1991). Children of alcoholics in the schools: Where are they? Their representations in special education. *Psychology in the Schools, 28,* 116–123.

Stewart, D. W., & Shamdasani, P. N. (1990). *Focus groups: Theory and practice.* Newbury Park, CA: Sage.

Strayhorn, J. M. (1988). *The competent child: An approach to psychotherapy and preventive mental health.* New York: Guilford Press.

Streissguth, A. P., Aase, J. M., Clarren, S. K., Randels, S. P., LaDue, R. A., & Smith, D. F. (1991). Fetal Alcohol Syndrome in adolescents and adults. *Journal of the American Medical Association, 265*(15), 1961–1967.

Streissguth, A. P., Sampson, P. D., & Barr, H. M. (1989). Neurobehavioral dose-response effects of prenatal alcohol exposure in humans from infancy to adulthood. *Annals of the New York Academy of Sciences, 562,* 145–158.

Tappan, M. B., & Brown, L. M. (1989). Stories told and lessons learned: Toward a narrative approach to moral development and moral education. *Harvard Educational Review, 59,* 182–205.

Tetenbaum, T. J., & Pearson, J. (1989). The voices in children's literature: The impact of gender on the moral decisions of storybook characters. *Sex Roles, 20*(7/8), 381–395.

Tobler, N. S. (1986). Meta-analysis of 143 adolescent drug prevention programs: Quantitative outcome results of program participants compared to a control or comparison group. *Journal of Drug Issues, 16*(4), 537–567.

Tucker, N. (1981). *The child and the book: A psychological and literary exploration.* Cambridge, England: Cambridge University Press.

Urbain, E. S. (1982). *Friendship group manual for social skills development (elementary grades).* Available from Eugene S. Urbain, Wilder Child Guidance Center, 919 Lafond Ave., St. Paul, MN 55104.

Van Evra, J. (1990). *Television and child development.* Hillsdale, NJ: Erlbaum.

Vandergrift, K. E. (1980). *Child and story: The literary connection.* New York: Neal-Schuman.

Velleman, R. (1992). Intergenerational effects—A review of environmentally oriented studies concerning the relationship between parental alcohol problems and family disharmony in the genesis of alcohol and other problems. II: The intergenerational effects of family disharmony. *International Journal of the Addictions, 27*(4), 367–389.

Vygotsky, L. S. (1978). *Mind in society: The development of higher psychological processes.* Cambridge, MA: Harvard University Press.

Walters, G. D. (1992). Drug-seeking behavior: Disease or lifestyle? *Professional Psychology: Research and Practice, 23*(2), 139–145.

Webb, T. E., & Van Devere, C. A. (1985). *Structured Pediatric Psychosocial Interview (SPPI) manual.* Akron, OH: Fourier.

Webb, T. E., & Van Devere, C. A. (1990). *Structured Pediatric Psychosocial Interview (SPPI) System manual.* Akron, OH: Fourier.

Wegscheider, S. (1981). *Another chance: Hope and health for the alcoholic family.* Palo Alto, CA: Science and Behavior Books.

Weintraub, S. A. (1990–91). Children and adolescents at risk for substance abuse and psychopathology. *International Journal of the Addictions, 25*(4A), 481–494.

Weissberg, R. P., Caplan, M., & Harwood, R. L. (1991). Promoting competent young people in competence-enhancing environments: A systems-based perspective on primary prevention. *Journal of Consulting and Clinical Psychology, 59*(6), 830–841.

Weissberg, R. P., & Gesten, E. L. (1982). Considerations for developing effective school-based social problem-solving (SPS) training programs. *School Psychology Review, 11*(1), 56–63.

Weissberg, R. P., Gesten, E. L., Leibenstein, N. L., Doherty-Schmid, K., & Hutton, H. (1982). *The Rochester Social Problem-Solving (SPS) Program: A training manual for teachers of 2nd–4th grade children.* Rochester, New York: University of Rochester.

Welch, R. A., & Sokol, R. J. (1992, April). Identifying the pregnant woman who drinks. *Contemporary Pediatrics,* pp. 95–107.

Wertsch, J. V. (1991). *Voices of the mind: A sociocultural approach to mediated action.* Cambridge, MA: Harvard University Press.

White, R. (1959). Motivation reconsidered: The concept of competence. *Psychological Review, 66,* 317–330.

Wilkinson, L. C., & Spinelli, F. (1983). Using requests effectively in peer-directed instructional groups. *American Educational Research Journal, 20,* 479–502.

Wirt, R. D., Lachar, D., Klainedinst, J. K., & Seat, P. D. (1984). *Personality Inventory for Children.* Los Angeles: Western Psychological Services.

Woodside, M., Henderson, B. W., Jr., & Samuels, P. N. (1991). *Parental consent: Helping children of addicted parents get help.* New York: Children of Alcoholics Foundation.

Yager, S., Johnson, R. T., Johnson, D. W., & Snider, B. (1986). The impact of group processing on achievement in cooperative learning groups. *The Journal of Social Psychology, 126,* 389–397.

Zahn-Waxler, C. (1991). The case for empathy: A developmental perspective. *Psychological Inquiry, 2,* 155–158.

Zahn-Waxler, C., & Radke-Yarrow, M. (1990). The origins of empathic concern. *Motivation and Emotion, 14*(2), 107–130.

Zahn-Waxler, C., Radke-Yarrow, M., Wagner, E., & Chapman, M. (1992). Development of concern for others. *Developmental Psychology, 28*(1), 126–136.

Index